After Taxes
Managing Personal Wealth

After Taxes
Managing Personal Wealth

Geoff Stevens

The Golden Dog Press
Ottawa – Canada – 1996

ISBN 0-919614-68-X (paperback)

Canadian Cataloguing in Publication Data

Stevens, Geoff, 1943–
  After taxes : managing personal wealth

ISBN 0-919614-68-X

  1. Finance, Personal–Canada. I. Title.

FC179.S55 1996   332.024′01   C96-900862-7

Cover design by The Gordon Creative Group of Ottawa.

Typesetting by Carleton Production Centre of Nepean.

Printed in Canada.

Distributed by:

  Oxford University Press Canada,
  70 Wynford Drive, DON MILLS, Ont., Canada, M3C 1J9.
  Phone: 416-441-2941   *   Fax: 416-444-0427

The Golden Dog Press wishes to express its appreciation to the Canada Council and the Ontario Arts Council for current and past support of its publishing programme.

Table of Contents

Tables and Illustrations

Introduction

Most of us have worked hard for what we own and, unless we're retired, continue to do so. Many of us, however, even if retired, don't have the time, inclination or experience to keep most of what we ear from the taxman, or to have it grow as quickly and safely as possible.

Money is my business. I've been giving people and organizations advice on how to use their money for more than 30 years. I've learned a few things in that time and I propose to share that knowledge.

This material will appeal to professionals and small business owners/partners. It will also be of interest to those earning $50,000, those with unearned income of $10,000, those with $25,000 in RRSPs and, in particular, anyone with any of the above characteristics over age 50.

While solely responsible for the accuracy and adequacy of the material appearing herein, I cannot be liable for errors, omissions or misrepresentations. Before taking any significant action as the result of anything in these pages, the reader is urged to seek competent legal or accounting advice.

I've had a lot of fun putting this together and I'm looking forward to your feedback.

Geoff Stevens   November 1996
Ottawa   6th Edition

Income Taxes

1. Federal Budget '96

Federal Finance Minister Paul Martin presented his third annual budget to Parliament on March 6. There were no major surprises, good or bad. The Liberals' main aim is to continue lowering spending, hence lowering the annual deficit, which is scheduled to drop from last year's $32 billion to $24 billion this next fiscal year.

Despite a credible job in reducing spending since the Liberals came to office almost three years ago, the accumulated national debt will nonetheless top $600 billion later this year.

Mr. Martin did not announce any changes to personal income tax rates, or the taxable income brackets they apply to. Nonetheless, there were a number of changes announced that will affect almost all Canadians. Here is a roundup of the major announcements, in no particular order.

1.1. RSP Contribution Cap

The present RSP contribution limit of $13,500 is being capped at that level until well into the next century. Indeed, it is now doubtful that we shall ever see a higher limit before most of us retire!

At the same time, the Budget removes the seven year maximum carry-forward provision allowing contribution room to build up if not used. While this may sound attractive to some taxpayers, the move seems designed to favour Revenue Canada more than individuals, since it is usually procrastinators who don't take advantage of their RSP contribution limits.

Now, those same procrastinators will have nothing nudging them to make those contributions towards their retirement nest eggs. Consequently, it will be Revenue Canada who save all those tax dollars on that gigantic pool of unfunded contribution room that has been building in recent years.

1.2. RSP Incomes to Begin Sooner

Until now, RSPs had to be collapsed by the end of the year in which the annuitant turned 71. This is being changed to age 69, with the benefit to Revenue Canada of earlier taxation of moneys that have been building up.

Individuals will no longer be able to make contributions to their RSPs beyond age 69.

Those turning 69 this year will be allowed to defer taking income from their RSPs until next year (at age 70). Those turning 70 this year (along with, of course, those turning 71) must collapse their RSPs before the end of this calendar year. Those turning 68 this year must collapse their RSPs by the end of next year.

The government assumes that financial institutions will allow GICs to be collapsed before the maturity date for those individuals affected by this change (Ha! Ha!). Fortunately, individuals buying GICs from life companies (known as deferred annuities) <u>before</u> Budget night are exempted, even though virtually all such deferred annuities, unlike bank and trust company GICs, are redeemable before end of term anyway!

Those folks being forced to buy an income product(s) too early because of this change in government policy, will be partially mollified to know the government has not changed the minimum RIF annual payout formula. The formula will be found in our *GASletter Collection*, fifth edition, page 49.

As a side note, RSP/RIF administration fees are no longer tax deductible. Our advice to owners of plans that levy fees outside the plans is to negotiate with their financial institution to have the fees deducted from inside the contents of the plan(s).

1.3. Federal Civil Service

Plans to cut another 5,000 civil service jobs were announced in the Budget, in an extension to a downsizing effort that will chop 45,000 jobs. As well, the government announced plans to create three new 'agencies' in the areas of national parks, food inspection, and national revenue collection, that could see as many as 50,000 civil servants transferred out of the public service.

Federal civil servants, whose salaries have been frozen for the past six years, will be able to bargain next year for more money. Ottawa will lift the wage freeze beginning next February, when collective bargaining with the country's remaining 200,000 unionized civil servants will resume.

Annual wage increments, suspended two years ago, will be resumed, and performance pay for senior civil servants, suspended in 1991, will be reintroduced. Both of these measures will begin this June.

Binding arbitration is being suspended until 1999, which the government justifies by citing national interests. "We cannot leave determining the results of collective bargaining to a third party unaccountable to Parliament", said the minister responsible for the civil service. This would imply the government expects considerable difficulty in completing the downsizing that has seen, so far, 17,000 jobs eliminated, on the way to total cuts of some 50,000 positions.

1.4. Offshore Investments

In yet another attempt to control and tax ever increasing amounts of capital leaving Canada for investment abroad, the Budget announces plans to force Canadians to report any investment outside Canada which exceeds $100,000. In last year's Budget, measures were introduced forcing expatriate Canadians collecting Old Age Security (OAS) to file statements of world-wide income, thus placing their OAS receipts in jeopardy of the Clawback tax.

With Canada as one of the highest taxed industrial nations causing suspected billions of dollars of capital to take flight offshore, Revenue Canada believes it has been losing huge amounts of income tax by those Canadians who, under the law, should be, but aren't, reporting world-wide income.

I fail to see how mandatory reporting of investments abroad will force much tax out of those who haven't been reporting income from those investments in the past. After all, if it is a Canadian's objective to avoid tax by not reporting offshore income, why should such Canadians suddenly feel compelled to report the very existence of such investments to Revenue Canada?

It will take far sterner measures before Revenue Canada can get its fair and due share of income tax from foreign investments than what will fall out from measures announced to date.

Meanwhile, those Canadians who have invested in life insurance contracts purchased outside Canada are not, in my opinion, affected by any of the measures announced to date.

1.5. Banks prohibited from selling insurance

In a surprise move, the Finance Minister preempted a Finance Department position paper expected to be published in April that was widely expected to favour banks selling insurance directly to consumers through their branch networks. The prohibition would seem to be more of a victory for massive insurance industry lobbying, than as a rational response to competitive market demand and supply pressures.

The banks were very much looking forward to selling insurance through their branches, believing they had a captive market every time their clients walked into their branches for other reasons. The banks will now have to wait until the next revision of the Bank Act, which won't take place for another five years. Insurers are, of course, ecstatic over the announcement.

1.6. Labour fund tax breaks cut

Ottawa is cutting tax breaks that have fuelled the growth of labour-sponsored investment funds. Labour fund purchasers have been getting a 20% federal tax credit, with most provinces matching the credit. The federal credit is reduced immediately to 15% for any new purchases till the end of 1996, with a further reduction, to as low as 10%, for purchases made after 1996.

1.7. Revamped OAS/GIS

Ottawa plans to revamp the Old Age Security and Guaranteed Income Supplement for low-income seniors. But the change won't occur for another five years, and today's seniors will not be affected. In the Budget, the Finance Minister proposes to replace the OAS/GIS system with only one 'seniors benefit'.

At the time the new system comes into being, the present age credit for those over 65 and the $1,000 pension income 'deduction' would be eliminated.

The new seniors benefit will be tax-free. At present, GIS is tax-free, but OAS is taxable as ordinary income up to a recipient's total annual income of about $53,000. Between $53,000 and about $85,000, a senior presently is taxed at an effective rate of about 70%, until there's no OAS left.

The new seniors benefit will automatically be split 50/50 between a couple, unlike the present OAS and GIS.

At present, maximum payments under OAS/GIS are $10,420 to a single pensioner, and $16,900 to a couple. In 2001, the new benefit would be $11,420 and $18,440. These seniors benefit amounts would then be reduced as pensioners' other income rises, based on joint couple income.

A single senior would effectively lose <u>all</u> of the seniors benefit when he/she had about $52,000 or more of other income. A couple would lose all of their seniors benefit once their joint income reached $78,000 or more.

Both the seniors benefit income and the income test will be fully indexed for inflation, as is OAS presently.

Those now 60 or older will be able to choose between the current system and the new one. Singles and couples with about $40,000 of income or more will likely find the <u>current</u> system is better, according to an actuary quoted in the Financial Post following the Budget. That's because the OAS clawback threshold (currently $53,000) will be higher than the new benefit's income test, said the actuary.

1.8.   Personal Income Tax Changes

The Finance Minister very proudly announced he was not introducing any income tax increases in this budget. True enough. But what he failed to discuss was the increased income tax we are all being forced to pay through 'inflation creep'. That's because our income tax system is only partially indexed for inflation.

While our incomes are supposedly rising to keep pace with inflation (actually, it's the other way around: inflation is caused by rising pay for the same amount of work), we are all slowly creeping up into higher income tax brackets. For example, when tax reform was implemented in the late 1980s, the thresholds for the tax rates were $27,500 and $55,000.

Thus, a person earning, let's say, exactly $27,500 in 1989 paid a maximum combined federal/provincial tax rate of 'only' 27% on their entire taxable income. Assuming that person's pay had increased since 1989 to cover only the effects of inflation, to, let's say, $35,000 today, they would be paying tax at the rate of 44% on all of their income exceeding $29,590, the current threshold for the lowest tax bracket. In other words, the $29,590 has not increased nearly as fast in relation to the base $27,500 as have salaries risen to account for inflation.

Thus, the individual cited in the preceding paragraph has lost 44% of his pay increases to the taxman, even though his pay increases were only enough, before tax, to cover the effects of inflation!

This 'hidden' tax grab is enormous, and most Canadians aren't even aware it's taking place. And it hasn't been debated by Parliament in over six years!

1.9.   Child Support

Thanks mainly to the publicity surrounding the Thibodeau Supreme Court case, the Budget announced that payers of child support under court-approved maintenance agreements will no longer be tax deductible, and that recipients of same will no longer have to include such payments as income on their tax returns.

This will come into effect with court orders dated May 1, 1997, or later. This change will <u>not</u> affect existing maintenance agreements. Watch for courts being choked with petitions for new maintenance agreements next year!

1.10. Charitable Donations

The annual limit on donations is being increased, starting with the 1996 tax year, from 20% to 50% of net income, and to 100% in the year of death. This will be a major shot in the arm for Canadian charities looking to high-income earners for sizable gifts and bequests.

1.11. Other Personal Tax Changes

Changes are proposed for 1996 and later years to the education tax credit, the equivalent-to-married tax credit, the limit on transfer of tuition fees and education tax credits to supporting parents, grandparents and spouses, the annual and lifetime limits on contributions to Registered Education/Savings Plans, deductible child care expenses, and the Working Income Supplement.

2. Ontario Budget

In early May, the Ontario Conservative government announced its first full-fledged budget. Beginning July, Ontario taxpayers will see larger paycheques, and starting next January, Ontario corporations will also pay less tax. This budget was certainly a 'good news' budget, the first in which a province unilaterally cut tax rates across all income levels.

The Ontario Finance Minister is betting that the tax cuts will work their way down into increased stimulus for the economy, still recovering from the recession and the previous socialist administration.

Starting 1 July, taxpayers will see Phase I of the promised 30% cut in personal income taxes. The provincial rate will be reduced from the present 58% of the basic federal rate to 56%. Phase II, starting next January, will see the rate fall to 49%, meeting the government's election campaign promise to cut taxes by 15% in its first budget.

Further cuts will be phased in in 1997 and 1999 taking Ontario down to 40.5% of the federal rate.

Everyone, regardless of tax bracket, will get the break, but higher-income earners will see some of their savings going towards a new 'fair-share health levy', which will be incorporated into the existing taxable income surtax. It will affect anyone with incomes of $52,315 or more a year.

Once fully implemented, Ontario will have the second lowest provincial income tax rate in the country, although other provinces may, in the interim, lower their rates as well.

For corporations, the government also kept its campaign promise to cut payroll taxes, eliminating employer health taxes from the first $400,000 of annual payroll. This cut will be phased in over three years, beginning July 1. While the cut will apply to all employers, it will obviously impact small business the most.

The cuts enumerated above are a key element in Premier Mike Harris' government's promise to eliminate the annual deficit by the year 2001. His government believes tax cuts will spur the economy. According to Finance Minister Ernie Eves, the cuts 'will prove a simple truth: the best job creation program is a tax cut for every Ontario taxpayer'.

Here are some examples of how the tax cuts will affect several hypothetical individuals:

- A $25,000 a year employee will save $59 in tax this year and $263 in 1997.
- A $50,000 a year employee will save $177 this year, and $799 in 1997.
- At $75,000 per year, an employee will save $399 this year, and $1,424 in 1997.
- At $100,000, an employee will save $366 this year and $1,674 in 1997.
- At $150,000, the savings are $500, then $2,681 in 1997.
- Self-employed people will save the same as employees this year, but will save even more beginning next year as the employer-health-payroll-tax exemption kicks in.

3.   Reminders to Retirees

Many retirees now lose the 'age exemption' on their tax returns. The age exemption is now income tested. This means that anyone age 65+ will lose part or all of the value of the exemption depending on the amount of net income reported. The threshold begins at an income of as little as $26,000. The exemption is lost entirely when income exceeds as little as $49,000. This measure means that a senior with income as low as $49,000 loses an exemption worth just under $1,000 in taxes. That is equivalent to a 2% income tax increase! The age exemption transferred from a spouse is not affected because, by definition, if the amount can be transferred in the first place, then the spouse does not have enough income to affect the amount of the exemption still available.

1994 was the last year a pensioner could contribute up to $6,000 to a spousal RSP from qualifying pension income.

The above measures by themselves significantly increase the income tax burden on middle income pensioners. For someone with a gross taxable income of as little as $60,000, the above measures, all by themselves, add no less than $5,000 annually to their tax bill (68% of $6,000 + $950).

Since tax reform was introduced in the mid-80s, it has been very important to take advantage of as many income-splitting techniques as possible. With Revenue Canada's implementation of the measures reviewed above, it becomes even more important for families to plan and effect as many income splitting techniques as possible. The federal and provincial marginal tax rate on a retiree with as little as $60,000 per year effectively becomes 70%, with a further tax cost of at least $4,000 per year in the loss of the spousal pension RSP provision. If you are not sure whether you could benefit from income splitting, read up about it in the many articles we have written herein.

While income splitting has its greatest benefits among those over age 64, it is important that families under that age employ income splitting techniques rigorously, if only to lessen the need for income splitting once you have reached retirement. Over and over again, we meet people who have worked hard during their careers to raise a family and to put some assets aside for retirement only to discover, after retirement when it's too late, that had they employed income splitting during their careers, they would be paying substantially less income tax.

4. Tax Gap Widens

The disparity between U.S. and Canadian taxes continues to grow. This is because Canadian income taxes will continue rising, even if there were no increases in this year's budgets. The primary cause is that in Canada, unlike in the U.S., our tax brackets are only partially indexed for inflation. Indexing is only on inflation which exceeds 3%. Thus, although all of our incomes theoretically increase to keep up with inflation, the tax brackets don't. Over time, we are pushed into higher tax brackets, while our disposable incomes stay the same. The average tax burden in Canada is projected to rise from the present 38% of gross domestic product to 39.5% in 1997. The corresponding U.S. figures are 30% and 31%.

5. Marginal Tax Rates

Taxable Income	Marginal Fed + Ont. Tax Rates 1996
< $30,000	27.4%
$30,000–$51,000	41.9%
$51,000–$59,000	44.4%
$59,000–$66,500	51.0%
> $66,500	52.3%

The above does not include the Clawback tax. For those over 64, and with taxable income between $53,215 and $83,535, add 15% to the above rates. A pensioner with a taxable income of as little as $66,500, after losing the 'age exemption', pays no less than 70% of his last dollar in combined federal and provincial income taxes, before provincial sales taxes, Goods and Services taxes, municipal taxes, and sin taxes on any alcohol and tobacco. No other industrialized nation on earth taxes its seniors as heavily as does Canada!

6. 70% Tax Rate!

Are you over age 65 with an income in excess of $53,000? Hang on to your chair, 'cause you are paying no less than 70% in federal/provincial income taxes on most of your income between $53,000 and $85,000! (The 70% consists of: 29% basic federal levy; plus 16% basic provincial levy; plus 8% of various federal and provincial surcharges; plus 15% federal Clawback tax; plus the equivalent of a 2% tax through elimination of the 'age amount'.)

One important way to minimize the 70% tax bite is to 'income-split' with one or more family members. Don't have any family members to 'income-split' with? Then there's not much you can do. You can no longer make $6,000 spousal RSP contributions. You can't even give it away, since the charitable donation tax deduction we enjoyed before Tax Reform has been converted to a tax credit worth only about $0.50 in saved tax per dollar of contribution.

We are seeing more and more affluent Canadians considering leaving Canada before they get taxed to death! Only France has a higher tax grab than Canada.

7. Tax Credit Limits

The Tax Credit Amounts have been announced for 1996. Because these are adjusted only when inflation for the preceding 12 months exceeds 3%, and because inflation for the past year has been barely 2%, the Tax Credit Amounts for this year remain the same as they were for 1995. Because inflation has been under 3% for several years, the Tax Credit Amounts remain the same as they have been since 1992.

Even though our incomes theoretically have advanced by the amount of inflation each year, Tax Credit Amounts remaining constant for five years in a row mean we are all creeping into higher tax brackets and, therefore, paying more in tax, even though our real incomes have remained flat. These income tax increases have not even been debated in Parliament!

Here are the Tax Credit Amounts for this year, as well as for the previous several years for comparison purposes:

Tax Credit Amounts

	1992–96	1991	1990	1989
Basic Personal Credit	6456	6280	6169	6000
Age 65	3482	3387	3327	3272
Disability	3482	3387	3327	3272
Medical expense threshold	1601	1570	1542	1500
Married Credit	5380	5233	5141	5000
For spouse with income under	534	524	514	500
Dependent Child Credit				
For each of the first 2	417	406	399	392
Thereafter, for each	834	812	798	784
with income threshold of	2670	2617	2570	2500
Refundable Child Tax Credit	597	585	575	565
+ for each child under 7	211	207	203	200
OAS/FA Clawback threshold	53215	51765	50850	50000
Clawback Rate	100%	100%	67%	33%
Tax Bracket Limits				
Lowest: 17% federal; under	29590	28784	28275	27500
Middle: 27% federal; under	59180	57568	56550	55000
Upper: 29% federal; over	59180	57568	56550	55000

8. Alternate Minimum Tax (AMT)

AMT is an outgrowth of Mulroney's 1984 campaign promise to levy a minimum tax on affluent Canadians. It concerns anyone with gross income, from all sources, of $40,000 or more. 'All sources' include: gross capital gains; dividends from Canadian corporations or small businesses; net rental income (or loss); retiring allowances; earned income such as salary and commissions; and interest. The first $40,000 of income is exempted. Tax credits are available for what used to be known as the personal deduction, for charitable donations and medical expenses. Notably absent from AMT deductions are RRSP contributions and rollovers, transfer of spousal credits, capital gains exemption, and employee stock option deductions. Having arrived at taxable income for AMT as above, a flat rate of 17% is applied and the result is compared to ordinary federal tax on taxable income net of dividend tax credits. If AMT is greater, it becomes federal tax. If regular tax is greater, AMT of up to seven years previous may be deducted to reduce it to the level of the current year AMT. The resulting tax is subject to provincial tax and surtaxes. If your income exceeds $50,000, you may be subject to AMT. If so, you would be well advised to prepare a pro-forma statement early in the tax year to determine the potential impact of AMT. There would remain time to alter strategies to minimize AMT.

9. Tax Tips

Do you owe the taxman? Do you have any other consumer debts such as department store, oil company or mortgage accounts? Why not pay down your consumer debt first? Revenue Canada will be happy with a monthly or quarterly payment program, and currently charges only 11% (for the 4th quarter, 1996) on the outstanding balance (versus 18%+ on most charge/bank cards). Why not arrange with your taxman a repayment schedule that's mutually satisfactory before paying down your other debts? This strategy also makes sense if you are pre-paying your estimated tax liability through instalments. Remember too, that Revenue Canada's current policy is to start to pursue you for owed amounts only 90 days after date of assessment/reassessment. So, you have at least 120 days from filing date before you need make your first payment. If you owe, filing date should be April 30, not one day sooner or later! During that 120+ day period, Revenue Canada still only charges you 11% on the assessed outstanding amount. A reasonable loan rate compared to credit cards! Interest paid by Revenue Canada on refunds sent to you after April 30 is reportable by you on your subsequent tax return. Interest payable on overdue amounts owing Revenue Canada, on the other hand, is not deductible!

Thinking of de-registering part or all of your RRSPs (as opposed to annuitizing)? Then expect to have the trustee of your RRSP withhold 10% on amounts less than $5,000, 30% for amounts great than $15,000 and 20% for amounts in between. This is the Revenue Canada prescribed formula, and applies to each transaction. So, if you find these rates of tax pre-payment too high, or, if you simply don't like pre-paying taxes, either de-register towards year-end and/or break up the desired amount into several transactions of less than $5,000 each.

Medical Expenses should be claimed by only one member of a family. The person claiming should be the person with the lowest net income of at least $6,500. Here's why: under tax reform, medical receipts generate federal tax credits equal to 17% of the excess over 3% of net income (or $1,500, if less). In a province with a 50% tax on top of the federal rate, this means an effective tax of about 26%. But since it's a non-refundable credit, it's important the right person claim medical expenses. To get maximum credit, the individual claiming should have the lowest net income in the household. Revenue Canada has long allowed pooling of medical receipts within a family. Also, many medical expenses are claimable as non-refundable tax credits which are not covered, or only partially reimbursed, by medical insurance plans, such as eye glasses. What's more, insurance plan premiums, not including provincial and/or employer group insurance premiums, are claimable. Thus, Blue Cross and travel insurance premiums are claimable. While it's not necessary to submit insurance plan premium receipts when you submit your return, it's important you keep them for subsequent audit. You must, as always, submit receipts for services and products such as prescription drugs. Medical expenses and premiums may be claimed for any twelve month period ending in a tax year. If you have expenses spanning the beginning of a tax year, play around with your receipts until you have the maximum for any twelve month period. Conversely, if you know you will, or already have, high expenses towards the end of a calendar year, it may benefit you to save some of the larger ones for the next tax year.

Charitable Donations/Gifts to Canada: Like medical expenses, these should be pooled and claimed by only one member in a family. The reason in this case is that the non-refundable tax credit is only 17% on the first $200, and 29% on the excess over $200. Therefore, if donations and/or gifts to Canada, a province, or a university are spread among two or more family members, each $200 of donations over and above the first loses 12% in federal tax credits, or, in a province with a 50% tax rate, about $36 in lost tax credit. If donations don't total at least $200 for the household, consider saving them for a future year, since donations and gifts can be carried forward up to five years. For either medical or charitable claims, remember not to 'waste' non-refundable credits by an ineligible person making the claim. If the total at line 335 of your tax return, minus the allowable portion of medical receipts, exceeds line 260, then you have worthless receipts for that year.

Carrying Charges: Safety Deposit box rental costs are deductible. So are interest expense charges when buying CSBs by payroll deduction. So are interest expenses incurred on loans to finance pension buy-back schemes. If you have borrowed from a life insurance policy, the interest cost is deductible if anyone in the household is earning interest or dividends, or is holding onto stocks, bonds or mutual funds. Tax-return preparation costs, where no advice on investments is given (i.e. with most H&R Block returns) aren't deductible. Carrying charges should be pooled and claimed by the individual in the highest tax bracket since carrying charges directly reduce taxable income.

Tuition Fees of $100 or more for any post-secondary course are tax-deductible if you have the proper receipt. Driver-ed course fees are eligible. Fees must be used by the student to reduce his/her tax to zero. If any fees are left over, left-overs may be used by either parent after the student fills out the back of the tuition fee receipt.

Single Parents of one or more children age 17 or less may claim any one child as 'equivalent-to-married' depending on the child's income. Any child qualifies; it does not have to be the oldest. The child claimed as the married equivalent can change from one year to the next.

The *'Equivalent-to-Married'* amount can be used by a single (or divorced, separated, or widowed) person supporting a close relative. See Tax Guide for more.

Child-Care Expenses may be claimed by the lower-income spouse for those expenses directly related to caring for children to allow the spouse to earn income.

Dividends: In some cases, it may be better for you to report all taxable Canadian dividends received by your spouse. You should do this if, by doing so, you can claim the 'married amount', or increase your claim for the 'married amount'. If you are unable to take better advantage of the 'married amount' by so doing, perhaps because your spouse has other income, and if you find yourself in a higher tax bracket than your spouse, you should dispose of the shares producing such dividends and have your spouse re-invest in the same stock. This is because the dividend tax credit is worth more to those in the lowest tax bracket than to those in the middle or highest brackets.

Foreign Taxes: If you paid foreign taxes on foreign investment income that you received, you may be able to claim the foreign tax credit that applies to countries with which Canada has a tax treaty. The U.S. is such a country.

Annuity Payments: Interest from annuities (deferred or immediate) held with life insurance companies qualifies as either interest income or pension income. This is an excellent way for those over age 59 to take advantage of the first $1,000 pension income exemption if they do not have any other qualifying pension income (CPP and OAS do not qualify as pension income for the exemption).

Retiring Allowances: Severance pay and other forms of retiring allowances may be rolled over into RRSP(s) at the rate of $2,000 per year of service while belonging to a pension plan, plus $3,500 per year of service while not belonging to a pension plan. This formula applies up to and including 1995. There is no rollover for years after 1995. Make sure the years of service shown on your retiring allowances tax slips are correct, since that is the figure Revenue Canada's computers will use to calculate the maximum roll-over amount you are entitled to.

Disability: If you, or any member of your family that you are supporting, suffer from a severe and prolonged physical or mental disability, you qualify to claim a disability amount, if you can get a medical practitioner to certify the disability is severe and prolonged. Many doctors have been cowed by Revenue Canada into not signing such declarations; many other doctors are only too willing to certify such statements when the disabled person is unable to carry on the routine activities of daily living without outside help.

Interest Earnings: If you are in a higher tax bracket than someone else in the household, it will be to your advantage to have that family member declare your interest income. It does not matter whose name is on the T5 slip as long as a case can be made that it was the taxpayer claiming the interest who earned it. Thus, most spouses have no difficulty swapping T5 slips since either spouse can claim the funds in the account(s) or investment(s) was that taxpayer's property. Similarly, accounts held for children will not usually be reported by either parent if the funds so held are clearly earmarked for the eventual use of the child, and income does not exceed $2,670/child.

Tax Shelters: All tax shelters being reported on tax returns must have their unique tax shelter numbers shown on the return. Otherwise, Revenue Canada will automatically deny the claim(s).

Commissions/Rental Income/Self-Employed Income: If you received any of these, you are allowed to claim expenses incurred in order to earn such income. See elsewhere herein for more.

Office at Home: Expenses incurred in operating an office at home are deductible in certain circumstances. They cannot be used, however, to create or increase a loss from corresponding income. Such losses may, however, be carried forward to a year when they can be deducted from self-employed or commission income.

CCA or Depreciation: The same rule as in the last paragraph applies to CCA or depreciation when calculating net income from self-employment or rental income.

That is, depreciation cannot create or otherwise increase a loss from self-employment or rental properties.

Income Splitting: There are three broad income tax brackets, approximating the following: income up to $30,000 is taxed at 27%; income above $60,000 is taxed at 53%; income between these two amounts is taxed at 42%. This includes federal and provincial taxes and surtaxes for a resident of Ontario. If you are in one tax bracket while your spouse is in another, one of you is paying too much tax. You should take steps to correct this situation to the extent possible by income splitting. Considerable tax savings are possible by so doing. See elsewhere herein for ways to income split between family members.

10. Taxman's Bias

Many folks have long believed that the taxman was biased against one-earner families. If you and your spouse have decided one of you will stay home to raise children, watch out! Not only will you as a family suffer while trying to make ends meet on only one income, the taxman will take more of your hard-earned dollars away in tax than if the two of you had made the same gross income. This discrimination has been with us since the introduction of the graduated tax structure over 50 years ago. Because of the graduated nature of the system, tax rates increase at a faster rate than income, so that an individual with taxable income of as little as $65,000 pays no less than 55% of his/her last dollar in income tax. But, a couple sharing that same income pays only 27% in combined federal/provincial tax on their last dollar of income.

A married couple resident in Ontario with only one income earner with an income of $65,000 pays about $22,000 in taxes, CPP and UI premiums. A couple earning $30,000 each would see total taxes and premiums of only $15,300. Thus, two people each earning $30,000 will have more take-home disposable income than a one-earner family with a gross of $65,000.

Prior to 1993, the tax system was biased only against legally married couples, as opposed to couples married common-law. But as many of the latter have discovered during recent tax seasons, they too are now being treated as married couples have been for the past 50 years.

The above makes even more mandatory the need for periodic family tax planning, and to take maximum advantage of income splitting techniques between members of a family where one member has substantially higher income than others.

11. Assessment Notice Wrong?

Have you received your assessment notice and it's wrong, or you disagree with it? Most of the time, Revenue Canada will be right. But if you're convinced you are right, then contact your District Tax Office. If it's a simple matter, a phone call (to 598-2275 in the Ottawa area) will usually suffice. For your own protection, you should record the name of the individual you spoke with, and the date and time. If the matter is more serious, or if you have to supply additional documentation, write a note to your District Tax Office, or bring it in in person. In Ottawa and area, the District Office is at 333 Laurier St. West, between Bank and Kent, K1A 0L9. Whether you mail material, or visit their office, copy everything. It isn't strictly necessary to use registered mail, although it doesn't hurt.

If you haven't resolved the matter to your satisfaction after about 80 days from the mailing date shown on the upper left corner of the assessment notice, you should file a notice of objection, in duplicate. Keep a third copy. If you use the mail for a notice of objection, register it. Or visit the District Office and present your objection by hand. If you do the latter, have Revenue Canada stamp your third copy as your proof that you made the 90-day deadline.

You will, usually within 3–4 weeks, receive acknowledgement Revenue Canada has received your objection and you will be contacted 'in due course'. While your objection is being processed, your account payable is put into suspense although the interest clock keeps ticking. In other words, until your objection has been decided upon by Revenue, their computer will not chase you for any amounts they feel you owe them. However, if you still owe them after they have decided on the objection, you will have been docked interest throughout the whole objection period, unless you subsequently win an appeal. Be prepared to be patient for six months or longer to hear about your objection. If you still don't agree with Revenue Canada's position after they have processed your objection, you then have the right to appeal to the Tax Court of Canada. However, you must file your appeal with the Tax Court within 90 days of Revenue Canada's last Notice of Assessment, or Re-Assessment, or Notice of Determination by the Minister.

If the amount of tax under dispute, not including interest and/or penalties, is under $7,000 for any one tax year, you may use the informal procedure of appeal. If your tax under dispute is over $7,000, you may still use the informal procedure, but any successful judgement will be limited to the first $7,000 of tax for any one year. If you wish to appeal tax amounting to more than $7,000, you must use the formal procedure of appeal.

The informal procedure requires no filing fee, and you can plead your case by yourself, without representation. If you wish, you may bring along representation in the form of a lawyer or tax specialist. If your case is even only partially successful, the Court may award you part or all of your expenses in mounting your appeal. If you lose all of your case under the informal procedure, the Court cannot award costs to Revenue Canada.

Should you wish to use the formal procedure, there is a filing fee depending on the size of the appeal, and legal representation will be expected, although not absolutely necessary. If you lose, in part or whole, you may be forced to pay Revenue Canada's costs as well as your own. Whatever costs you incur in objecting and/or appealing a notice of assessment or re-assessment is tax deductible in the year incurred. Interest on amounts owing Revenue Canada while an objection or appeal is being heard is not subsequently deductible. Interest earned on any refunds, even from an appeal or objection, is taxable. You may obtain forms for filing an appeal from the Tax Court. In Ottawa, the Court is located on the 2nd floor, 200 Kent, at the corner of Laurier. If you wish to appeal a tax court decision, you may go to the Federal Appeals Court. If you don't like their verdict, you may then go to the Supreme Court of Canada. Either of these Courts are expensive, and either may refuse to hear you without even giving any reason for their refusal. When dealing with either of these courts, legal representation is a must if you don't want to lose your shirt!

12. Tax Audits

Any taxpayer is subject to audit anytime up to three years after the mailing date on an assessment notice, or at any time if Revenue Canada has reason to believe there is fraud. There are some types of taxpayers who can practically forget about ever getting audited. There are others who stand an excellent chance of being audited, frequently. Those who stand little chance of being audited are those on fixed incomes, such as pensioners. Even those pensioners with sizable investment income from banks, trust companies and life insurance companies, stand little prospect of being audited if they have religiously claimed all income reported on tax slips. This is because all financial institutions must now, by law, carry SI numbers for all of their clients. Such institutions regularly report to Revenue Canada by computer. It is a simple matter for Revenue Canada to match up these reported incomes with those reported on tax returns. Where there are discrepancies, usually caused when a taxpayer changes address from what the financial institution had on their records, it's easy for Revenue Canada to churn out a new assessment notice to reflect the income that wasn't reported. Those who stand a large chance of being audited are those who are self-employed and who are claiming expenses, or those operating rental income properties, or those reporting cash receipts, such as taxi drivers, waiters, and barmaids. Those receiving commissions from employers who file payroll records with Revenue Canada have little chance of an audit if they claim little or no expenses. Those claiming much more than 20% of their commissions as expenses can expect to be audited at least once every three or four years.

When Revenue Canada decides on an audit, they will usually cover more than one, and up to three tax years. They can't go beyond three unless they get your written permission to do so or unless they believe you have committed fraud. Revenue Canada considers it a worse offence to fail to report income than to over-report expenses. Income is fairly black and white. Allowable and reasonable expenses, however, are open to interpretation. Any taxpayer should refrain from the temptation of not reporting income. Even those earning income by illegal means are best advised to report such income since Revenue Canada must consider such information confidential. Here are some tips to keep in mind to better weather an audit:

- if cash is part of your business, keep a good log
- if you deduct expenses, keep receipts
- if you claim auto expenses, keep a mileage log

Who is more likely to face an audit? The following situations stand a very good chance of generating what Revenue Canada calls a 'desk audit', where Revenue Canada writes the taxpayer a letter asking for further details including, when necessary, receipts and/or logs (as in, for example, the claimed use of an automobile):

- claiming an office at home
- claiming an auto cost or other deductions when the taxpayer is an employee
- claiming deductions for tax shelters where the tax shelter identification number has not been provided on the tax return
- claiming business losses to cover employment income

- claiming significant interest income when some of that income is from non-traditional sources, as in, for example, a private loan
- claiming travel and convention expenses, especially when such travel is to exotic places outside North America, or when such expenses end up being a large portion of total expenses
- claiming that you are self-employed when, in fact, you have received a T4 slip from an 'employer'. This often occurs with part-time university teachers
- claiming large medical expenses, especially if they involve an attendant at home, structural alterations to a house, or special schooling for a disabled child
- claiming the Disability Amount without submitting a Disability Certificate completed by a physician
- claiming large charitable donations, especially of the 'in-kind' type, if the property in question has not been certified by the Cultural Property Review Board
- claiming a capital gain on property that was owned in 1971, which can result in an argument between Revenue Canada and the taxpayer on what the true value of the property was in 1971
- claiming moving expenses where such expenses end up representing a large proportion of the taxpayers gross income

Surviving an audit is usually quite routine, if somewhat nerve wracking. Most audits are settled very quickly when the taxpayer provides a missing document in substantiation of a claim. However, if more than two or three of the above situations occur on the same tax return, the odds rise on the likelihood of a detailed 'office audit'.

Where more than one or two missing documents are at issue, be prepared for the audit to take months, and sometimes even years to straighten out!

13.   Didn't File a Tax Return?

Haven't filed a return because you don't owe any tax? OK, but have you taken into account the bewildering array of tax credits that are available at both the provincial and federal levels that you may be entitled to, but which you virtually need a computer program to find out if you are? We were surprised yet again this year how many people had refunds coming to them that were much larger than clients were anticipating, primarily because of the tax credit system. The size of the credits and their nature are too complicated to get into here, but if you haven't filed just because you think you don't owe anything, you may be missing out!

14.   The Clawback Tax

The Clawback tax is a tax designed to claw back Old Age Security benefits (and Family Allowances). It is the most insidious tax we have ever seen or heard of in this country, because it takes back precisely what the government has been telling us we should save for, and it does so after we have become defenceless, at retirement. Since the 1950s, one government after another has encouraged us to plan for our retirements by deferring tax on what we contribute to RRSPs. At no time during the past 35 years have we seen any tax payer defer more than about 50% in tax what he/she contributes to RRSPs. The average has been more like 30%. Yet, those were sufficient inducements to cause many taxpayers to take government literally and pile up sizable nest eggs for retirement in the form of RRSPs, planning to augment their OAS and CPP with annuity or RIF income after retirement.

Precisely when it is too late to do anything about it, taxpayers are discovering only at age 66 (when they do their tax returns for the year they turned 65) that income in excess of $53,000 is being taxed at from 60 to 70%! Under tax reform, there is nothing a prudent and well-meaning taxpayer can do to lower his/her taxable income. Taxpayers can no longer contribute pension income to their RRSPs, nor can they lower taxable income through charitable donations, as they could just a couple of years ago.

Many taxpayers are discovering too late that they have saved far too much in RRSPs, and that much of their RRSP accumulations will be taxed at something like 60% when they received a tax concession of perhaps only 30% at time of contribution. It's bad enough government reneged on its pledge of universality. It's inexcusable to sneak such a tax onto the backs of those no longer in a position to do anything. Almost as bad as the hidden nature of the Clawback tax itself, is the way we are all edging into higher tax brackets, even if our real disposable income stays flat.

15.   Tax Gripes

I get many complaints about the tax system every year. I list the more common with help from Arthur Drache, probably Canada's leading tax lawyer (whom I have consulted on occasion).

The 'Equivalent-to-Married' Exemption: If you are a single parent supporting a child over age 17, you get no tax relief under this exemption, even if the child is attending high school. A Tax Court judge has ruled this contrary to the Charter of Rights. Revenue Canada has appealed.

Supporting Parents: If your parents have little or no income and you support them financially, you can claim some tax relief if they live in Canada. But you don't get any tax breaks if they live outside Canada.

Free Loans to Government: If you have overpaid your taxes, on which you have not gotten any interest while the government has used your overpayment, Revenue Canada won't pay you interest on what you're owed until 45 days have passed from April 30, or from the date you file your tax return (whichever date is later). On the other hand, if you owe the taxman, your interest starts to accumulate from April 30 or, in the case of people who should have made instalment payments earlier during the tax year, from the date the instalment payment should have been made. This applies even if the instalment payment was caused by receipt of income late in the tax year that you had no way of knowing earlier in the year you would be receiving.

Timing of Tax: If you earn interest on money owing to you, as on for instance a GIC, you must pay tax as the interest is earned, even though the money is not paid to you. But if you receive a lump sum payment in a year that relates to prior years activities, like a retroactive pay increase, the whole amount is taxable in the year you receive the lump sum. You cannot spread it back over the years you earned it.

Relying on Revenue Canada: If you receive advice from Revenue Canada which you follow, you are still liable for taxes and interest even if the advice turns out to be wrong. Tax Courts have consistently said advice from a Revenue Canada bureaucrat, no matter how incompetent, cannot over-ride the law.

Paying for Tax Returns: Individual taxpayers cannot deduct the cost of having their returns prepared, even though complex rules are making correct preparation of returns increasingly difficult. Yet, the cost of preparing returns is a normal business expense and is therefore deductible for businesses. In the vast majority of cases, the cost of preparing the business owner's personal returns gets included in the cost of preparing the business tax returns. In our case, our clients get to deduct the cost of our preparing their tax returns, since we charge for investment advice, not the actual preparation of the return.

Employee Expenses: Employees usually cannot deduct the expenses related to their jobs. Yet almost every employee has such expenses. The most obvious, of course, is the cost of travelling to and from work. On the other hand, such expenses incurred by business owners get written off as deductions from taxable income by the businesses. Until a few years ago, there was a general deduction of $500 available to all taxpayers for employment related expenses. That was done away with during tax reform in the name of equity.

The Standby Charge: Most people understand the logic that employees or shareholders who get company cars should pay tax on the benefit they receive. But they cannot understand why the benefit is computed on the original cost, instead of the original cost being depreciated, the way other assets are, over time. So, a person driving a company car that cost $20,000 and is now five years old will get dinged the same stand-by charge on his/her T4 slip from his employer as someone who is driving a brand new $20,000 car.

Averaging: Many folks experience fluctuations in income from year to year, especially self-employed or commissioned sales types. Anyone who has given even a cursory look at our progressive tax system would agree that we need some form of averaging to make the system fair. Supposedly, the government when it introduced tax reform several years ago, pledged fairness. Anything except fairness could be used to describe the inequitable taxes someone who has 'lumpy' income from one year to the next faces. Such a taxpayer pays far more in tax than someone who has a fairly predictable, even if rising, income. While some form of income avereaging was around for decades, it was done away with during tax reform.

Inflation I: Indexing of the tax system is a key element of fairness in any tax system. The decision of government to annually index the system only by the amount that inflation exceeds 3% per year undermines the fairness of the system and imposes a hidden tax increase on all taxpayers as our incomes increase to keep pace with inflation. This is not only unfair, in my opinion, it is very deceitful. A good example of the unfairness is that when the Clawback tax was originally proposed, it was to apply only to the rich. With inflation de-indexing, the Clawback tax now applies to those with a current income of only $53,000 per year, hardly high income these days. A study was done a few years ago that showed the Clawback tax would rob someone of <u>all</u> OAS income when that person had an income in today's dollars of only $40,000, in the year 2005!

Inflation II: While indexing, as inadequate as it is, helps taxpayers, many deductions and exemptions are not indexed, and have not been changed in 20 years. Examples include the tax-free amount students can receive as scholarships; the limit

($1,000) below which personal property is not subject to capital gains tax; the tax-free limit ($25,000) of employer-provided term life insurance. Other tax items have been increased lately, but nowhere near enough to have caught up with inflation over the past 20 years.

16. Tax Deductible Expenses

Tax deductible expenses will be of interest to those allowed to claim expenses from taxable incomes. This includes self-employed professionals, business people, commissioned salespeople, and people with second jobs. Many of the following expense items are also deductible by persons operating rental properties. The chart below is a partial list of deductible expense items that, over the years, Revenue Canada has allowed in computing taxable income.

Tax Deductible Expenses

Entertainment:	**Office Expenses:** (at home too!)
o Theatre	o Mortgage Interest
o Lunches	o Rent
o Coffee Breaks	o Municipal Taxes
o Parties (incl. at home)	o Buy/Sell Costs i.e. legal
o Meals, including spousal	o Insurance
o Flowers, Plants	o Utilities
o Tips	o Advertising
o Bar Bills	o Postage
Travelling:	o Equipment
o Auto	o Supplies
o Taxis	o Telephone and Long Distance
o Meals, Coffees	o Answering Machine/Service
o Tips, Parking	
Inter-Spousal Wages, Commissions, Gifts	Licences and Dues
Reference Books and Materials	Automobile (see article below)
Bank and Other Charges (incl. Accounting/Legal)	Social Club Expenses (but not Membership)
Overtime Meals (even when alone)	Courier Charges
Babysitting, Child Care	Coin Telephones
Periodicals	Goodwill Items, Gifts, Greeting Cards

This is not an exhaustive list, but is published to jog the reader's memory to ascertain if he/she has thought of these. These change from year to year, and a number are of the gray variety, that is: may be allowable in one taxpayer's circumstances, and not in another's. While Revenue Canada doesn't expect a full accounting when you file your return, they may ask for such during a subsequent audit. It is important you keep as many receipts as possible to support your claims. Some items, such as parking meters and coin telephones, don't lend themselves to receipts. But a well-kept diary helps substantiate expenses not backed up by receipts. Such a diary also helps to keep track of, and to justify, entertainment and auto expenses. Remember: if you don't claim on a gray expense, you'll never know if it was deductible!

17.   Tax Reform and Automobile Expenses

This will be of interest to those allowed to deduct automobile expenses from taxable incomes. Individuals allowed to so claim are listed in the article above. Those who use an automobile for business purposes have always been able to deduct expenses relating to the operation of their vehicle from taxable income. However, to curb abuse, the Finance Department introduced rules during tax reform that significantly reduce amounts that can be deducted. This article highlights those rules.

Maximum capital cost for depreciation is $24,000. If you borrow to buy, maximum deductible loan interest is the lesser of interest paid or $300 per month. The same rationale applies to leased vehicles. The maximum lease cost is the least of:

a) the actual lease cost;

b) $650 per month; or

c) $\dfrac{\text{lease cost} \times \$24{,}000}{\text{List Price (+ PST)} \times 85\%}$

Operating expenses (e.g., fuel, repair, maintenance) continue to be prorated as before tax reform on the ratio of business use to total kilometers driven. Fixed expenses (e.g., depreciation, lease costs, licence fees, insurance and interest), on the other hand, are now prorated twice if business use is less than 24,000 km per year. Fixed expenses are first prorated by the ratio of business use kilometers, then, by the same formula again, but with total kilometers for both business and total use limited to 24,000. Thus, for a car driven 20,000 km and used 50% for business, the prorating factor is 50% × 10,000 km divided by 20,000 km, or 25%. But for a car driven 36,000 km and used 50% for business, the prorating factor is 50% × 18,000 km divided by 24,000 km (the maximum), or 37.5%. Total annual business use has to equal at least 24,000 km before the second factor is eliminated. Insurance premiums and licence fees are now considered to be fixed expenses, subject to proration. However, all parking expenses, including those at normal place of work, remain fully deductible. As a result of these rules, the following should be kept in mind:

- Record keeping is more important than ever. A complete and accurate log of business travel is a must.
- Since the 24,000 km business use limit is crucial for prorating fixed expenses, it is important that business travel be on only one vehicle in a two-car family, when possible. Spreading 30,000 km of business use over two vehicles will not yield anywhere near the same deductions as the same use on one vehicle (the more expensive one!)
- Keep one car in a two-car family almost solely for business.
- In a one-car family, consider taking the bus, if convenient, and claiming personal travel on public transit. Or consider more taxis/limousines, the cost of which continues to be deductible when for business, if supported by receipts.

Instead of claiming all of the expenses associated with running a vehicle, consider a flat rate deductible equal to $ 0.31 per km which may be used for travel instead of detailed expenses, where supported <u>by a travel log</u>.

18.   Mileage Deductions

For years, I have advised readers who are entitled to claim auto expenses against their income on their tax returns that they could claim $ 0.31/kilometre in lieu of claiming actual costs determined by receipts. Now comes word that federal bureaucrats are now allowed to claim $ 0.37/kilometre on their expense statements, while Members of Parliament have voted themselves a raise to $ 0.367/kilometre. While Revenue Canada seems to be in no hurry to raise the $ 0.31 allowed to taxpayers, it is now my advice that, beginning with this taxation year, taxpayers claim the higher amount of $ 0.37/kilometre.

19.   Foreign Investment Taxes

Each year, when I help our investment clients with their income tax returns, I am asked about foreign investment income taxes, and how Revenue Canada handles these. Fortunately, most foreign investments are in the United States, where the Internal Revenue Service has mandated that a flat 15% withholding tax be remitted by the holder of the investment, and that the investor be issued with a tax reporting slip indicating what the withheld tax is.

Because of the Canada–U.S. Income Tax Treaty, taxpayers of one country with income from the other will get a tax credit for any taxes withheld at source, simply by claiming same on their respective tax returns. No special filing is required with the country that has withheld foreign income tax.

If you are contemplating a foreign investment in securities outside North America, but through a North American based investment broker/company, then withholding taxes will be taken care of automatically by the investment trustee regardless of whether the trustee is located in Canada or the U.S. Thus, for example, any mutual fund issued anywhere in Canada or the U.S., even if it transacts in Asian or European securities, will be forced by Canadian or American authorities to withhold appropriate foreign income taxes on capital gains, dividends, or interest, and to report same to the client/taxpayer. The client/taxpayer will then receive credit for these taxes withheld by the financial institution by simply including a copy of the relevant slip(s) with his/her tax return.

Capital gains earned on U.S. investments will not have any taxes withheld.

20.   Save Those Receipts

Do you qualify to deduct expenses from otherwise taxable income at tax time? If so, save those receipts! Self-employed people, or professionals, or business owners (including landlords) often forget to request receipts when disbursing cash for payment of goods and services they use or consume while going about their business, resulting in lost tax deductions. Examples of deductions frequently missed include: long distance charges, parking, gas fill-ups, oil changes and other smaller auto repairs or maintenance, including car washes, lunches and coffee breaks, postage, greeting cards, paper clips and other smaller office supplies. Even parking meter or coin telephone calls are deductible, even though receipts won't, of course, be available. It's so easy to forget asking for receipts for such items, since individually, none are usually for more than $10 or $15. They can add up, to many hundreds if not thousands of tax-deductible dollars per year at tax time. If you are in a 41% or higher tax bracket, they represent significant after tax dollars in your pocket or business.

How can you ensure you are not missing any receipts? First, by making it a habit to ask for a receipt any time you reach for cash to pay a bill, no matter how small. And, second, by developing and maintaining a record-keeping system. It doesn't have to be very fancy, nor does it have to be computerized. A simple diary religiously maintained on a daily basis will usually suffice. Record who you're seeing, where, and for what. Include stops at stores, restaurants, gas stations and other places where you're spending money, including brief notes regarding parking meters and coin telephones, in the form of cryptic notations or shorthand. If you insist on using credit, consider getting a separate card for business purposes, although credit cards are frowned upon by establishments for smaller items. Use the diary to record mileage and taxis. If visiting the same place frequently, you won't have to measure mileage more than once. Getting into the habit of asking for receipts every time you spend money on a business-related transaction, coupled with a simple yet reliable record keeping system could save you lots of dollars at tax time!

21. Filing a U.S. Tax Return?

More and more of our clients are having to file U.S. tax returns as they spend increasing amounts of time down south each year. As well, we have seen some Americans living in Canada who must also file U.S. tax returns, even if they haven't lived in the States in decades.

Are you a potential U.S. tax filer, and aren't sure whether you should file? Better be safe than sorry, since the penalties can (if rarely) be severe.

Filers have until April 15 for the U.S. For non-residents, this is automatically extended to June 15.

Every year, the American I.R.S. mounts a Canadian road show to explain U.S. tax rules. Sessions begin on the East Coast in March, and move on to Toronto, Vancouver, Calgary, Edmonton and Montreal by mid-April.

If you're a 'Snowbird', you may have a requirement to file if you had a 'substantial presence' in the U.S. last year. This usually affects people only if they spend more than four months down south each year. But it's not that simple. Did you spend between 30 and 182 days in the U.S. last year? If so, add up those days, add in one third of the days you spent in the U.S. during 1994, and one-sixth of the days in 1993. If the total exceeds 182, the IRS wants, and expects, to hear from you. This means you have to file something with the IRS, but not necessarily a tax return. If you can show you had a 'closer connection' to Canada than to the U.S., all you need file is what is known as an NR1040 form, where 'NR' stands for, you guessed it, Non-Resident.

If you believe you are in a grey area, and don't want to spend the time attending one of the IRS seminars, then call their Ottawa office at 613-563-1834. I have dealt with this office on many occasions on behalf of my clients, and I can only say I wish Revenue Canada were half as polite and one quarter as knowledgeable!

22.   Capital Gains: An Introduction

The following is the best intro to the complex tax topic of Capital Gains I've seen. It's reprinted from a brochure published by Commercial Union Life. My thanks to Mr. Lester Heldsinger of CU Life for permission to use their material. While the subject of capital gains and losses is a complex one, it's worth getting to know what the concepts mean and how you can avoid making costly mistakes.

Recognized for tax purposes in 1972, capital gains and losses occur when capital property is sold. Property that is sold but is not capital property is simply recognized as income. Unfortunately, there are no clear rules defining capital property although the courts have developed guidelines over the years. You may need to seek professional advice if you're uncertain. It is important to note that there is a fine line between property sold from a business and profits included as income and the profits that can be claimed as a capital gain. **Example:** If you speculate on real estate and you buy and sell a number of properties, your gains on the sales will probably be income rather than capital gains. If, however, your purchase was an isolated transaction and you were to hold the property for a long period of time, any gain on a sale is likely to be a capital gain. Gains or losses are taxable or deductible not only upon the sale, gift or other disposition[1] of property, but also upon the death of an individual taxpayer.

22.1.   Capital Gains

Capital gains are taxed only in the year that the disposition takes place. The basic capital gain calculation is easy to understand: **CAPITAL GAIN** equals **Proceeds of Disposition** (normally the sale price) minus **Selling Expenses** (e.g. repair costs) minus **Adjusted Cost Base (ACB)**.[2] In most cases, the ACB is simply the cost of the property, but the figure can be changed in various ways.

Although taxed at a lower rate than regular income, capital gains taxation is progressive as far as individuals are concerned. See elsewhere herein for the marginal tax rates for various income levels.

22.2.   Capital Losses

It is important that when talking about capital losses we distinguish between ordinary capital losses and allowable business investment losses.

Ordinary capital losses occur when the capital gain calculation produces a negative amount; that is, the adjusted cost base is greater than the proceeds of disposition minus the selling expenses. Just as capital gains are less heavily taxed than regular income, capital losses are less useful to the taxpayer than regular (or business) losses.

---

[1] **Disposition:**

  Actual: results from any transaction or event entitling a taxpayer to proceeds of disposition, e.g. includes sales, exchanges, redemptions, transfers, etc.

  Deemed: examples include: change in use of property, loss of Canadian residence status, property owner's death, transfers by way of gift, etc.

[2] **Adjusted Cost Base** (ACB): The original cost of the property is very often used for the purpose of compiling any capital gain and loss. For depreciable property the ACB equals the capital cost of the property at that time and for non-depreciable property (e.g. real estate property) the ACB is the cost to the taxpayer plus and minus certain adjustments.

An allowable capital loss is three quarters of a capital loss and this amount can be off-set against taxable capital gains. This loss, however, <u>cannot be used against any other income</u>. These allowable capital losses can be carried back or forward and they are then adjusted for any change in capital gains taxation rate.

Allowable business investment losses are an exception to the general rule in that these losses can be used against ordinary income. A capital loss on the shares or debt of a small business corporation is called a "business investment loss". Three-quarters of this amount, the *Allowable Business Investment Loss* (ABIL), can be deducted against any other income such as employment income or investment income. However, the amount of the ABIL which can be deducted against other income must be reduced by any capital gains exemption claimed in prior years. The availability of an ABIL is an extra incentive to investment in private Canadian businesses.

<u>As with regular business losses, these losses can be carried back</u>, and used to off-set income in any of the three previous years; or <u>they can be carried</u> forward and used to offset income in any of the next seven years.

22.3. The Role of Life Insurance

When you die, you are deemed for tax purposes to have sold all of your capital prop-erty, thus, <u>triggering a capital gain on all of the increase in value which has accrued since you purchased it</u>. Where property is left to your spouse, the gain will be put off until your spouse's death, at which point the entire capital gain will be taxed in your spouse's hands. The significance of the tax liability as related to capital gains can be substantial. Many estates are comprised of primarily non-liquid assets, and <u>the burden placed on heirs by this tax liability could force the untimely sale of these assets. Life insurance is undoubtedly the most effective estate planning tool that can be used to either minimize or eliminate this tax liability</u>. The life insurance indus-try has, over the years, produced products that are not only price competitive but also flexible enough to meet constantly changing needs.

23. Income Splitting

Skip this section if you don't want to reduce your income taxes, or if you don't have anyone to split your income with. With the latest federal and provincial budgets, tax rates are higher than they were before tax reform. As can be seen elsewhere herein, Canadians in tax pay a minimum of 53% of all income exceeding $59,000. Indeed, someone receiving OAS actually pays 68% of all income above $59,000 up to about $80,000, thanks to the infamous claw-back tax! On the other hand, those with incomes of less than $30,000 pay only 27% of their last dollar as tax. In fact, someone over age 65 can have $11,000 tax-free! It is quite possible to have a household where one taxpayer is in a 68% tax bracket while at least one other family member pays no tax at all. If one person in such a household can shift, say, $1,000 in taxable income to another, the tax savings amount to 68%, or <u>$680 in after-tax dollars!</u> This shifting of taxable income is known as income splitting.

There are a number of perfectly legal techniques for income splitting which usually takes place between spouses. However, any two people can income-split, including common-law spouses, parent/child, and even trusting friends. What's important is that one of the two is in a higher marginal tax bracket than the other and, by splitting some of the income, net after-tax savings are equivalent to the marginal rate differential multiplied by the income shifted; i.e. if $10,000 is shifted by someone in a 68% tax rate to someone with a rate of only 27%, the <u>after-tax saving</u> is no less than $4,100! These after-tax savings are not only available for the current tax year, but for every year down the road until governments reduce the increments between tax brackets and/or until the techniques described below are ruled invalid.

Before outlining the more popular techniques, caution: the federal government knows it is losing substantial revenues through income splitting, particularly between spouses and between parents and children. They have reduced the attractiveness of cross-investments by family members with so-called attribution rules, discussed in the next article. So, how to split income? Some of the more popular methods include:

Spousal RRSPs: probably the most effective single technique available to the largest number of taxpayers. Up to $13,500 of earned income may be invested in the lower-income spouse's RRSP with the tax deduction claimed by the higher-income spouse.

Salary/Wages/Commissions: the higher-rate taxpayer pays a consideration to a lower-rate taxpayer for work or services performed or rendered. The person paid must, of course, have done something to justify the consideration; the consideration must be reasonable in the circumstance; the consideration must be deductible from taxable income by the payer; the transaction should be documented. Most commonly used by self-employed or commissioned taxpayers who are allowed to claim expenses, and/or by taxpayers with investment income to secure help/advice/assistance to manage their investments. Common examples include a spouse acting as secretary to the other spouse, or a parent paying a child to help maintain a rental property.

Two-Income Households: lower-income earner 'banks' entire after-tax income for subsequent investment income and consequent taxation at lower rates, while higher-income earner pays all household expenses.

Child Benefits: while not significant in any one year (about $400 currently), these can be invested by one parent such that the intended eventual owner is identified as the child. Tax on any resultant income is attributed to the child rather than the parent. Over a dozen or more years, such a strategy can result in a pool of capital easily worth $10,000 per child.

Splitting CPP Benefits: two married people combine their CPP benefits and then split 50/50. See elsewhere herein for details.

Asset Purchase/Sale: a taxpayer lending/giving funds to a lower-rate taxpayer for subsequent investment income may be affected by income attribution rules (see below). Such rules do not apply, however, if a taxpayer buys assets from another. For example, a spouse can purchase another spouse's asset(s) whereby the selling spouse now has the funds to purchase income-producing assets. This technique is often used by a family to re-structure asset investments to minimize taxation on the family unit as a whole. Let us assume the high rate spouse has bonds earning 10% who is in a 68% tax bracket, and who has a partner (spouse, child, friend) in a 27% bracket with tangible assets (as in, for instance, a cottage or principal residence). The bond-owner is really only earning about 3.2% after tax (and before inflation). The bond-owner would sell the bonds and buy the other's asset (or portion) with the seller re-investing the proceeds. Assuming a re-investment at the same rate, i.e. 10%, the seller now nets over 7% after tax! This technique is also employed by high-tax-rate dividend earners.

Cash-Value Life Insurance: regardless of who is insured, the <u>owner</u> should be the lower-income taxpayer, while the <u>premium</u> payer should be the higher taxpayer. Thus, when taxable cash is subsequently taken out, as at, for instance, retirement, those taxable benefits are accrued to the lower tax rate payer (note: this does <u>not</u> apply to death benefits, which are tax-free to the beneficiary in any event). Current owners of older cash value insurance contracts should review their tax positions and whether the ownership is by the lowest tax rate family member. Life insurance contracts may be absolutely assigned ('given') between most family members with <u>no</u> tax liability to the original owner.

As can be seen above, someone with taxable income of as little as $59,000 is paying no less than 53% on his or her last dollar of income (<u>before</u> applicable Clawback tax)! So, if that taxpayer has someone at home with taxable income below $59,000, there is a splendid opportunity to save plenty of tax dollars by income splitting. Neither the 1996 or 1995 budgets have affected the wide range of family income splitting techniques that are still valid, and more valuable than even before.

One income splitting technique that we're seeing more and more of is: **Nepotism!** That's where you hire a family member to help with your business, or with matters directly related to your earning commissions, or, where your employer insists, where you maintain an office at home. Your child over 18 can also be hired to augment/replace your baby-sitter where what you pay your child, within certain limits, become tax-deductible child care expenses to you.

We've seen children as young as five or six placed on the family payroll if they can lick stamps, stuff envelopes, or swing a broom. You can pay each of your children up to $2,670 per year without losing any of your child dependency tax credit claim. You can also pay your spouse (or your equivalent to spouse child, if a single parent) up to $534 where that spouse has no other income, and you still keep all of the tax benefit of a married dependent claim! Just make sure the work you are paying wages for is reasonable under the circumstances, and that the work does get done!

24.   Attribution Rules

Where funds are transferred between two parties and taxable income is generated by the recipient, there may be taxable income attributed back to transferor by Revenue Canada (see table above).

25.   Declaration of Taxpayer Rights

Many readers have expressed concern with what they can expect when communicating with Revenue Canada about their tax situations. Herewith from Revenue Canada's own policy: The constitution and laws of Canada entitle you to many rights that protect you in matters of income tax. You are entitled to know your rights. You are entitled to insist on them. You are entitled to be heard, and to be dealt with fairly. Helping you exercise your rights remains an important role of the staff of Revenue Canada at its district offices and other locations. Fair treatment of a complaint is one

Attribution Rules

Type of Transaction	Spouse	Child, sibling niece/nephew under 18	Child over 18 or close relative
Gift	Investment income or losses and capital gains or losses attributed to transferor.	Investment income or losses but not capital gains or losses attributed.	No Attribution
Sale	Must elect fair market value, or prescribed rate, whichever is less; otherwise investment income + capital gains or losses attributed.	Sale must be at fair market value, else investment income — but not capital gains or losses attributed to transferor.	No Attribution
Loan	Must bear interest at prescribed rate, else investment income or losses and capital gains and losses are attributed.	Must bear interest at prescribed rate, else investment income or losses but not capital gains and losses are attributed.	Ditto to para. on left.

Notes: There will be no attribution when transferring to earn business income. Attribution rules may apply to property transfers between close business associates who are not family members.

of your greatest rights. Fair treatment in all dealings with Revenue Canada means important rights to:

Information: You are entitled to expect the government will make every reasonable effort to provide you with access to full, accurate and timely information about the Income Tax Act, and your rights under it.

Impartiality: You are entitled to impartial determination of law and facts by departmental staff who seek to collect only the correct amount of tax, no more and no less.

Courtesy and Consideration: You are entitled to courtesy and considerate treatment from Revenue at all times, including when it requests information or arranges interviews and audits.

Presumption of Honesty: You are entitled to be presumed honest unless there is evidence to the contrary.

Fair treatment under the constitution and laws of Canada includes important rights to:

Privacy and Confidentiality: In addition to other constitutional and legal rights, you have a special right that personal and financial information you provide to Revenue will be used only for purposes allowed by law.

Independent Review: You are entitled to object to an assessment or reassessment if you think the law has been applied incorrectly. To protect this right, you must file your objection within 90 days of assessment or reassessment. Filing objection starts an independent review by departmental appeals officers. If they don't resolve the matter to your satisfaction, they will explain how you can appeal to the courts.

An Impartial Hearing Before Payment: Until you have had an impartial review by the Department or a court, you may withhold amounts disputed in formal objections. If you appeal to a higher court, you will be able to provide equivalent security instead of paying those disputed amounts. Certain exceptions, set out in legislation to guarantee these rights, are applicable to frivolous appeals to the courts, or where collection is clearly in jeopardy.

Bilingual Services: The Official Languages Act gives you the right to communicate with and receive services from Revenue Canada in either official language.

You are entitled to every benefit allowed by the law. You have the right to arrange your affairs in order to pay the minimum required by law. You can also expect your government to administer tax law consistently, and to apply it firmly to those who try to avoid paying their lawful share.

26.   Good Reads

If you want to learn more about Canada's tax system, a paperback by Linda McQuaig, *Behind Closed Doors*, is excellent. Written from a middle-income earner's point of view, the book describes the evolution of the system, paying particular attention to the Carter Royal Commission recommendations of the 1960s, and Wilson's tax reform of the late 1980s. Very readable. Sticker price about $8.99.

If you're determined to do your own return but find Revenue Canada's Tax Guide just doesn't have enough information, then get a copy of the *CCH Tax Guide*, revised every year and usually available early in the new year. Chock full of examples and lots of tips on tax planning, this is the guide Revenue Canada's own staff use when dealing with the public! Sticker price about $15.

For those concerned about Revenue Canada taxing real property, excluding principal residences, as announced in their 1992 budget a paperback by John Budd published by McGraw-Hill Ryerson at $12.95 called *Second Property Strategies*, is a must. Written for the layperson with lots of easy to follow examples.

Royal Trust has published a 49-page tax and estate planning guide called *The Cottage: Keeping It In The Family and Away From the Taxman.* Like *Second Property*, this is not a do-it-yourself guide, but more a list of points to consider discussing with your financial advisor. For a free copy, write to Royal Trust Image Services, Attn: Cottage Succession Booklet; 115 Thorncliffe Park Dr, Toronto M4H 1M1. Most of their branches will <u>not</u> have copies.

Spending a lot of time in the U.S.? Have assets down there? Then you should be worried about taxes, and the different treatments accorded various income types, and asset types between the two countries and, in the U.S., the various States and municipalities, not to mention U.S. death taxes. Published by CCH Canadian, *Canada/U.S. Transfers* makes fascinating reading. It's difficult to follow because the tax systems in each country are so dissimilar. But the book should give the reader a better appreciation of the need for expert advice to prevent double- or over-taxation of either income or assets, or both. Steep sticker price of $34.95 is tax-deductible by those who have investment properties. Call your local CCH Canadian office and ask for Book # 4045. Should be available in your local library.

Personal Finance for Canadians, by Kathleen Brown (Prentice Hall Canada, $26.75). Reads like a community college text; good source for technical details of financial planning including time/value of money.

It's Your Money, by Brian Anderson And Chris Snyder (Metheun, $16.95). Good overall text dealing with wide range of topics.

How to Beat the Taxman All Year Round, by Brian Costello (Stoddart, $14.95). Entertaining style characteristic of broadcaster/journalist Costello is a bit hard to take, but 118 tips are reliable and substantive; lots of white space!

The 1995 Home Tax Plus (Merisel, $49.95) is an update on Costello's earlier tax works. Paperback updated versions of his *Your Money and How to Keep It* ($12.95) and *Making Money From Your Mortgage* ($14) are good value.

The Money Coach; Your Game Plan for Growth, Tax Relief and Security, by Riley Moynes (Copp Clark Pitman, $10.95). Up-to-date, well laid out and sensible.

Planning For a Successful Retirement and *Retirement As You Like It*, both free, both published by the Canadian Life and Health Insurance Association. The first is written for a younger audience while the latter is aimed at those planning on retiring within 5 to 10 years. Both excellent and can be ordered by calling 1-800-268-8099.

The Wealthy Barber; Everyone's Common Sense Guide to Becoming Financially Independent, by David Chilton (Stoddart, $15). A combination of a novel and a guide to financial planning; has been on the best seller list for well over a year. Some of the best advice around.

The Money Doctor by Ken Wharram (Macmillan, $15). A good intro reference source; includes material on divorce and wills.

The Kitchen Table Money Plan, by Barbara McNeil and Robert Collins (Harper Collins, $15). Easy-to-use reference, short chapters, good index.

The Deloitte Touche *Canadian Guide to Personal Financial Management* (Prentice-Hall, $17). Updated annually; has been around for years; prepared by a team of C.A.s; lots of room to record your own info and objectives.

How to Survive Without a Salary, by Charles Long (Warwick Publishing Group, $13).

The Counsel Self-Help publishers, Vancouver, have put out a wide array of self-help publications on everything from divorce to probate to wills to power of attorney to selling your home. Usually written by lawyers, or specialists within the topic matter, material is always easy to read and comprehend by the layperson; lots of examples; blank pre-approved forms for many provinces included or available as kits separately; usually between $10 and $15. *GASletter* uses this material more than any other source. Their list of titles is too long to publish here; just about any bookstall or stationery carries these on a revolving rack; seldom does any one book store have all of their titles in stock at any one time.

We're often asked to recommend reading material to help women with their financial planning. Here are four books:

The Retirement Answer Book, by Gail Vaz-Oxlade (Stoddart Publishing, 181 pages, $9.95).

Balancing Act: A Canadian Women's Financial Survival Guide, by Joanne Thomas Yaccato (Prentice Hall Canada, 272 pages, $16.95).

Financial Strategies for Women: The Basics, by Shirley Neal (Women's Investment Network Inc., 159 pages, $12.95).

Becoming the Wealthy Woman, by Henry Cimmer (Springbank Publishing, 223 pages, $15.95).

27. Tax Shelter?

Considering the purchase of one of the numerous tax shelters available on the market? Some advice:

- The most common deduction arises from the interest cost on the money you borrow to invest with.
- Other deductions include Capital Cost Allowance and other special depreciation deductions, as well as soft costs. Soft costs are the costs of doing business when the promoters of the tax shelter create the limited partnership syndication. All of these costs have the effect of increasing initial losses, which in turn affect the amount of capital gains exemption available by affecting CNIL.
- Research is key to purchasing a good limited partnership.
- Assess the investment on its own business merits. A tax shelter will reduce your taxes, but a dollar of cash is always better than a dollar of tax deduction. Make sure your investment will provide the rest of the cash necessary to cover the expense.
- The investment should give a profitable return at some point in time, preferably when you are in a lower tax bracket, not a higher one.
- It should be a quality product, with a market demand, offered with management expertise, experience and a proven track record.

An example of what not to do: the author in the mid-seventies bought two tax shelter units in a 'made-in-Canada' movie for a total of $10,000. This tax shelter saved him over $4,000 in tax immediately. Since then, the investment has returned less than $3,000 in royalties. There is no market to sell the investment on. Not one of our better ideas.

28. Life Insurance as Tax Shelter

A tax shelter that anyone, even those who are uninsurable, can take advantage of is 'tax-exempt' life insurance. In a single contract, you can get life insurance protection plus tax-free investment earnings. And you can do so with contracts on any close member of your family, not just on yourself. One of Canada's top accounting firms, Coopers and Lybrand, recently recommended, in their annual tax planning checklist, exempt whole life contracts as an excellent long-term investment either for taxpayers or their beneficiaries. Not only can these policies be borrowed against, usually at favorable rates compared to conventional bank loans, they offer the significant advantage of virtually tax-free compounding at current rates of return over a long term. Such contracts may be a very powerful tax planning tool, especially when integrated with the plans of other family members, particularly spouses, children and grandchildren. Exempt life insurance combines the attraction of tax-free benefits to beneficiaries upon death coupled with tax-free accumulation of cash values while the assured remains alive. This tax shelter is particularly attractive to those who have already used up their RRSP limits, or for those who want to leave their children tax-free investments, or to those who know their estates will have significant income tax on death. Exempt life insurance is a tax planning tool that should not be overlooked, particularly by those in higher tax brackets.

29. Support Payments

When it comes to tax treatment of support payments between ex-spouses, the traps are many for the unwary. Arrangements usually allow one party to deduct the payment made from taxable income while the recipient includes such in calculating taxable income. Because of this, there will be dissimilar incentives on the part of both giver and recipient as to respective declaration of amounts disbursed or received. To be taxable or deductible, payments must be made as a result of a court order or under a written agreement between the parties. The parties must be living apart from each other pursuant to a written separation agreement. Payments must be periodic, not lump sums. A financial agreement, of and by itself, is not sufficient. There must be a written agreement that the parties are separated. Payments over and above those called for under a court order or written agreement are not deductible nor included as taxable income. On the other hand, payments that fall short of what are called for under order or agreement may not be over-stated for tax purposes to the amounts specified in the order/agreement. The temptation by the recipient to claim an amount different from that being claimed by the donor should be resisted unless the recipient has incurred legal or other expenses deductible from support payment income. This is especially so since Revenue Canada now electronically match tax returns from former spouses quite easily. If in doubt, secure professional advice to prevent costly misunderstandings with your not-so-friendly taxman.

If your ex-spouse has moved to the States, child support payments you receive here in Canada are free of Canadian (and U.S.) income tax! You are supposed to report such income, but you then get to deduct it on line 256 of your T1 tax return. And what if you pay support to someone who's moved south of the border? Normally, there's a 25% withholding tax you're supposed to deduct and remit to Revenue Canada. But, this amount may subsequently be recaptured, at least in part, at tax filing time, if the country you're sending support payments to has a tax treaty with Canada. But there are no withholding requirements for support payments you send to the U.S. and, unfortunately, you can't deduct the payments from your Canadian taxable income, either. So, arrange that your support payments are sent to a Canadian address, if possible!

30. Farming

Quite a few of our clients and subscribers own farms. Others plan to acquire one, if only as an investment in some cases, and if only as a retreat/retirement location for others. For many years, losses from farms were fully deductible from other taxable income, allowing many 'gentlemen' farmers, the author included some 25 years ago, to reap substantial tax concessions from 'operating' a money-losing farm. In effect, the federal, and therefore, provincial, governments subsidized such operations with tax dollars. It is still possible to deduct losses from unprofitable farming from other taxable income, but the rules have been tightened up in recent years. If farming is in your plans, then you should read on. Revenue Canada now distinguishes between full-time farmers, part-time farmers, and hobby-farmers. Each is entitled to claim losses, but in a diminishing scale of eligibility and under different litmus tests.

A full-time farmer has no difficulty claiming losses from other taxable income (presumably investment income, or from earned income on weekends and night-work), if he or she keeps a decent set of books. Part-time and hobby-farmers must, however, in order to claim losses, be able to demonstrate to Revenue Canada's satisfaction that they had an expectation of eventually making a profit. Hobby-farmers, as well, are restricted to the first $2,500 of losses plus half of the next $12,500 to a maximum of $8,750 per year. The litmus test of profit expectation down the road will be more severe on hobby farmers than on part-timers. If only as a wise business decision in any case, the potential farmer is well advised, as is any business person, to draw up as comprehensive a business plan as possible when starting out, revising and updating that plan anytime there is significant variance from the original plan.

Profit expectation of would-be part-time and hobby-farmers is further evaluated by Revenue Canada by looking at the time spent farming, the person's prior experience in farming, the amount of capital employed, and the extent (i.e. acreage) of the business. Just because your neighbour got away with a loss claim doesn't mean you will, nor vice versa.

Activities defined by Revenue Canada, or by the Tax Act, as farming are surprisingly wide ranging. Operations that are considered working farms include exhibiting livestock, poultry, or racehorses, fur farming, fruit growing, bee keeping, raising trees, fish or wild game farming, greenhouse operation, market gardening, operating a nursery or chicken hatchery all qualify! Even if deducting losses from other taxable income is now somewhat curtailed by the above rules, there is still considerable financial attraction to those wanting to operate a working farm because on sale, the owner of such an operation qualifies for a $400,000 taxable capital gain exemption in addition to his/her $100,000 personal capital gains exemption. So, for a married couple, up to $1 million in profit from the sale of a farm, profitable or otherwise, is tax free!

31.   Salary or Dividends?

The recession has made tax planning that much more valuable, especially for small business owners. There are many things to consider when establishing a tax strategy, but for business owner operators, probably the most important consideration will be whether to pay oneself salary or dividends.

Salary is employment income which is subject to tax. It can consist of true salary, commissions, or bonuses declared by year-end and paid within 180 days of year-end. The amount of salary paid directly affects RRSP contribution limits, CPP contributions (and, therefore, benefits at retirement), UIC (and UI benefits, if unemployed), and in many provinces, health insurance plans.

Dividends, on the other hand, are distributions of company profits to shareholders. Because corporate income tax has been paid by the company on its profits, the federal Tax Act allows that dividends will be taxed at a lower rate to individuals than will the same amount of salary. This is to avoid double-taxation. The Tax Act achieves lower tax on dividends to individuals by means of the dividend tax credit. Because of the dividend tax credit, an individual could receive up to $25,000 of dividends each year tax-free, if there was no other income.

Unlike salary, dividends don't enter the computations for determining how much can be contributed to RRSPs, how much UI premiums have to be paid, how much

CPP will expect in premiums, nor how much the payroll health tax will amount to. Therefore, careful planning will be necessary by the owners of small businesses where such owners also work for the business. This planning will be influenced by how much the share owner/employee will want to put aside in his/her RSP nest egg, whether he/she will want to be covered by UIC, whether he/she expects to need any CPP benefits at retirement (and whether, in fact, there will still be a CPP payment stream when he/she retires), and how much payroll tax to pay for provincial health premiums.

To use *GASletter*/Stevens Financial Services as an example, the owner operator doesn't consider CPP benefits, for which he won't qualify for another seven years, as being that worthwhile, and so wants to pay the minimum in CPP contributions. He also knows that in Ontario, self-employed individuals are covered under provincial health plans for free, as long as income remains below $40,000, so medicare payroll taxes have been held to a minimum (i.e. zero). Since shareholders of more than 40% of a company's stock are exempted from UIC payments, he has elected to keep out of the UI system, and is therefore unprotected in case of 'layoff'! So, he pays himself just enough in self-employed commissions so that income tax is offset by tax credits, and pays himself the balance of his remuneration by way of dividends, taxed at a low 'small-business' rate by the companies he owns. Meanwhile, retained earnings within the companies that have not been paid out by way of dividends are accumulating within the companies, which will eventually be his 'retirement savings plan'. And instead of having regular employees on the payroll, his 'staff' consists of contracted self-employed who make their own CPP arrangements at tax time, and who aren't covered by UIC.

As can be seen from the above, there is an almost unlimited number of permutations and combinations available to the owner/manager of a corporation as to remuneration and deductions for welfare, health and savings programs. For such owner/managers, careful planning can reap substantial tax and other benefits.

32.   Individual Pension Plans

After years of uneven pension laws in Canada, the Federal Government has finally moved in the direction of equity. In a sweeping set of revisions to the Pension Standards Act, which included revised and improved RRSP contribution limits and deductions for most income earners, discussed elsewhere herein, the government has introduced a new Individual Pension Plan feature that appears to provide long overdue tax relief and increased retirement benefits for some owner managers and many higher-income employees and professionals.

In the past, a high-income person working, for example, for the federal civil service, would be permitted a substantial pension plan where yearly contributions would far exceed his RRSP contribution limits. However, a self-employed individual, or one on commissions, or a professional, was for all practical purposes limited to the much lower maximum RRSP contribution limits even though he might have the same or even higher income than the more fortunately placed civil servant just mentioned.

Pension tax reform, including increased RRSP contribution limits has dramatically altered the rules governing tax assisted retirement savings schemes. One innovation allows owner managers and higher-income employees the opportunity to have an Individual Pension Plan, or IPP, customized to their requirements.

The basic benefit in an IPP is that it permits greater contributions into a tax-sheltered plan than would be possible with an RRSP. There are a number of factors which make an IPP attractive to only a small segment of the working population. For example, an employee should be at least five years away from 'retirement' and not contemplating a change in employers for a similar period of time, since IPP start-up costs would likely outweigh the benefits compared to more traditional RRSP contributions. Also, a person should be at least 38 years of age, otherwise, again, RRSP contributions are likely more effective than an IPP. Income should exceed $100,000 per year, consistently. Lastly, and this is where the high-income civil servant would be at a disadvantage, at least for the next few years, the employer must be willing to offer this benefit.

An IPP's benefits vary from case to case. However, as an example, a 45-year-old, earning $100,000 per year, would have an IPP worth over $500,000 by age 65, compared to not much more than $300,000 under conventional RRSP contribution limits at current interest rates.

An IPP may also be customized to the individual's estate planning needs. Like RRSPs at life insurance companies, IPP's are creditor proof when a family member is named as beneficiary, for the same reason: all IPPs must be with life companies. As well, contributions are not subject to provincial employer health taxes, a decided advantage in some provinces, such as Ontario, which now collect a payroll tax in lieu of individual OHIP premiums.

There are drawbacks to IPPs, namely: they are totally locked in unlike most RRSPs. They can only be used to fund retirement, unlike many RRSPs that are subsequently cashed to fund maternity leaves, sabbaticals and unemployment. There are set-up and administration costs, as well as registration and reporting formalities. Each individual's tax situation must be examined in detail by an expert before a plan is initiated. Not all observers agree that an IPP is more advantageous than individual RRSPs. Nevertheless, IPPs appear to represent a major step toward pension equity.

33.   Interprovince Move Cuts Taxes

Combined Federal/Provincial income tax rates in several provinces now exceed 50%. Indeed, Ontario is now at 54% on income exceeding $60,000. For those individuals expecting receipt of large amounts of taxable income, it may pay handsomely to plan a move to a less onerous taxation province, such as Alberta, where the combined Federal/Provincial rate is only 46%.

I sometimes see people receive large one-shot sums for loss of employment (only part of which can be rolled-over tax-free to an RSP), or as a result of a specific transaction (e.g. book royalty; sale of a business). When received, these amounts must be added to the individual's other taxable income for the year of receipt, and taxed at that person's top marginal tax rate. If the payment can be taxed as a resident of a low rate province by virtue of a little tax planning and a move, then substantial amounts of income tax can be saved.

For example, the tax that would be saved on a $1 million taxable receipt by moving from Ontario to Alberta would amount to no less than $80,000 (even more if you moved to the Northwest Territories: $100,000). These tax savings would more than pay for the actual moving costs, both to the low tax-rate province, and back again. Now that 75% of all capital gains are taxable at a person's top marginal tax rate, the same rationale applies to capital gains.

Note that you don't have to sell your principal residence or your business in order to take up residence in another province. All you need is an address where you were on December 31. Many years ago, this author was representing a high-tech company when he found himself visiting Edmonton on December 31. At tax time, he filed as a resident of Ontario, and then remembered several months later he was in Alberta on December 31. He wrote a short note to Revenue Canada and a few weeks later, received a notice of re-assessment based on Alberta residency, and a nice refund cheque!

Note also that if you earn income at the new location, your moving costs are tax deductible! Ditto if you move back whence you came!

34.   Stop Free Loans to Federal Government

Earlier this summer, we read all manner of accounts how Revenue Canada were so pleased to announce they had mailed refunds totalling so many billions to taxpayers. Fact is, almost everyone who receives a tax refund is guilty of poor financial planning. Fact also is that where a taxpayer is getting a refund, it means the federal government has been using their money for most of the year, interest-free!

It's worth noting the government tilted the playing field even more, recently, when legislation was passed saying Revenue Canada owes you interest only 45 days after the filing deadline (or the filing date, if you're late), while you, on the other hand, owe interest from the due date (i.e. April 30). So, now, Revenue Canada are using your refund money for most of the tax year interest-free, and won't pay you interest on your refund until mid-June!

The playing field tilted even more in Revenue Canada's favour recently when, thanks to the last Federal Budget, Revenue Canada now charges you 2% more on what you owe the government, compared to what they will pay you on overdue refunds!

What all of the above boils down to is that over-paying your taxes before filing your return is just about the worst investment you could possibly make, even if you do get a large charge out of getting a refund cheque. Because it's not a tax refund, it's a refund of your money which the government just happens to have been using without paying you one cent for that privilege!

If your only source of income each year is from an employer, and you have no significant deductions, then your refund cheque is probably going to be for less than $100. No problem. But if you're like most people, you will have made RSP contributions, charitable donations, made support payments to a former spouse, or operate a business, each of which will likely cause you a substantial refund (read: more than $100!) each year. There's no reason why you should allow that to continue! All you have to do is contact your district tax office, who will allow you, after providing an explanation, to adjust your source deductions at your place of employment. Similarly, if you are retired, and have been in the habit of making quarterly instalment payments, only to have much of those instalments returned to you each year, cut back on the amount you send in each quarter, even if it means ignoring Revenue Canada's suggestive letters!

Past experience shows, however, that despite such advice as the above, countless Canadians love over-paying during the year, and providing the government with interest-free use of their money, if only because they get a real kick out of getting a refund check. If this applies to you, ask yourself: Would you consciously overpay your monthly mortgage payments in the hope you'll get an interest-free refund when your mortgage is paid up?

35. Profit Expectation Key for Business

Starting a business from a hobby usually results in deductions of losses from other taxable income during the early years. Revenue Canada takes the position that a business which does not have a profit expectation is, in reality, only a hobby. Therefore, if you have recently started a business, or intend to, make sure that you operate your business from day one with the expectation of making a profit, even if you subsequently turn a loss for the first few years.

Renting out a spare bedroom will be considered by Revenue Canada as purely a hobby if you can't show that you had reasonable expectations of making a profit from the operation, even if your plans were temporarily derailed by unexpectedly high mortgage interest rates! If you expect that your new business will show a loss for the first few years before then becoming profitable, it is imperative you draw up a business plan showing in as much detail as possible just how you will be eventually profitable. Without such a business plan, and in the event of an audit, you will likely be adjudged by Revenue Canada as indulging a hobby as opposed to running a bona fide business.

36.   Are Taxes Higher Elsewhere?

We've often stated herein that income taxes in Canada are about the highest in the world, exceeded perhaps only by France. Recently, a study was conducted by Ernst and Young, a major international accounting firm, of what individuals pay in the Group of Seven countries, plus a few others. Here's a breakdown (all figures expressed in Canadian dollars except for the U.S.):

U.S.: The top federal marginal rate is 39.6% on taxable income exceeding $250,000, although state and local taxes can add 12% or more to that. Capital gains are taxed at two rates: long-term gains are taxed at 28% while short-term gains (realized on investments of less than 1 year), are taxed at the top marginal rate. Both interest <u>and</u> dividends are taxed at 39.6%, although some state and local debt securities are tax exempt. Estate taxes can be as high as 55%, although a credit of $192,800 is available to offset these.

Britain: Income above $52,000 taxed at 40%. Capital gains also taxed at 40%, although first $12,700 of gains tax-free each year. Inheritances in excess of $328,000 taxed at 40%.

France: Income exceeding $75,000 taxed at 57%. Capital gains taxed at 19%, except for some (speculative) real estate gains, which are taxed at 57%. Estate taxes as high as 60%. First $2,200 of interest and dividends each year tax-exempt.

Germany: Top tax rate is 53% on income exceeding $117,000. First $5,800 of interest, dividends, royalties, and real estate income each year exempt. Estate taxes are as high as 70% if the heir not related to the deceased; otherwise 35% after an exemption on the first $240,000.

Italy: 51% on income exceeding $244,000, not including local taxes, which can add 16%. Interest and dividends taxed at top rate. Capital gains taxed at a flat 25%. Inheritances taxed at a maximum of 33%.

Japan: Top tax rate is 65% on income exceeding $325,000, including regional and local taxes. However, first $49,000 of income taxed at only 20%. Dividends taxed at flat 35%. Capital gains taxed at top marginal rate. Estate taxes range from 10% on $12,000 to 70% on $16+ million.

Australia: Top marginal rate is 47% on amounts exceeding $49,500. Capital gains fully taxed, though adjusted for inflation. Dividends taxed fully as income, less an allowance for dividend-tax-credit. Interest, royalties, and real estate income fully taxed at top marginal rate. No estate taxes.

Sweden: Top rate is 50% on incomes exceeding $36,500, including local taxes. Capital gains taxed at 30%. Swedish corporation dividends are tax-free. Inheritance tax is 30%.

Isle of Man, Cayman Islands and most other 'tax havens': no taxes of any kind to non-resident owners of investments located therein; minimal income taxes of usually less than 5% on resident incomes; minor inheritance taxes on residents.

CANADA: By comparison, income exceeding $60,000 taxed at 55% (differs slightly by province); interest, royalties, and dividends fully taxed as income at top marginal rate, though a small tax credit is given on Canadian dividends; 75% of all capital gains taxed at top marginal tax rate. Seniors over age 65 pay an extra 15% on top of 55% (i.e. 70% total) until their income exceeds $85,000. Estate taxes run to 70% on registered 'retirement' assets, plus up to 5% for probate fees, depending on province of domicile.

You be the judge! For income earners, it can be argued there are more heavily taxed jurisdictions than Canada. But for seniors, taxes of 70% on income exceeding only $60,000, plus a further inheritance tax of up to 75% are easily the most onerous of the countries surveyed.

37.   Airline Points Taxable

In a recent Tax Court decision, Revenue Canada was upheld in trying to tax the value of free airline points when cashed in by an employee for personal or family use. We know lots of people (ourselves included) who are entitled to personally trade in points accumulated on airline trips paid for by their employers or their personally owned businesses for 'vacation' trips for themselves or family members free of further cost.

Revenue Canada has been attempting to force such individuals to claim as a taxable benefit the value of the transportation so obtained otherwise free of cost.

The Tax Court did mollify taxpayers by coming up with a formula for estimating the value of a free ticket for inclusion as a taxable benefit that ends up being much less onerous than what Revenue Canada was pushing for. What Revenue Canada wanted was to tax the replacement cost of the free ticket with equivalent service class, at full cost.

For example, say enough points were converted to end up with an economy class ticket that would otherwise have cost $1,000, Revenue Canada was determined to include $1,000 as a fully taxable benefit (at the taxpayer's top marginal tax rate).

What the Tax Court has ruled, instead, is that because such free tickets often have exclusions and restrictions, the amount to be computed for inclusion as a taxable benefit is the cost of the cheapest advance-purchase ticket available for that route. Typically, an economy class ticket costing $1,000 covers a route for which a discounted ticket would cost only $200 to $400.

Should you start to claim the value of your free tickets as a taxable benefit on your tax returns?

We would say no, since it would seem to be more properly the employer's responsibility of calculating and reporting the value of free tickets, since most employers have access to the employee's 'frequent flyer' point totals. Bet you, however, Revenue Canada would not agree with this interpretation. But ignorance continues to be a good defence at audit time!!!

38.   Car Allowances

Beginning 1996, Revenue Canada now allows those that are permitted to claim auto expenses to claim $0.33 per kilometer instead of calculating actual operating costs. The old rate, for a number of years, had been $0.31.

Readers will recall an article in last year's edition in which it was revealed Members of Parliament had voted themselves an increase in their mileage allowances to $0.367 per kilometer, while federal bureaucrats were given a raise to $0.37 per kilometer on their expense statements. It was my advice in that article (reproduced in the *GASletter Collection*, 5th ed., p. 18), that until Revenue Canada raised their rates, taxpayers who are allowed to do so should claim $0.37 per kilometer, with effect from 1995. That advice remains constant, despite what Revenue Canada has just announced. I feel if the federal government itself can claim $0.37, then taxpayers should also!

Meanwhile, for those employees whose employer-owned vehicles have all operating expenses (including personal mileage) paid for by their employers, Revenue Canada announces that with effect from 1996, the value to be computed for inclusion in taxable income as a taxable benefit to the employee is at the rate of $0.13 per kilometer, versus $0.12 previously. Sounds reasonable.

39.   Canadians Poor Tax Planners

Most Canadians were found to be docile taxpayers, not the aggressive tax planners today's high tax rates demand, according to survey results. They even seem ready, as with many other aspects of Canadian life, to bear their allotted tax burden without much of a struggle.

More than half the respondents said they had no plans to take advantage of any tax shelters (such as RSPs) this year, while almost half said they probably hadn't fully used the tax shelters available in previous years. In fact, the survey found most Canadians don't spend much time, at all, planning their income taxes. When looking for tax advice, most don't seek professional help, but instead rely on friends, newspapers, or other sources of information available for example on book shelves.

The results should be very disconcerting to firms that sell tax advice, and to Ernst and Young in particular, the firm that commissioned the survey.

While Ernst and Young admitted there wasn't much someone earning less than $30,000 could do in the way of tax planning, they went on to state that those earning a high taxable income (i.e. over $60,000) were likely missing many dollars of tax savings by not seeking professional advice.

So when's the best time of the year to do some tax planning? Definitely not February, or April either. In our experience, our clients make the most effective tax plans in November/December, for the future, not the past. In other words, the best tax plans are hatched in a proactive manner, not in a reactive knee-jerk to an expected large tax bill.

40. Federal Government Retreats on Year-Ends

In his February 1995 Budget, the federal Finance Minister proposed to do away with the ability of unincorporated businesses to have fiscal year-ends other than December 31. For decades, such businesses were able to effectively defer, by up to eleven months, the reporting (and hence, the taxation) of taxable income to the owners of such businesses.

Perhaps because the federal government is so desperately short of ways to raise yet more income tax, the Minister proposed to force all unincorporated businesses to declare their fiscal years, for income tax purposes, to end on December 31. This would have forced many businesses to declare taxable income much earlier than many owners had expected, or been able to pay tax on.

After a huge hue and cry from the business community, the federal government has relented, at least partially. Now, unincorporated businesses will be allowed to keep their previous year-ends, but will have to go through a complicated formula to calculate how much income should be brought forward to the previous tax year for the purpose of calculation of current tax. Most such businesses will be forced to retain professional help to get through the next business tax reporting cycle, ending this April 30.

41. Canada/U.S. Tax Treaty

The tax treaty between Canada and the U.S. was finally ratified late 1995, bringing many welcome changes to the taxation of assets and income earned in one country by taxpayers of the other. The pact is the result of nearly five years of discussions and negotiations between the two countries, and should go a long way to improving free trade of capital and individuals between the largest two trading partners in the world.

The major changes affecting individuals include:

- Canadians owning U.S. real estate, shares of American companies and bonds from U.S. issuers get substantial relief from the threat of U.S. estate taxes when they die. Rebates on such estate taxes already paid since 10 November 1988 may now be obtainable. Until now, estates of Canadians with U.S. property faced both Canadian capital gains tax and U.S. estate tax, with no offsetting credits. Under the treaty, estates worth less than $US1.2 million will face U.S. tax only on U.S. real estate and personal business property, the former exempt up to a value of $US600,000. Where U.S. estate tax is paid, Revenue Canada will grant offsetting credits against Canadian tax related to the deceased's U.S. holdings.

- As of 1 January, the two countries have revamped taxation of public pension payments to cross-border retirees. Up till January, retirees paid tax only in the country where they lived, based on half their payments. Under the new treaty, Ottawa now levies 25% withholding tax on CPP/OAS to Canadians living in the U.S. Canadians receiving U.S. Social Security in Canada, on the other hand, now face a 25.5% U.S. withholding.

- Canadians visiting U.S. casinos now get to deduct gambling losses from any winnings that face U.S. tax (losses presumably including travelling costs!). Canada does not currently tax winnings.

- Canadians leaving large bequests to charities or schools south of the border can now get additional deductions for U.S. estate tax purposes and increased Canadian tax credits.

- As of 1 January, withholding tax rates on cross-border payments are reduced from the previous 10% to 6% on corporate dividends and from 15% to 10% on interest paid to individuals. The dividend tax change applies only to recipients holding at least 10% of the issuing company's shares as in, for example, an owner operator of a U.S. based company.

- As of 1 January, the 10% withholding tax on payments of royalties for computer software, patents and technological information is abolished, a welcome move for Kanata high-tech workers/investors. Such payments continue, of course, to be taxable in Canada.

42. Federal Court Rules On 'Expectation of Profit'

Revenue Canada has long allowed deduction of expenses from revenues in bona fide businesses, even allowing the offset of self-employment losses against otherwise taxable income from other sources. However, in allowing losses from businesses to be deducted from other taxable income, Revenue Canada has also long expected the business operator/owner to have a reasonable expectation of some day making a profit from the business.

In recent years, in attempts to raise more tax revenues, Revenue Canada has been putting pressure on business loss declarers to show that they have indeed an expectation of making a profit. They do this, among other means, by asking the taxpayer for a detailed business plan that shows, presumably, a profit down the road. We have seen in our own tax practice many taxpayers being denied the carry over of such losses against other taxable income when, not surprisingly, the taxpayer could not satisfy Revenue Canada of the business profit potential.

The inability to turn a profit on an otherwise bona fide business most often has occurred, during the past decade, in rental properties. Too many people have been swayed that they could buy a duplex or similar building, spruce it up with the proceeds of remortgaging, renting it out, racking up losses that were transferrable to other taxable income for the first few years, and then, once the property became profitable, selling it for tax-free capital gains. Many factors have transpired to foil the rental property purchaser from eventually making a profit, including frozen rents in rent-controlled provinces, higher than expected maintenance costs, obstreperous tenants, and much higher than planned mortgage interest rates.

The saga of rental property owners failing to turn a profit on their tax returns has caused Revenue Canada to re-assess countless thousands of such hapless taxpayers. But one of them has fought back by appealing his tax reassessment. And guess what? The Federal Court recently ruled in favour of that disaffected taxpayer, finding that the taxpayer's lack of sophistication as a new business operator should not be held against him by Revenue Canada.

In the case in point, Tonn v. HMQ, the taxpayer purchased residential property in Scarborough with 100% financing in the late 1980s. Tonn was not a sophisticated real estate operator, and did not do any elaborate economic or market analysis before purchasing the property. He bought because he simply believed that he should purchase the property to gain income, seeing it as a long-term investment.

As it turned out, Tonn did not receive the rental income he had been hoping for, and expenses were higher than forecast. Tonn claimed business losses for three successive years running, which Revenue Canada eventually denied on re-assessment on the basis that 'he did not have a reasonable expectation of profit'.

In deciding in favour of the taxpayer, the Federal Court has sent a message to Revenue Canada that the latter should not second-guess the business judgment of the taxpayer when the expenses claimed are clearly incurred in order to generate income.

While many of our readers are operating rental properties, this court decision affects anyone who starts any kind of a valid business and incurs losses during start-up, and not just rental property owners. No longer can Revenue Canada with impunity deny such losses just because the taxpayer is not able to show a reasonable expectation of profit in the time limits Revenue Canada deems reasonable.

43.   Better Break for Donations

In the last Federal Budget, it was announced that the limits on charitable donation claims on tax returns was being increased. Not only can charitable gifts now amount to as much as 50% of annual income (up from 20%), but the maximum that can be claimed in the year of death is raised to 100% of income, with a one-year carry back of up to an equal amount.

In other words, if no charitable donations were claimed in the year immediately prior to death, then in the year of death, charitable contributions of up to twice income can be made and claimed in the year of death, with a carry-back of half the amount to the previous year by way of re-assessment.

This will be a significant boon to charitable organizations, since it will now make very worthwhile the naming of charities as beneficiaries of bequests under wills and estates.

Those individuals who know ahead of time their estates will be faced with heavy taxes in the year of their demise (by, for example, capital gains taxation of accrued gains on cottages or stocks) will now be able to lessen the tax burden by making provision for their favourite charities in their last year alive, either by gift while on their death beds, or by wills.

Conventional financial planning wisdom holds that large charitable donations should be made while a person is alive, in order to spread the maximum charitable donation out over a five-year carry forward. Under the new rules, it will now make even more sense that large charitable donations be made, including in the year of death.

44.   Tax-Free Income

Yes, Virginia, there is such a thing in Canada!

Not too many types of income are free-of-tax, but some are. And while most of us won't see many of these but once or twice in a lifetime, it might be worthwhile to run down what's still untaxed in this country.

All gifts and inheritances are free of any type of tax, both to the recipient and to the donor/giver. There may be some accrued taxes payable by the donor if the asset is transferred with accrued profits, such as capital gains taxes payable on the profit accrued on a cottage at time the gift is made. But unlike the United States, there are no succession or estate or income taxes payable by virtue of the gift itself. Note further that there may be probate and other legal costs if a gift is made by way of an estate at death. These probate and legal fees do not apply, however, to bequests made by way of beneficiary designation with a life insurance company contract (any type of life insurance company contract qualifies, including investment contracts!).

The Income Tax Act exempts from tax the first $10,000 of any death benefit payable to an employee's spouse. This is usually a lump-sum 'death-severance payment', which is payable for example by the federal government (as an employer) at the rate of one times salary. This Tax Act provision should not be confused with life insurance, which is paid tax-free. And if paid by way of a named beneficiary, the life insurance escapes probate and legal fees, whereas if the life insurance is paid into the estate, then the life insurance is subject to probate and legal fees.

Lottery and other gambling winnings are still free of tax in Canada, unlike in the U.S., where many Canadian gamblers have discovered the Internal Revenue Service withholds tax from significant winnings. And in Canada, we often hear of instant millionaires being created by lottery winnings, unlike in the U.S., where winnings are often spread over 20 and more years. That's because of the tax grab in the U.S. A U.S. major lottery winner pays much less income tax on a large win if that win is spread over a long period of years (that's also why major winners of Canadian 'skill-testing question' contests will usually have their prizes paid out over many years, because of the tax such skill-testing contests imply).

Prizes for 'meritorious achievement in the arts, the sciences or service to the public' are usually free of income tax. So, if you happen to pick up a Nobel prize, you won't have to pay tax on the funds that go with it. Similarly, the first $500 of any scholarship, fellowship or bursary, each year received, is free-of-tax.

There are also a few work-related types of income that are tax-free. If you are a volunteer fire fighter, the first $500 per year is tax-free. If you are a member of the clergy, and you have a congregation, an allowance you receive for accommodation will be tax-free.

Some types of employment-related benefits are considered free of income tax. For example, club membership fees will be tax-free to you if the club membership is considered to be beneficial to the employer.

Some private business entrepreneurs and farmers can still take advantage of up to $500,000 of tax-free capital gains when they dispose of qualifying assets.

The biggest single tax break available to everyone continues to be the individual basic tax credit, which means that every Canadian, no matter what age or medical health, can make up to $6,456 of income tax free each year. This continues to be a huge source of income-splitting potential, where a high-tax-bracket individual splits some of his/her taxable income with one or more family members who have less taxable income than $6,456. This applies to children, for example, or teenagers who do not yet have lucrative jobs, or disabled dependents still living at home (regardless of age!).

Employees of the United Nations and many of the UN's agencies receive income that is not taxed anywhere in the world, even if resident still in Canada.

Hundreds of thousands of parents each month receive a 'Child Tax Benefit', which is free of income tax.

Most welfare income is still free of tax. However, the receipt of such income will generally affect the eligibility for most non-refundable tax credits.

Gains on principal residences are still tax free, unlike in the U.S.

Investors get a tax break on their capital gains, in that only 75% of such gains are actually taxed, even though much of the capital gain may have been due to inflation while carrying the investment over a number of years.

The first $200 realized profits each year in foreign-exchange transactions are tax-free. And if you own Canada or Newfoundland War Savings Certificates, profits are tax-free (we saw a bunch of these just recently!).

For many people, still, the first $1,000 of pension income is tax-free, although such recipients begin losing the tax-free status if their other income exceeds approximately $25,000. Interest on life insurance company GICs (known as deferred annuities) qualifies, still, as pension income, which comes in handy if someone over age 65 does not have a pension.

Many other pensions are free entirely of income tax. Payments to victims of the Halifax explosion of 1917, payments made by Germany to victims of Nazism, service pensions (Canadian and most other foreign service pensions too!), and RCMP pensions are all exempt from income tax.

Many awards made by courts are not taxable, if the award is not related to earning income. Thus, a successful suit for wrongful dismissal will have a tax-free component related to 'pain and suffering', or 'damage to reputation', and a taxable component related to loss of earned income while looking for a replacement job.

Most people are aware they can leave their RSPs/RIFs to a spouse tax-free. Most are not aware that they cannot leave such assets to others tax-free. But there is a provision for leaving RSPs and RIFs to minor children, and/or to financially dependent and disabled adult children! Thus, in families that are unfortunate in having a disabled adult child, we often advise the parents to leave their RSPs/RIFs on the death of the second parent to the disabled child, making up the deficiency to the other children through bequests of non-registered assets. (Note that RSP/RIF income is taxable to the recipient, even if the recipient is disabled.)

The splitting of RSPs/RIFs between spouses on marriage breakdown is tax free, although most financial institutions, to keep the folks at Revenue Canada happy, will insist on a copy of a court order before accomplishing the split.

Disabled taxpayers effectively get to keep an extra $4,000 of annual income free-of-tax, and if they don't have enough income to shield under this provision, another family member is usually able to claim that deduction.

While the above is not an exhaustive list of tax-free income, it does give some idea of what the most frequent ones are. As can be seen from the range of tax-free incomes still possible, we spend a lot of our time in financial planning in helping families identify how and why they can take advantage of these 'loopholes'!

45.   Income Tax Rates Down

This is the year many Canadian taxpayers have been waiting for: decreased income tax rates!

The federal government hasn't announced any changes for 1996. Many provinces have, thanks to the belt tightening many began several years ago. And while the federal government is staying pat for this year, there's a federal election due in two years. So watch for decreased federal income tax rates in the Finance Minister's next Budget, due February 1997.

Five provinces have announced tax cuts this year, including Ontario, British Columbia, Saskatchewan, Nova Scotia and Alberta. The only province to raise taxes is Newfoundland, which has added a new surtax on high-income earners.

Even though most of Ontario's tax decreases are not scheduled to come into effect until 1997 and later, this year's Ontario tax decrease, at 2% (from 58% of basic federal tax down to 56%) is still the biggest tax break in any province in 1996.

But those with $60,000 or more of taxable income in Ontario won't get the full tax reduction relief because of what the Ontario government calls the 'fair share health care levy'.

Because of the magnitude of tax cuts in 1997 and later, it would be wise tax planning in Ontario to maximize deductions (e.g. RRSP contributions) and/or minimize income for 1996.

The table below shows the top marginal tax rate by province for salary, pension and interest income. Dividend and capital gain income are taxed at slightly different rates.

Although top marginal tax rates are flat or down in all provinces save Newfoundland, don't forget you face a hidden tax increase because of inflation. Federal tax brackets (and, hence, provincial tax brackets) and personal tax credit amounts are adjusted for inflation only when inflation exceeds 3% in a year. Since inflation has not exceeded 3% a year since 1992, tax brackets and personal amounts have not been changed since then, even though inflation has caused all of us to be making 20% more income with no increase in spending power.

But that 20% extra income just to make up for inflation is taxed! So, for a top tax bracket employee, he/she would have had to receive pay increases of 50% during just the last five years to make up for the loss of spending power caused by inflation and income tax! And, for a senior who is losing OAS at the rate of 70% because of the Clawback tax, he/she would have had to have increases in pension and other income of at least 75% since just 1992 to take care of inflation and income tax!

46. Top Marginal Tax Rate

Province	Tax Rate*
B.C.	54.2%
Alberta	46.1
Saskatchewan	52.0
Manitoba	50.4
Ontario	52.9
Quebec	52.9
New Brunswick	51.4
Nova Scotia	50.3
P.E.I.	50.3
Newfoundland	53.3
Yukon	46.6
N.W.T.	44.4

*For incomes of usually more than $60,000.

47. Camp Fees Deductible

With summer over for another year, many parents will have sent their kids to camp. Few such parents are aware that their summer camp fees are usually tax-deductible as child care expenses.

Many more children are now eligible since the last Federal Budget raised the age for child care expenses for children from the previous 14 years of age to 16.

Camp fees are eligible child care expenses if they meet the usual rules, namely that the claimants must be earning income (or attending school), and that the lower-income spouse be the beneficiary of the claim.

There is no restriction on the type of camp. We've seen sports camps, music camps, even 'daycare' camps such as the ones operated by the YM/YWCA.

The maximums for child care expenses that can now be claimed are $5,000 per year per child under age seven at the end of the year for which you are filing a return, and $3,000 per child for children aged seven to 16, inclusive.

48.   Tax Calculator

Thanks to Ernst and Young, the accounting firm, here's a quick tax calculator, showing what provincial and federal tax bites come to for an individual with a $75,000 taxable income. The second column shows what that same taxpayer's marginal tax rate is at a $75,000 taxable income level. In other words, the second column shows what the rate of combined federal/provincial income taxes would be for this individual's next dollar of income in excess of $75,000.

	Tax Payable	Marginal Rate
B.C.	26,256	50.9
Alberta	24,948	46.1
Saskatchewan	28,145	52.0
Manitoba	27,717	50.4
Ontario	26,907	52.9
Quebec	30,368	52.9
New Brunswick	27,263	49.9
Nova Scotia	26,534	48.6
P.E.I.	26,534	48.6
Newfoundland	28,402	53.3

2

Retirement

1. Government Benefits — 1996

Contemplating retirement? Already retired? Here's what you may qualify for if you've contributed to CPP long enough. Figures are monthly; apply for all of 1996 (exception: OAS); and are for all provinces except Quebec.

Retirement Pension at 65	$727
Disability Pension	871
Disabled Contributor's Child Benefit	164
Surviving Spouse Pension: before age 65	400
after age 65	436
Orphan Benefit	164
Lump Sum Death Benefit	3,540
Maximum CPP Contributions in 1996	
payable if: self-employed	1,786
an employee	893
Old Age Security (4th qtr 1996; age 65)	400

Benefits under CPP/OAS must be applied for. They do not start automatically. Do you qualify for the maximum CPP pension? Don't answer too quickly. Most people simply don't know. And don't rely on that periodic employer's statement that usually says something like 'If you qualify, your CPP pension at age 65 could be $$$'. If you haven't done so recently, you should request a computer printout from the CPP. For an application form, call 1-800-277-9914. Allow six weeks for the printout.

2. The Canada Pension Plan

CPP is an integral part of Canada's social security system. Under the plan, millions of members of the labour force acquire and retain, during their productive years, protection for themselves and their families against loss of income due to retirement, disability or death. The CPP is one of the key areas covered in general financial planning. This summarizes current legislation. See elsewhere herein for levels of benefits by category.

2.1. Contributions

Contribution Period: Contributions began to be payable in 1966. Eligible individuals must begin to contribute one month after their 18th birthday. Contributions stop the earlier of: a) death; or, b) the month retirement pension starts, or the individual reaches age 70. The contribution period does not include any month when a member is disabled as defined under the CPP.

Record of Earnings: Every three years each member receives an updated statement of contributions and earnings from Health and Welfare. If you want to know what your benefits are, request a statement from the local Health and Welfare office (in Ottawa: 990-1500).

2.2. Disability Benefits

'The disability must be a physical or mental impairment that is both severe and prolonged'. Severe means inability to regularly pursue any substantially gainful employment. Prolonged means such disability is likely to be of indefinite duration or to result in death. Therefore, CPP members who have a mental or physical condition which seriously affects their ability to earn an income for longer than temporary (not defined by the government) should apply. Individuals under 65 who become disabled can receive benefits if they: a) are considered disabled under CPP legislation; b) have contributed to CPP in at least two of the last three years, or five of the last ten; and, c) have not received a CPP retirement benefit for longer than 12 months. When an individual reaches 65, the disability pension will be converted to a retirement pension. A disabled contributor may receive both a survivor pension and a disability pension, if both spouses contributed to the plan. A disabled contributor's children (natural or adopted) can qualify for a disabled 'Contributor's Child Benefit' if they are: a) under 18; or, b) between 18 and 25, and in full-time attendance at school or university. A child may receive two benefits if both parents were CPP contributors and are either deceased or disabled. Disability pension may be payable from the fourth month after the individual becomes disabled and can only be paid retroactively for a maximum of 12 months.

2.3. Retirement Benefits

CPP contributors may start retirement pension between ages 60 and 70. If a contributor chooses to retire at other than age 65, the retirement benefit will be: a) decreased by 0.5% per month for each month remaining to age 65; or, b) increased by 0.5% per month for each month since age 65, with a maximum retirement age of 70. For a pension to start before age 65, contributor must wholly or substantially have ceased working. After age 60, either spouse may apply to split the other spouse's CPP income. This generally results in a reduction of taxes paid by both spouses and an increase in their disposable incomes (see elsewhere herein for more).

2.4. Survivor's Benefits

On the death of a contributor, a Survivor's Benefit becomes payable to one or more of the following: a) the deceased contributor's estate; b) the surviving legal spouse; c) the surviving common-law spouse, if he/she lived with contributor at least 1 year; d) dependent children, including those 18 to 25 in full-time school or university. There are three types of Survivor's Benefits:

2.4.1. Surviving Spouse's Pension

Survivor benefits continue after remarriage. The amount of pension or benefit is related to the amount of the contributor's retirement pension. If the surviving spouse is:

Age 65+: the survivor benefit will equal 60% of the deceased's retirement pension.

Age 45–64: the benefit will be a flat rate plus 37.5% of the deceased's pension, to a maximum.

Under 45: if not disabled with no dependent children, the benefit will be reduced by 1/120th for each month he or she is under age 45 at time of contributor's death.

Under 35: if not disabled with no dependents, no benefit is payable until survivor reaches 65.

A contributor can receive both a retirement pension and a survivor's pension if both spouses contributed to the Plan. The amount of combined pensions depends on the contributor's age at the time he/she became eligible for each pension. The combined pension is subject to a maximum.

2.4.2.   Orphan's Benefit

When a contributor dies or begins receiving disability benefits, each child is entitled to a flat rate benefit per month, which continues to age 18, or to 25 if in full-time attendance at school or university. If both parents were contributors and are either deceased or disabled, a child may receive two flat rate benefits per month.

2.4.3.   Death Benefit

The Death Benefit is a lump sum benefit payable to, or on behalf of, the estate of a deceased contributor. It is the lesser of: a) six times the monthly retirement benefit that would have been payable to the contributor if he or she had lived; or, b) 10% of the current 'Year Maximum Pensionable Earnings'.

2.5.   Division of Earnings on Divorce/Separation

Note: A division of earnings will apply not only to credits but also to income. For example: A spouse can apply to receive a portion of disability benefits or retirement income received by a former spouse. The definition of spouse now includes a common-law spouse. A spouse only needs to apply to the Minister of Health and Welfare for the division and, except where a spousal agreement signed prior to 4 June 1986 precludes the division, the division may not be prevented by the terms of a spousal agreement. **Divorce after 1 Jan 1987:** As long as a couple lived together for at least 12 consecutive months, credits earned during marriage will be split. **Separation of spouses after 1 Jan 1987:** For legal spouses: The separation must have lasted at least 12 months, and if one spouse dies following the separation, an application for the division must be made within three years of death. For common-law spouses: Spouses must have lived in a conjugal relationship for at least 12 consecutive months.

3.   CPP Disability Benefits

In mid-1992, the federal government introduced legislation to rectify an unjust anomaly in the Canada Pension Plan. Until now, a disabled person had to have contributed to CPP in either two of the last three, or five of the last ten years, to be eligible to collect CPP disability benefits.

A relatively small number of Canadians have discovered they have not qualified. This has been because their disabilities have rendered them unable to work for more than 5 years but unable to substantiate their disability to the CPP administrator's satisfaction until recently. In other words, someone started with a disability that prevented working and, hence, contributing to CPP, with a disability that seemed in the early years mild enough to prevent qualification for CPP benefits. After 5 or more years of disability, usually under the care of a physician, such people then found themselves disqualified by virtue of the fact they had not contributed to CPP during the requisite time frames prior to applying. The new legislation corrects this unfairness by adding to eligibility anyone who had made the requisite CPP contributions prior to the onset of the disability.

If you think you qualify, call CPP (1-800-277-9914). At the same time, also ask for a CPP benefit statement, if you have not received one of their bi-annual statements recently. This will tell you how much you are entitled to receive. While press reports suggest only a few hundred Canadians would benefit from the change in CPP legislation, we ourselves have no less than two clients who appear to qualify for benefits. A third client has a son who would seem to qualify. Therefore, perhaps by coincidence, we know a high percentage of the folks the government expects this change to benefit. On the other hand, the press reports may be wrong! That's why we are including this article herein; we suspect many more Canadians than the government is letting on have been denied benefits because their disabilities were much longer endured before they could be considered eligible for benefits; so long, indeed, those individuals then found themselves shut-out because they hadn't (and couldn't) make the necessary contributions.

4.   Pension Reform

The Federal government now allows:

- A choice in 'retirement' age for CPP benefits of ages 60 through 70. Pension benefits at age 60 will equal 70% of those normally available at 65 and will increase by one half of 1% for each month above the age of 60 that 'retirement' is deferred. Thus, someone electing 'retirement' at age 70 would receive 130% of those benefits then available to someone 65.
- Splitting pension benefits and/or credits by marriage partners on either retirement or marriage breakdown.
- A more liberal definition of 'disabled' as well as increased payment to disabled contributors.
- Continuation of survivor benefits upon remarriage.

Old Age Security, currently $400/month, goes to all Canadians age 65, regardless of working history. OAS is not affected by the above measures. Both CPP and OAS continue to be inflation-protected through indexation.

Ontario has passed legislation affecting private pension plans. The major reforms include:

- An employee has vested rights to his employer's pension plan contributions after no more than two years of service.

- Upon termination, an employee has the choice of leaving his combined employee/employer pension credits with his old employer, moving them to his new employer's plan (at the new employer's discretion), transferring them into a 'self-directed' locked-in RRSP, or purchasing a deferred annuity.
- Employers must provide retirement benefits from their pension plans to employees who retire as early as 55.
- Survivor benefits continue on remarriage.
- Part-time employees have access to an employer-provided pension plan after no more than two years of service.
- Inflation protection of private pension plans is not yet mandatory.

So, when should a person start collecting CPP? This is a popular question, now that the Government allows us to choose our 'retirements' anytime between 60 and 70. For most readers, the maximum available will not significantly alter their lifestyles. Hence, the decision for most will be dictated less by necessity than by taxes, timing of other investments, and psychological motivation. Just when is the right time to start that CPP cheque? The Government no longer insists on complete retirement. 'Substantial' retirement seems the definition. This means a person stops contributing to CPP and also UIC, once CPP benefits are being received. These restrictions don't appear to prevent part- or even full-time employment after someone is considered 'retired' by CPP. A look at the mortality tables may help in the decision-making. A major life insurance company's mortality expectations discloses:

Life Expectancy			
At age:	60	65	70
For: Males	22.62	18.63	14.96
Females	26.32	21.98	17.87

Thus individuals of average health may expect future payments from CPP to total as shown in the table below (no allowance is made for present value, nor for inflation indexing)

Males retiring at	60:	$22.62 \times 12 \times .70 \times \$727 = \$138,136$
	65:	$18.63 \times 12 \times 1.0 \times \$727 = \$162,528$
	70:	$14.96 \times 12 \times 1.3 \times \$727 = \$169,664$
Females retiring at	60:	$26.32 \times 12 \times .70 \times \$727 = \$160,731$
	65:	$21.98 \times 12 \times 1.0 \times \$727 = \$191,754$
	70:	$17.87 \times 12 \times 1.3 \times \$727 = \$202,667$

Clearly, for once, females have an advantage! So do people with above-average health. Those with less-than-average health, i.e. those with shorter-than-average life expectancy, might be well-advised to begin drawing CPP at the earliest! To further complicate the decision, inflation is not now a problem although it was recently and might again be. Also, people are living longer, thanks to improvements in medical science, diets, exercise and habits. So today's 50-year-old, if still alive at 70, can expect to live several years longer than today's 70-year-old. Last, but far from least, is a psychological factor. When this writer turns 60, he will have contributed to CPP over a career spanning 40+ years. He will have, statistically, only about 23 years to get back his contributions, plus interest. On the other hand, he might get run over by a bus before he turns 60! So this writer is planning on getting as much out of CPP at the earliest, in case he beats the odds and dies early! Which begs the question: What will happen to the writer's 40 years of contributions if he dies at age 59? No longer married and with his children grown up, the writer's estate stands to collect $3,500 as a one-time death benefit, and only if his executor remembers to take the time to apply to the government for it!

5. Splitting CPP Benefits

This article will benefit those married and retired, or approaching retirement. As can be seen from tax tables (see elsewhere herein), there is a wide variance in marginal tax rates under Tax Reform between income levels. This is more apparent when one considers the first $7,000 or so of income is tax-free. This rises to $11,000 for those over age 64. Married couples, both retired, often find one spouse has a higher marginal tax rate than the other. This often occurs when one spouse has spent most of his/her working years at home raising a family. Under reform, many couples find one partner is taxed at 40% or more, even as much as 70%, while the other pays no tax at all! A useful and financially rewarding option of the Canada Pension Plan allows couples to 'split' their benefits. Here's how it works: suppose you are entitled to CPP of $500/month. Suppose your spouse, because she/he spent her/his working life at home, is not entitled to any benefits. You can ask CPP to split benefits such that you would receive $250/month each. 'But our cash flow remains the same' is your first impression. Not so, after taking tax savings into consideration. Let's assume you're in a 70% tax bracket, and your spouse, because she/he spent her/his career at home, isn't paying any tax. Splitting CPP shifts $250/month, or $3,000/ year of taxable income away from you and onto your spouse. At 70%, you've just saved yourself $2,200 in tax, which is the same as getting an increase in your income of over $7,000!! Splitting CPP is one of the last ways left to 'income split' between spouses. And it's easy. You and your spouse must each be over age 59; both of you must be essentially retired; and you must apply to the Canada Pension Plan (call 1-800-277-9914). Upon death or marriage dissolution, benefits are restored to each party's original entitlements.

6. CPP Reform

The federal and provincial finance ministers have released a discussion paper containing a number of options for reform of the Canada Pension Plan system. There is nothing therein that is new compared to what's been bandied about the past several years. But here is our prediction of what's likely going to be implemented:

- CPP contributions are likely to double over the next six years, from the present maximum of about $1,800 (split equally between employee and employer; paid in full by self-employed), to $4,000 per year.

- CPP benefits to the already retired will be cut approximately 10% over five or six years through the simple expedient of 'temporarily' de-indexing benefits from inflation increases. In other words, present dollar values will be maintained, but there will be no further increases to offset inflation until the cumulative decrease in real dollar values caused by inflation ends up amounting to some 10%.
- CPP benefits to disabled, widowed and orphaned recipients will be cut by about 15%, also through deindexing for inflation.
- The CPP lump-sum death benefit, now worth up to $3,540, will be removed entirely, as of the first of next year.
- CPP benefits for those still in the work force, once they do retire, will be cut 10%, in stages, over five years, by perhaps 2% a year, but in such a way that those who are already close to retirement will lose less than much younger contributors.
- The CPP retirement age, now 65, will likely be gradually increased over a twelve year period to 67, at the rate of two months of age for each calendar year elapsed. In other words, the retirement age in 1997 would be age 65 and 2 months; in 1999, age 65 and 6 months. This would be a fairer implementation method for those within a few years of retirement than simply increasing the retirement age overnight to 67.
- One likely change to the CPP system that has not received much publicity over the years of discussion leading up to the present, is in how the CPP pension asset pool is invested. At present, the CPP has about $40 billion, but it's all invested in loans to the provinces at money-market rates. The proposed changes to the contribution rates and payout levels are designed to increase the CPP asset base to well over $100 billion, and one of the strong suggestions in the consultative paper is that CPP administrators be allowed to invest the bulk of that on competitive investment markets, including Canadian and foreign equities. This should dramatically increase investment yields, and thereby reduce the amount of necessary contribution increases or benefit reductions otherwise necessary.

The federal government is likely to announce its desired options out of the ones listed in the consultative paper as part of the upcoming Budget. We hope they do not do so in isolation to their promised, but delayed, paper on the reform of the Old Age Security System and the Guaranteed Income Supplement System.

7.   Defining a Spouse

This article won't concern you if you've been happily married for a number of years, and, but once. Nor will it be of interest if you've never been married, nor co-habitated with anyone! However, if you're one of the growing numbers who have an ex-spouse, and/or if you've ever co-habitated with anyone without having been 'married', the following will be of importance. It attempts to set down the current definition of 'spouse' as decreed by pension plan authorities and the taxman.

Canada Pension Plan: Under current law, a spouse means:

- a legally married individual, or
- a person of the opposite sex who is co-habitating with the CPP contributor in a conjugal relationship at the relevant time, having so co-habitated with the contributor for a continuing period of at least one year.

RRSPs: For spousal contributions or death benefit or payout amounts, a new definition applies: The spouse of an individual means a person of the opposite sex who:

- is married to the individual, or
- has been living with the individual in conjugal relationship at least one year. This change permits tax-free transfer of RRSPs to RRSPs or RRIFs of a common-law spouse where the taxpayer dies before his/her RRSP has been matured. It also allows a common-law spouse to receive survivor benefits under an RRSP payout annuity/RIF.

Registered Pension Plans: Definition of spouse varies according to the jurisdiction that applies. This could be either the jurisdiction of domicile or the jurisdiction while making contributions. 'Jurisdiction' usually means 'province'.

Prescribed Annuities: Under current law, a spouse means:

- a person who is legally married and of the opposite sex
- a person of the opposite sex co-habitating with the particular person in conjugal relationship for at least one year.

Revenue Canada: The taxman has the following definitions:

- Spouse, on a tax return, is someone legally married to the taxpayer on December 31 of the tax year in question or is someone with whom the taxpayer has lived in a conjugal relationship for at least one year.
- A former spouse, for tax purposes, is someone once legally married to the taxpayer, or someone who previously co-habitated with the taxpayer for a minimum of one year.

Confusing? Probably not if you've been married to the same person for many years! If you've been co-habitating, or if you're supporting children from a previous marriage or relationship, or if you're contemplating a marriage breakdown, then it might benefit you to know the current law! That way, you can more adequately plan your financial affairs accordingly!

8. New Seniors Plan

If adopted as announced in the Federal Budget earlier this year, the new Seniors Plan will overturn several long-held principles in financial planning circles. The Seniors Benefit is scheduled to replace the present Old Age Security and the Guaranteed Income Supplement systems for those who turn 65 after December 31, 2000.

It will not affect those already receiving OAS, and those currently between the ages of 60 and 65 will have a choice between the new and old systems.

The new benefit will initially be a tax-free payment of $11,420 for a single senior, and $18,440 for a couple. This is a Finance Department projection of benefits in the year 2001, assuming an average annual inflation rate of 1.6% during the intervening five years. The payment is fully indexed for inflation. Thus, if inflation is different than the expected 1.6% annual rate, then the payment in the year 2001 will be higher or lower accordingly.

But, the Seniors Benefit will be reduced based on the recipients' other income, such as investment income, RSP withdrawals (including RIF and/or annuity payments), or payments from an employer pension plan or Canada/Quebec Pension Plan.

If single, the recipient will lose the entire Seniors Benefit at an income of $52,000 per year. If married, recipients will lose all of their Seniors Benefit on joint annual income of $78,000.

With the clawback based on all other income over and above the Seniors Benefit means you will face a double tax on income after age 65 over and above the Seniors Benefit. This double tax could amount to between 42% and 78% of each dollar of outside income until there is no Seniors Benefit left (at about $78,000 for a couple), or unless the couple's joint income was between $18,000 and $26,000, where the new benefit will closely match the existing OAS payout.

Single seniors will be hit even harder. At a time when they're alone, having typically lost their spouse. Many single seniors will find they are taxed even more heavily after retirement than when they were formerly working.

In this book, I have repeatedly warned about the perniciousness of the present OAS clawback regime, in which seniors over the age of 65 can find themselves paying effectively up to 70% of their taxable incomes between about $53,000 and $84,000 annually. The new clawback provisions of the new Seniors Benefit is even more onerous!

One strategy I have been advocating for a number of years, since the present OAS clawback was first introduced, will become very popular in the years ahead: to boost income in the years immediately before turning 65, and then reducing taxable income for the next five years or so (until age 69, by which time an income must begin from any remaining RSPs). All in order to boost the Seniors Benefit not otherwise clawed back by virtue of other taxable income.

The current rule of thumb in financial planning circles is to put as much as possible into RSPs while working. Since the introduction of the present OAS clawback, I have maintained that is the wrong strategy.

I have advised numerous clients and readers that the correct strategy, at present, is to limit the amount of one's RSPs at age 65 such that income from them, when added to other taxable income, does not create a clawback situation.

The clawback rates for the new Seniors Benefit are even more onerous than the present clawback rates. Hence, it will become even more important that taxpayers do not find themselves with too big a pile of RSPs by the time they reach age 65.

As a rough rule of thumb, I reiterate the advice given here often in the past:

- Continue making RSP contributions if you are presently in the top tax bracket.
- But if you are in the lowest tax bracket (i.e. under $30,000 annual taxable income], consider deferring claiming your contribution deductions until you are in a higher tax bracket.

- And if you are in the middle tax bracket, you need some professional advice!
- But if you know now that your combined income with your spouse will exceed $78,000 after age 65, then by all means continue making and claiming your RSP contributions, since you will end up losing <u>all</u> of the Seniors Benefit, anyway!

Another conventional financial planning rule of thumb is to live on non-registered funds immediately after retirement, saving RSPs until the last possible moment (which was previously age 71, now age 69 under the last Budget). This advice too has fallen by the wayside.

Since the introduction of the present OAS clawback system, we have advocated that retirees should live on their RSP incomes <u>before</u> age 65 if only to reduce their pile of RSPs that would have to eventually produce an income by no later than age 71.

With the new Seniors Benefit clawback, this advice is even more important:

- Live on your RSPs after retirement, <u>but before</u> age 65, prior to depleting your non-registered assets.

And where one spousal partner is under age 65, and the other over age 65, it is doubly important the under age 65 person deplete his/her RSPs before age 65, if only to forestall the clawback after both partners have turned 65.

Another conventional financial planning rule of thumb is to defer CPP as long as possible, preferably to age 70.

But precisely because of the existing OAS clawback, it has been our advise to take CPP as early as possible, even as early as age 60, if only to reduce the amount of taxable income. This becomes even more important advice for those who will be receiving the new Seniors Benefit.

For several years, we have been advising our clients that the main purpose of their RSPs should be to finance their retirements <u>before</u> age 65! This will become even more evident to those slated to receive the new Seniors Benefit.

Yet another financial planning myth will be exploded by the new Seniors Benefit clawback: that it always makes sense to make spousal RSP contributions. Under the new rules, spousal RSP contributions will have made sense during working years only if:

- one retired spouse is under age 65 and <u>not</u> in the highest tax bracket, <u>or</u>
- if one spouse alone will have at least $78,000 in post-age 65 taxable income while the other (regardless of age) is <u>not</u> in the highest tax bracket.

Spousal RSP contributions will continue to make sense where one spouse is younger than the other. Not because the recipient spouse will withdraw the RSPs at a lower tax bracket than when the original contributions were first made, but because the younger spouse will have more years to withdraw the RSPs before age 65 when any withdrawal gets hit by the new Clawback tax.

Clearly, financial planning is even more necessary, especially for those not yet age 65, but contemplating retirement!

1. RRSPs

Registered Retirement Savings Plans were introduced in the 1950s. Originally meant to encourage systematic savings of tax deferred income until a person retired, RRSPs are widely assumed to be cashable at lower tax rates after retirement. RRSPs are increasingly used to: finance sabbaticals; tax average widely varying incomes; supplement UIC when out of work; spousal income-splitting; and tax-shelter income from job termination benefits and superannuation refunds. RRSPs are big business. Over five million Canadians own one or more. Over $200 Billion is invested in them. Every kind of financial institution offers them. They are available in many forms including bonds, equities, gold certificates, mortgages, life insurance, deferred annuities, and Registered Retirement Income Funds (RRIFs).

Why does the government encourage us to save tax-deferred dollars? CPP and OAS were never envisioned as the total retirement income package, even when someone had a healthy private pension plan. Government doesn't want us to rely only on its assistance in retirement. Government also makes more in taxes by encouraging us to defer income till later. If a 30-year-old invests $1 at an average of 10% annually, the taxman will be able to get his share of a $25+ taxable income by the time that person reaches the age of 65. Thanks to inflation and the claw-back tax, a 65-year-old will often find himself in a higher tax bracket than when he was 30 (or even, sometimes, 50!).

2. Where Should RRSPs Be Kept?

Virtually every type of financial institution offers RRSPs. Newspapers are full of adverts in February extolling the virtues of this or that plan. Last-minute RRSP scrambles often result in long lines in front of tellers who often know little more than what the contribution limits are and how to fill out forms. For growing numbers of people, RRSPs already represent their largest single investment. We frequently see clients with $100,000 plans and even $500,000! Yet, most people treat their RRSPs in a cavalier fashion, like opening up a chequeing account. They often do so without any long range goals or plans and they often make unwise investment decisions. We have one client who bought gold certificates several years ago and is still hanging on to them hoping to break even soon. Another who bought Kanata hi-tech stock now worth $ 0.20 on the dollar. A third who converted the mortgage on her residence into an RRSP and paid $3,000 for the privilege! Except for the sophisticated, knowledgeable investor who can afford to take a gamble on losing a good chunk of his capital, the average owner should invest in high-grade bonds (i.e. GIC equivalents, known as accumulation or deferred annuities in the life insurance industry) or very well managed Mutual Funds. The latter should also offer death benefit and maturity guarantees.

Everything else being equal, RRSPs should be invested with larger firms, partly because of safety of capital, but more importantly because that's where most of the expert advice resides. Speaking of advice, anyone over age 50, or anyone with $25,000 of RRSPs should have a professional advisor thoroughly knowledgeable and up-to-date on RRSPs, taxation, annuities and RRIFs. After all, RRSPs are meant primarily for retirement. Safety and growth of capital coupled with tax considerations and payout/income provisions are of paramount importance. In our experience, few advisors are qualified and up-to-date in these areas because tax laws and product offerings change so frequently.

Other factors that will influence the choice of an RRSP trustee are: the trustee's rates for guaranteed investments; its track record and contractual provisions for its Mutual Fund offerings, if any; whether or not the RRSP contract is creditor- and probate-proof; what kind of direct beneficiary provisions will be effected in the event of premature demise; and the geographical extent of the trustee's branch network.

Guaranteed interest rates for multi-year contracts should be of the compounded variety. Many banks and trusts still only advertise simple interest, while virtually every major life insurance firm offers only compounded interest. The difference can be substantial. A five-year simple interest contract with 10% annual payout yields 50%. The same term contract with 10% annually compounded yields 61%+! Avoid 30–180 day terms or daily interest accounts unless you expect rates to rise in the short term. As an individual is likely to move after retirement, the financial institution should have offices across the country, and internationally as well.

If you're concerned about creditors having access to your RRSPs, go with a life insurance company. Only their contracts can be made creditor-proof, even from Revenue Canada! (Exception: In certain 'Family Law Reformed Act' provinces, and Ontario is one of them, a spouse may have a valid claim upon marriage breakdown or death, regardless of the beneficiary.) Only a life insurance company can guarantee a death benefit directly to a beneficiary, bypassing probate (exception: that spouse mentioned above may have a valid claim to part of an RRSP after death, <u>regardless</u> of beneficiary designation). Because most RRSP holders buy income contracts (annuities and RRIFs) from life insurance companies, many of the larger firms offer bonuses or discounts to those people who already have their RRSPs with them before annuitization. These can often add 2% or more per income payment for as long as the payments last. I have seen some contracts 40 years old and going strong!

In fairness to the reader, I make a large portion of my income from brokering client investments with large life insurance companies. I'm biased, but justifiably so. Never has a Canadian legal reserve life company ever defaulted on any financial obligation, and the industry goes back to 1847! Also, most of the knowledgeable advice on matters discussed herein resides within insurance firms. It's possible nowadays to find a competent individual within such a company without being expected to buy life insurance!

3. RRSP Contribution Limits

The calculation for RRSP contribution limits is as follows: up to 18% of earned income, up to $13,500 <u>less</u> Pension Adjustment, for those who belong to a pension plan, regardless of whether contributions were made to the pension plan. <u>Earned income</u> is the aggregate of net salary or wages, royalties from authorship or invention, alimony or maintenance receipts, supplementary UI benefits, net research grants, net business and/or commission income, net rental income, less business losses, rental losses, alimony or maintenance paid. RRSP contribution room is now based on entitlement from the previous year. In other words, what you may contribute during 1996 is based on your earned income for 1995! T4 slips now show the Pension Adjustment amount to be used to calculate RRSP contribution room for the year after the tax year reported on the T4. Starting in 1992, assessment notices report contribution limits.

3.1. RRSPs from Unearned Income

You can no longer contribute up to $6,000 of pension income to your spousal plan.

3.2. New RRSP Provisions

For those with earned income, unfunded but earned RRSP contribution room may be carried forward indefinitely. The amount of such unfunded room that may be 'filled' and claimed in a tax return in any one subsequent year is limited to the greater of 3.5 × the dollar limit for that year (ignoring the 18% factor) or the individual's personal limit (taking 18% into account) for the current year and the six previous years. This is a powerful way to reduce taxes in a future year where income is in a higher tax bracket than most other years. This should prove beneficial to those such as authors or sports stars who receive a large lump sum, but only periodically. However, the temptation to pass up making a contribution in the current year with the thought that the employee might be in a higher tax bracket down the road is extremely dangerous: such dreamers rarely, if ever, catch up.

4.   RRSP Strategies

The new RRSP contribution limits have been in effect long enough to have lead us to some conclusions. The limits and rules now in effect are discussed elsewhere herein. This article assumes the reader is familiar with them.

4.1.   For Those Still Earning Income

If you are in the lowest tax bracket, i.e. if your taxable income is under about $29,000, there isn't much point in contributing and using your contribution to further reduce your taxable income at tax time, since you may never be in a lower tax bracket. Indeed, there is every possibility you may be in a higher tax bracket when you have stopped earning income, so that when you withdraw your RRSPs, they will end up being taxed at a greater rate than the tax savings realized at contribution time. We are not advocating that you don't set aside as much money as you were planning to put into an RRSP for your eventual retirement, only that you don't put it into an RRSP, or, if you do, that you don't claim the deduction in any year when your taxable income is less than $29,000. Even if you do make an RRSP contribution you no longer have to claim that deduction immediately; you can save the deduction for a year in the future when your taxable income exceeds $29,000.

The above is a radical departure from most conventional financial planning advice, and is dictated by my having seen many people put too much money, and sometimes at the wrong time, into RRSPs. Many think they were a great way of reducing taxes. Reduce taxes such RRSPs do, but only until those RRSPs are withdrawn. That's where the problem often occurs, when the taxpayer is defenceless against the Clawback tax. There are exceptions to the above general advice: if you know you will be going on a sabbatical, or on a lengthy maternity leave, or back to school, then making an RRSP contribution(s) while having a taxable income less than $29,000 may still make sense, if you can withdraw such RRSPs in a year when your taxable income will not attract any tax. For example, a university student with $3,000 of tuition fees can have a taxable income of up to about $10,000 without attracting any tax. A single person going on maternity leave can have a taxable income of up to over $15,000, again without attracting any tax.

For those with taxable income above the lowest bracket, that is, about $29,000, ensure that you won't be caught by the Clawback tax when you retire, before making and using your RRSP contribution. Anyone receiving Old Age Security (i.e. age 64+) with taxable income exceeding about $53,000 falls into a 70% tax bracket! Therefore, if you contribute to RRSPs when you are in the middle tax bracket, you are 'saving' 44% in tax of whatever you contribute to RRSPs currently, but may see 70% of those RRSPs disappear in tax on withdrawal if your taxable income, including OAS, is more than $53,000.

Although all of the advice in this article so far advocates against RRSPs for those situations described, let me repeat that I do not advocate that you spend the money that you would have contributed. Instead, find a good capital gain producing asset, such as a well managed mutual fund that concentrates on tax-reduced capital gains. Your retirement fund outside RRSPs will thereby grow much faster, in any event, than inside an RRSP.

For those earning income and married, another exception to the above guidelines will occur if your spouse will be in a lower tax bracket at the time of RRSP withdrawal than you are, either now, or at the time of withdrawal. For example, if your spouse has no taxable income, as is still frequently the case when one spouse stays at home, then a spousal RRSP will make sense, even if you are in the lowest tax bracket. But make sure, if you are in the lowest tax bracket, that you are liable for tax! If have seen not a few individuals, usually college students acting on their parents' advice, who have some taxable income from which they have contributed some funds into an RRSP only to discover at tax time that they had no tax liability, and that, therefore, their RRSP contribution had no effect on their tax liability. Now, thanks to the RRSP carry-forward provisions, such individuals can at least use their contribution in a later year.

4.2.   If You are Receiving a Pension

You can no longer contribute to a spousal plan.

Again, we repeat: don't make any RRSP contributions to your own plans if you are reasonably sure you will be caught by the Clawback tax! If you aren't sure where you'll stand at age 65 vis a vis the Clawback, do a little planning: calculate, in today's dollars, what your employment pension will be; add about $12,000 per year for CPP and OAS; add interest income on whatever GICs and CSBs you expect to have at that time (use 10% as a planning Rate of Return); plus add 10% of your current RRSP holdings as a return on your RRSPs without encroaching on capital.

If the total of all of that already exceeds $53,000, then you already are at risk of losing 68% of whatever more you contribute to RRSPs, thanks to the Clawback! The exception to this is if you anticipate your taxable income will exceed $85,000 per year at age 65, since those people will have no OAS left to claw back! As a very rough rule of thumb, if you are currently earning $50,000, have been with your present employer 20+ years, are at least ten years away from retirement, and belong to a fairly good pension plan (i.e. the federal civil service), then your RRSPs should not exceed $250,000 at retirement, and shouldn't exceed $100,000 currently, if you plan on making maximum contributions over the next ten years. If your RRSPs already exceed $100,000 with the characteristics just mentioned, some careful planning is in order to avoid getting caught in a 68% tax bracket at retirement.

Remember that income, when it's from a RIF or annuity, qualifies as pension income, the first $1,000 of which is tax-free! Remember also that the first $1,000 of interest from a life insurance company GIC outside an RRSP also qualifies as pension income subject to the $1,000 exemption. These are more technically known as deferred annuities; most are never later converted to annuities, but, instead, cashed when their usefulness is outlived.

5.   RRSPs and Border Hoppers

We're often asked by people considering leaving Canada what happens to their RSPs from an income tax standpoint when they make lump-sum withdrawals. The answer usually depends on whether the person is leaving the Canadian income tax jurisdiction and, if so, whether the new country of tax jurisdiction has a tax treaty with Canada.

Most people assume, incorrectly, that they would cease to be Canadian income tax filers by simply leaving the country. Determining one's Canadian income tax obligations is far from that simple. Revenue Canada uses a whole host of qualifications to determine tax status, including property ownership, ownership of bank and safety deposit box accounts, children attending school in Canada, even ownership of burial plots!

But assuming you are leaving the country, and no longer have to file a Canadian tax return declaring therein your world-wide income, what happens to RSP withdrawals? This depends on whether the country you are taking up tax filing obligations with (which is not necessarily the new country of residence!) has a tax treaty with Canada.

The U.S., Mexico, countries of the European Union (including the U.K., but excluding the Isle of Man!), and Australia all have such tax treaties. Most tax treaties call for the country where pension funds reside to withhold tax at the rate of 25% on withdrawals, which is then applied for as a tax credit on the tax return you would file in the new country.

But even if the country where you are taking up tax filing responsibilities does not have a tax treaty, the Canadian federal government will withhold 25% on payments from an RSP/RIF/registered annuity, once it (or, more properly, the financial institution holding your contract) finds you have become a non-resident.

Our advice to all such individuals wanting to minimize the amount of tax withheld and remitted to Ottawa is to withdraw all RSPs, in chunks no larger than $5,000 each, at the beginning of the next calendar year after you have left Canada, before the

				RIF Minimums			
Age	**Old**	**New**	**% Diff**	**Age**	**Old**	**New**	**% Diff**
71	5.26	7.38	40	83	14.29	9.58	−33
72	5.56	7.48	35	84	16.67	9.93	−40
73	5.88	7.59	29	85	20.0	10.33	−48
74	6.25	7.71	23	86	25.0	10.79	−57
75	6.67	7.85	18	87	33.33	11.33	−66
76	7.14	7.99	12	88	50.0	11.96	−76
77	7.69	8.15	6	89	100	12.71	−87
78	8.33	8.33	0	90	0	13.62	—
79	9.09	8.53	−6	91	0	14.73	—
80	10.0	8.75	−13	92	0	16.12	—
81	11.11	8.99	−19	93	0	17.92	—
82	12.50	9.27	−26	+	0	20.0	—

financial institution(s) have discovered you have left the country (most investment brokers are ideally situated to provide this service). The tax withheld (and, presumably, lost) will amount to only 10%. Do this only <u>after</u> you have cashed in all other Canadian property!

6.   New RIF Rules

Formerly, RIFs had to be exhausted by the owner (or spouse) at age 90. The new regulation is that RIFs be issued such that income will continue past 90. The <u>minimum</u> payout rules to age 71 remain the same; i.e. age 90 minus current age divided into the fund balance. The minimums for ages 71 through 77 have been increased. This will generate more income in the early years of the RIF, which will mean more taxes for those who only want/need the minimum payout, which in turn could trigger clawback of OAS. After age 78, minimum withdrawals are reduced compared to the old scheme. This reduces taxes in the later years, and allows for payments past age 90. In essence, the new rules take more taxes in the early years from higher minimums, while taking less tax from reduced minimums in later years. The very steep increases in minimums under the old rules during the last five or so years of a RIF will be reduced in 'steepness'. After age 93, the minimum will then be 20% per year of that year's fund balance. Thus, by age 96 or so, there will be negligible payments unless the owner has lucked into a high-yield long-term investment. New and old minimum payments as a percentage of RIF assets are shown in the table above.

7.   Life Income Funds

Until recently, people with 'locked-in' retirement funds (LIRAs or RRSPs) had no choice at retirement but to buy life annuities with this money. Thanks to progressive new legislation, Life Income Funds (LIFs) are now an attractive flexible alternative to life annuities.

When the term 'locked-in' is used in this discussion, we mean funds that cannot be spent by the owner before a certain age, usually 55. The funds in question are not locked-in to a specific institution or term; only the owner is 'locked-in' in not being able to personally touch the funds until that specified age.

Unlike a RRIF, a LIF can only be purchased with money from a locked-in RRSP, LIRA, select pension plans, or the commuted value of a life annuity (provided the original annuity was purchased with locked-in funds). Similarly, locked-in RSPs cannot be used to buy a RIF because, by its nature, a RIF can be collapsed in its entirety, which runs contrary to the underlying concept of both locked-in RSPs and LIFs.

Locked-in pensions and savings used to be quite rare. But they have gained in popularity. This is because of changes to the Pension Benefits Standards Act, which now allows any employee to move his/her pension entitlements to the financial institution of their choice, rather than leaving the entitlements with their former employer until retirement age. We now often see locked-in funds at time of severance, when a terminating employee is given, by law, the option of taking his/her pension entitlements with him. In every case we have ever seen, it has made much more economic sense for the terminated employee to take his pension with him, rather than leave it with the employer pension plan. This is because of the inherent conservatism of even the best pension plans. An individual, without undue risk, can always outperform a pension plan performance unless that individual sticks his/her pension entitlements into Canada Savings Bonds!

While LIF owners are required to withdraw a minimum amount each year, they are also prevented from withdrawing too much. This is to ensure the LIF owner has money left at age 80 to buy an annuity.

LIFs, like RRIFs, also offer the advantage of beneficiary designation and selection. Unlike most annuities and some company pension plans, when a LIF owner dies, funds remaining in the LIF pass either to the designated beneficiary if the LIF is with a life insurance company, or to the estate in all other cases. They are not absorbed by the issuing company, as are most annuities.

It is important to remember that a LIF is regulated by the province in which the locked-in funds were first registered, and not by the owner's province of domicile, or the province in which the LIF was purchased. Therefore, someone buying a LIF in a province other than the province where the locked-in funds were earned will be governed by legislation passed by the province where the funds were originally earned. Fortunately, the differences in legislation affecting LIFs does not vary greatly between provinces, and is not even worth discussing in detail herein.

In summary, then, LIFs are very similar to RIFs, with one key difference: with a RIF, the owner can purchase a life annuity at any time. With a LIF, on the other hand, the owner must purchase an annuity by no later than age 80. The main attraction to LIFs is that they provide flexibility to the owner between retirement age and age 80, whereas before the advent of LIFs, the only option was a life annuity.

As with RIFs and RSPs, LIFs with life insurance companies provide creditor protection and beneficiary designation, eliminating probate time and expense when compared to RIFs, LIFs and RSPs with banks, trusts, and other financial institutions.

8. Group RSPs Warrant Careful Study

If your employer offers to donate a matching grant to your group RSP, you'd probably be nuts to pass that opportunity by. But if your employer does not offer such an inducement, should you join a group RSP plan at work? There are a number of factors you should consider before jumping in.

Matching plans, where the employer kicks in a percentage of the employee's contributions, tend to be offered by small- to medium-sized employers who have no pension plans. Where there is no pension plan available, and the employer offers to match contributions, you should probably sign up.

The other type of group RSP plan is usually offered by larger firms, who already have a pension plan, and where the employer is making the group RSP available as a convenient method of payroll deduction for enforced savings. That sort of plan offers ease of administration for both employer and employee. That form of plan, often referred to as a supplemental plan, should usually be avoided because of the usually very poor investment opportunities offered by the plan's administrators.

Although we often see such plans offering mutual fund type investments, because the administrator offers no ongoing advice to employees, most employees end up opting for GICs, which today are paying as little as 4%. And because the employer is not matching any contributions (usually because the employer already offers a pension plan), the employer couldn't care less what the investment returns are the employees have been getting, since the employer will understandably claim the employee should know what type of investments to subscribe to.

If you have little experience in managing your own investments, the first thing you should ask the group RSP administrator is what type of advice they give, and how often. Your next question should be what their track record on performance has been. Only after you're satisfied with the answers to these two questions, should you then ask the administrator how much they charge as admin fees and as investment management fees.

But if you know what you're doing, a group RSP is very convenient, and should make you as much money as if you administered your own RSPs (which you're likely doing as well as group RSPs, in any case), particularly if you subscribe to a good investment and tax publication (like this one!).

9. RSP Season

Mercifully, the RSP season is over for another year. Mercifully, not so much because we've been busier than usual, but because of all of the advertising that bombarded our senses during the six to eight weeks of the season.

Our investment clients gave us almost $2 million during the first 60 days of 1996. But less than $100,000 of that was in the form of RSP deposits. The balance was in transfers from other institutions, and new non-registered deposits. Well over 90% of my business these days is in mutuals, and almost all of that is in Canadian Growth equity funds. The few GICs I handled were limited to short-term renewals of maturing GICs, where the owners are planning to cash in for purposes ranging from buying a new car to financing a cruise.

Why I'm so happy that the season is over is because of the overload of misleading hype put out by so many financial institutions, designed to lull unwary and ignorant investors into plunging into the wrong mutual funds, for the wrong reasons. Several concepts were touted as never before in these sales pitches that really bother us. They include: diversification; foreign fund limit maximization; and fund history. Let's dissect each one.

Diversification: claimed almost universally as what wise investors do. Well, the kind of diversification promoted during this RSP season was designed to entice investors to buy several different fund types, implying that by doing so, an investor would increase annual performance of his/her overall portfolio. Nothing could be further from the truth (except by accident). Here's why:

The mere act of buying a mutual fund in itself diversifies one's investments across a wide spectrum of underlying investments that comprise the fund. To this extent, diversification is a very wise move compared to buying individual securities on, say, the stock market. This is especially so if the fund chosen is well run and conservative in its objectives, and has minimum performance guarantees.

Where diversification is a mistake is in buying funds spanning several different sectors, just because the investor feels that by doing so, he/she is minimizing exposure to risk. Yes, the investor is minimizing risk; but purely by the act of minimizing risk, he/she is condemning himself to mediocre performance.

One can substantially reduce risk by retaining the services of an advisor who has a good track record making fund type recommendations (i.e. equities versus long bonds, versus money market, etc.). And one can further reduce risk by ensuring the mutual funds have guarantees. But reducing risk by spreading an investment over several fund types is bound to end up crimping the portfolio's overall performance.

Fund companies want their clients to invest over several fund types for two primary reasons: because it is very rare for any fund company to give ongoing economic analysis and fund type switch recommendations, most fund companies are only too well aware that if they recommend one specific fund type, sooner rather than later the investor is going to suffer a large downturn. So the fund companies protect themselves from unwanted investor dissatisfaction with downturns in specific fund types by recommending clients invest across many types. Then, when one type suffers a large reversal, the fund salesman can say: but look at your other fund types, aren't they doing OK? Trouble is, when the overall portfolio performance is examined, there just isn't much to be happy about.

Over and over, we meet traditional mutual fund clients who complain their overall portfolios just haven't moved the way they had expected. The underlying reason is almost always that the investor has followed the initial advice to diversify across several fund types, and then not known what to do, because the fund company did not advise its clients when the time was proper to get out of one fund type in favour of another.

And that leads to my second major advertising gripe: invest in foreign funds to take advantage of RSP foreign content limits. First off, we couldn't agree more that wealthy individuals should invest a good chunk of their assets outside of Canada. But that's a very far cry from investing up to 20% of one's RSPs via foreign securities bought by Canadian companies. RSPs are supposed to be for retirement. For most people, they will form the backbone of their retirement incomes. They should not, and usually cannot, suffer large losses in their RSPs. Only wealthy people can afford to gamble, and those people aren't relying on their RSPs for retirement.

So my standard advice is: within RSPs, stick as close to home as possible, where you will know a lot more about Canadian economic conditions than you will about conditions in any foreign country (including the U.S.!). If you have non-registered funds and you want to invest in a foreign country, fine, but do it through a foreign investment firm, where Revenue Canada will not know about, and, hence, not tax your profits, until you decide to report them.

Folks whose investments are limited to their RSPs simply are not well enough off to go investing anything in foreign markets.

The third bugbear I have is that most mutual funds are sold using their historical performance. The great bulk of mutual fund ad space is devoted to one-, three-, and five-year performance histories. Those histories say nothing about what those funds and fund types will do in the future. Yes, the small print invariably says something like 'past performance is not an indication of future performance'. But the implication is nonetheless very strong, and most investors who don't know better are lulled into the hope, if not outright expectation, that a fund's history will repeat after that investor buys in.

The fact is, history is seldom repeated, and when it is, it is usually accidental. The capitalistic society we live in is designed to go through cycles, even if most of us don't like them. Interest rates, inflation, unemployment, consumer confidence, political stability, equity and bond market performance, corporate profits; all of these and many other economic factors operate in a bewildering interplay that results in periodic recessions as well as good times. Fortunately, government monetary authorities are getting increasingly sophisticated in the tools and timing they use to dampen or quicken economic responses, so that the overall goal of slow but steady growth is now within reach. Interest rate policy, for example, first in Canada beginning four years ago, followed more recently in the U.S., was very successful in trampling down inflation.

Having said all that, there are still cycles in equity performance, bond performance, and interest rates, that can be predicted, with growing accuracy, by those who have the time, inclination, and aptitude to do a lot of reading. That's where I believe fund investors should spend their research time: instead of looking at fund company histories, they should seek out those money managers who have demonstrated a good long-term track record of guessing what will happen next, and making loud recommendations when the time seems right to get out of one fund type and into another.

While I do have a pretty good track record, I do make mistakes. Take my advice fully two years ago to favour Canadian equities over American equities. We not only misjudged the strength of the American economy, but further misjudged the appeal of Parizeau and Bouchard's rhetoric, the consequent political uncertainty, and the negative effect of that uncertainty on Canadian financial markets. But I did accurately predict when interest rates would peak, and at what rates, early last year, and were able to take satisfaction in seeing fully a third of our mutual funds get rolled over into long-term GICs.

By listening to seasoned money managers, investors can ensure they are ahead of the investor pack. Because my experience tells me that most investors are followers, as well as fund history buffs. Those investors, by the time they make up their minds to do something, have already missed most of the good action and profits. Procrastinators, for that is what such investors are, seldom are as profitable as those who are willing, following good counsel, to be in the vanguard.

10.   Unlimited RSP Carry-Forwards

In the last Federal Budget, the carry-forward provisions of unused RSP contributions was changed from a maximum of seven years to no limit. In other words, RSP contribution room may now be carried forward indefinitely.

In my newsletter discussing this provision at the time of the Federal Budget, I foresaw that the only beneficiaries of this new rule would be Revenue Canada.

Now, with no carry-forward time limit, it's my feeling that those who might previously have made a contribution just before expiry of the wven-year time limit now won't ever make the contributions.

The new unlimited carry-forward provisions do, however, open up some new and exciting financial planning opportunities, especially for younger people.

For years, we've been advising parents of young adults that their children should be filing tax returns, even if the children have no otherwise taxable income. In the past, this advice has been motivated by the myriad tax credits available to anyone who files a tax return.

Now, for younger people, there will be an added incentive to file a tax return, even if no tax is owing: building up RSP contribution room for the future!

And this opens up an income-splitting opportunity between generations: a parent now can make an RSP contribution in the child's name (even though the parent can't claim the deduction on his/her return). The growth of RSPs in the child's name occurs tax-free, while the parent is comfortable knowing he/she made a tax-free contribution to the child's eventual retirement.

The bottom line to the advice above is that filing tax returns for young adults can result in significant future tax sheltering opportunities, even if the RSP contributions are not made and claimed until the child is in a high tax bracket, all for the sake of doing some paperwork (i.e. filing a tax return) to allow Revenue Canada to build an earnings history for the child.

Another use of the unlimited carry-forward provisions for RSP contributions is for people approaching retirement who know they will be hit by the new Seniors Benefit clawback.

It may make more sense for such people to defer making and claiming an RSP contribution(s) during the later stages of their working careers in order to save such contribution room until they have reached age 65.

The article above on the New Seniors Benefit sheds more light on this.

Non-Registered Investments

1. Investing

Until interest rates dropped below 10% in 1992, investors fell into one of two camps: the conservative who was quite happy with pure interest on guaranteed investments such as GICs, CSBs, and term deposits; and the cautious who was willing to take minimal risk to achieve better rates of return than were available through risk-free investments.

Another type of individual considers him/herself an investor but is really a gambler or speculator. This individual invests directly in the stock market, venture capital funds, non-personal-use real estate, rare metals, or other commodities such as coins and postage stamps. We have no interest in speculation, having been burned years ago. So little will be said herein about speculative 'investments', except by way of example.

With interest rates at 30-year lows, with inflation at less than 3%, and with the Canadian economy recovering from recession, investment performance criteria used during the 1980s have gone out the window. Many folks now approach investment decisions with a completely open mind. Others are adversely affected by their historical bias against any risk. Herein, I try and analyze various types of investments in relation to these changed circumstances.

I should point out at the outset that, as the largest independent investment broker in Eastern Ontario, most of my clients have the bulk of their investments in long-term GICs/term deposits of at least five years duration, with many for 15, 20, and even 30 years. The average rate of return is better than 10.5% compounded annually. Of the $30 million I administer on behalf of my clients, at least 90% of the investments I handled up to 1991 were in GICs with the balance in mutual funds.

Although I have experienced an average 15% compounded annual growth with the mutual funds I represent, most of my clients felt more comfortable with GICs when they were guaranteed as much as 13% on long-term fully insured investments. Frankly, so did I! When long-term GIC rates dropped below 10% in 1992, I noticed a dramatic shift away from traditional interest bearing deposits to mutual funds. Perhaps the migration has been influenced by years of advertising by traditional mutual funds of their superior performance compared to GICs. Perhaps it was a realization by many of our clients that the bulk of their investments were in long-term guaranteed deposits earning better than 10% with little to lose with some mutual funds. Perhaps it was a realization by many that eventually the recession would end and the economy would rebound, along with mutual funds. In any case, what happened was that in less than six months, the market switched from 90% GICs/ 10% mutual funds, to the opposite extreme of 10/90.

While some of my clients were too conservative when interest rates were attractive, I suspect some of my clients are now too hesitant about investing in GICs because they perceive interest rates as being too low. Yet, historically, the real rate of return on GICs has seldom been as high as now. Even though long-term GICs are fetching barely 6% today, because inflation is at 2%, the real rate of return is about 5%, as high as we've seen in at least a decade. The difficulty, as many of my more astute clients have perceived it, is that inflation could rear its ugly head again before their GICs mature, catching them holding 7% contracts while rates climbed back into double digits. Most of my clients are delighted to have bought five-year GICs at 11% with several years remaining, when they can get less than 7% today. They don't want to buy today at 6% only to find their positions reversed two or three years hence.

The recession just ended was the worst economic downturn since the depression of the 'thirties. As with previous recessions, while ours began after the American recession began, so our recovery began after the American recovery. As previously, our recession was deeper than the American recession. Again as in the past, our present recovery will be stronger than the current American recovery.

What does all of the above mean?

For the cautious investor (read: saver) who has been holding short-term GICs/term deposits/CSBs, the damage has already been self-inflicted. Those people are already in serious trouble, even if many of them still don't know it. While their taxable interest income has dropped substantially saving them many tax dollars, and even pushing some of them into lower tax brackets, their net after tax interest income has dropped by more than half in less than two years. If such a person were living on his/her interest income, then even with inflation down to 2%, their real disposable income has dropped substantially. If such an investor was counting on continued high interest rates to achieve a certain amount of absolute growth in his/her nest egg, growth will have slowed appreciably because of their mistake in choosing short terms.

Those wise enough to have invested for the long term at 10%, 11% or even 12% are now literally laughing all the way to their bank (or investment broker!). With inflation at 2%, such investors (not savers!) are experiencing real growth in their assets of 10% or better, compounded annually (before income tax).

What to do?

Those with well-balanced portfolios of long-term GICs with staggered maturity dates will have little to lose by investing their maturing GICs in performance-guaranteed mutual funds which are fully insured as to capital in the event of death or the mutual fund company's financial difficulty. For the next two to four years, we are likely to see avereage annual compounded growth of 15% in such mutual funds, which is a continuation of our own experience over the past 15 years. And, holding some mutual funds, you will be much better positioned to take advantage of higher interest rates whenever an upturn in rates takes place.

For those suffering from their mistake of investing in short-term GICs, you have the painful choice between continuing to re-invest your maturing GICs in short terms of no more than one year at 4%, or taking what you perceive to be a chance in mutual funds. You cannot take the chance of investing in long-term GICs for fear of missing the upturn in interest rates, whenever that will happen. And happen it will, although we don't see rates going back up to 10% or better until at least 1998.

For those who insist on investing directly into stock markets, venture funds, precious metals, and so-called tax shelters, I am not even going to wish you good luck. To outperform mutual funds, you will need more than good luck; either an 'inside tip' or divine intercession! My advice: spend some time at the race track, or buy a bunch of lottery tickets, instead. Your odds will be better, and you'll get rid of the gambling itch that much more quickly and painlessly! And have fun!

Many mutual funds have been recently advertising the performance of their international segments. I believe the time for best returns on international mutual funds, when compared to the likely return on Canadian funds has already peaked and passed. The same applies to bond funds, real estate funds, mortgage funds, and precious metals funds.

Some experienced investors consider me 'contrarian'. This term means that, while most people are buying a certain type of risk investment, I am selling so I can reap the profits to invest in something else. I am a firm believer in always being ahead of the markets, and not reacting to the current 'news'. That is the basis of my success: being able to predict which market segments have peaked, and which are about to go up. Those who buy or sell in reaction to what they perceive others are doing are almost always too late, and will almost always lose money. That's why, in my observation, at least 90% of individuals lose money on the stock market. They are continually trading based on stock broker comments about recent past performance. In other words, too many individuals play the stock market based on comments from their brokers that 'a lot of people have been doing well by buying . . . .' By the time such people have bought, the contrarians have usually left with their profits, leaving later investors to buy at too high a price.

I do have some clients who manage their own individual investment portfolios, and who have done better than I have. Invariably, such successful market punters are either retired, or have lots of time to research on a daily basis individual security histories and prognoses, and have been doing it for many years. Those individuals would, in our estimation, account for less than 1% of all stock market players.

For those contemplating buying into a venture fund: you have more money than you know what to do with, and enjoy throwing it away on long shots!

I have added a third family of mutual funds, this one 'off-shore' on the Isle of Man, United Kingdom. Like the other two I already offer, it is fully insured as to capital in the event of death, and has optional performance guarantees. This fund family will be attractive to those who believe they have enough invested in Canada and want to diversify their holdings into the international arena.

It is operated by one of the oldest and strongest financial institutions in the world, Royal Life PLC, London, England, via their subsidiary, Royal Life International (a sister company to Royal Life Canada). Because of its location on the Isle of Man, investors in Royal Life International are exempt from UK or Isle of Man income taxation. As with other 'tax-haven' investments, Canadians do not have to report any profits on their tax returns until the investments are cashed, unlike what they have to report on profits made on their North American investments (as with, for example, annual accrued interest). This delay in reporting profits to the Canadian taxman can be very attractive for those in high tax brackets who expect to fall into lower brackets later, for example at retirement.

Investing off-shore can also provide a hedge against revaluation of the Canadian dollar, as well as providing funds for the frequent overseas traveller or someone who intends to take up domicile in Europe. But the investor can also lose if currency revaluations go in the opposing direction to that desired.

I chose the Isle of Man in general, and Royal Life International in particular, because of the reputation of both, because of the ease of communication (voice and fax) in the same language (albeit with accents!), and because of the stringent regulatory behaviour of Isle of Man authorities. While there are at least 30 countries today offering tax-haven status, I feel the Isle of Man is one of, if not the, best. And being so close to the heart of the world's insurance markets, London, England, I felt this was the best combination of location and fund manager of any off-shore investment. Indeed, I would rank this combination as favourably as a top financial institution in New York City (which is not a tax haven).

We are the first to admit there is at present only a very limited market for off-shore international investments by Canadians. Most such investments have loads (i.e. commissions or fees), and the potential investor should, therefore, be prepared to remain with the investment somewhat longer than with North American investments. Notwithstanding, the profit potential is higher, and more immediate than most Canadian investments of a similar commodity. Coupled with significant income tax savings, off-shore investments will be attractive to high-tax-bracket and high-net-worth individuals.

Although (or perhaps, because) Royal Life International is located on the Isle of Man (in the Irish Sea, between Liverpool and Dublin), they offer just about any of the mutual funds that are sold across national frontiers. These include most of the well-known multi-nationally available funds, such as Barings, Jardine Matheson, Fidelity. Several currencies are available to choose from, including U.S. dollars, U.K. pounds, and European ECUs.

Most people believe it takes at least six figures to invest off-shore. Not so! You can invest as little as $10,000 in a variety of investments with a number of life insurance companies every bit as strong as Canadian insurers, with your investment guaranteed and insured just like here in Canada. At least until such time as the investment is sold, there are no tax implications with Revenue Canada. Since the investment is with a life company, the investment is also creditor-proof. Since the investment is in an off-shore tax haven, there are no taxes to worry about in the off-shore country.

One conclusion reached from the above is that interest rates have fallen so far since they peaked in late 1991, they are now at 30-year lows. Indeed, a GIC at 6% is hard to find, while mortgages are now being offered at as low as 7%, the lowest since the mid-1950s. At the same time, the Canadian economy is now clearly recovering from a severe and long-lasting recession, such that investment in high-quality, well-managed and conservative mutual funds are likely to return far more than GICs at minimal risk. I also saw that investments in venture capital funds, precious metals, real estate funds, mortgage funds and individual stocks on the stock markets was a form of gambling, with such speculators often driven by short-term profit expectations (i.e. greed), in which the vast majority lose money.

2.   An Investment Guru Says ...

Sir John Templeton, the now-retired former owner of the Templeton Group of mutual funds, was quoted recently with these long-term investment views:

Invest for Maximum Total Real Return: Anyone who fails to recognize the effect of taxes and inflation on their portfolio fails to recognize the true nature of investing — and is severely hampered. It is vital to protect purchasing power. One of the biggest mistakes people make is putting too much money into fixed-income securities.

Invest, Don't Trade or Speculate: If you move in and out of stocks every time they move a point or two, or if you sell short, deal in options, or trade in futures, the market will become your casino. Like most gamblers, you will eventually lose. Remain open-minded about different types of investing. Don't rule out sitting on cash, because cash sometimes enables you to take advantage of investment opportunities.

Buy Low: That may be obvious, but it's extremely difficult to go against the crowd and buy when everyone else is selling and things look darkest. But, if you buy the same securities everyone else is buying, you'll have the same results as everyone else. Bernard Baruch (an early 20th-century Wall Street baron and intimate of Winston Churchill's) was quite succinct in saying 'Never follow the crowd'. So simple in concept. So difficult in execution.

Buy Value, Not Market Trends or the Economic Outlook: A wise investor knows that the stock market is really a market of stocks. While individual stocks may be pulled along momentarily by a strong bull market, ultimately it is individual stocks that determine the market, not vice versa.

Diversify: There is safety in numbers. No matter how much research you do, you can't predict or control the future. A hurricane or earthquake, a strike, or an unexpected technological advance by a competitor can cost a firm millions. Then, too, what looked like such a well-managed firm may turn out to have serious internal problems. So you must diversify.

An Investor Who Has all the Answers Doesn't Even Understand the Questions: A cocksure approach to investing will lead to disappointment, if not outright disaster. The wise investor recognizes that success is a process of continually seeking answers to new questions.

Don't Panic: Sometimes you won't have sold when everyone else is buying, or you'll be caught in a market crash like 1987. But don't rush to sell the next day. The time to sell is before the crash, not after. If you didn't own your present portfolio after a crash, would you go out and buy it after a crash? Chances are you would!

Learn From Your Mistakes: The only way to avoid mistakes is to not invest — which is the biggest mistake of all.

There's No Free Lunch: Never invest on sentiment, such as in the company that gave you your first job, or that sold you your first car. And never invest solely on a tip. You'd be surprised how many well-educated and successful people do this!

3.   Why Renting Beats Buying

Canadians have had a love affair with real estate since at least the end of the second World War. Is it any wonder? For most of the post-war economic boom, real estate has more than kept pace with inflation. In recent years, Canadians are waking up to the realization that the real estate boom has flattened out. Indeed, many Canadians are only just now realizing that the values of their properties have actually decreased during the recent economic recession, and that, at least on paper, they have lost between 5% and 20% of their values in just the past 2 to 4 years.

Many Canadians are also waking up to the fact that the Canadian federal government is now preaching austerity, and seems on the verge of actually practising it. Therefore, in some localities, especially Ottawa, there will be wholesale federal civil service layoffs, leaving a glut of empty houses on the market. Empty for two reasons: some civil servants, just out of work, will no longer be able to pay for their mortgages, and will walk away from their debts. Another reason is that many civil servants, having been given a golden handshake to retire early, will be moving to the sunbelt, and will turn their properties over to real estate agents with instructions to sell at just about any price.

Canadians, who have always been told to buy real estate as a good investment, are now realizing there are better ways to use their capital than in investing in real estate, whether for principal residence purposes, or for speculation in, for example, cottages.

Those who have always believed owning a home is a quick and easy way to build equity are learning fast that good mutual funds are even better ways of wealth building, without the hassles of cutting the grass, or fixing the roof!

While many homeowners can crow about their tax-free capital gains accruals, many renters have been making good use of their assets for more dynamic ventures by using funds that would have gone towards repairs, maintenance, property taxes, decorating, and monthly payments on that mill-stone, the mortgage. I'm even seeing many seniors, who've lived in their homes all of their married lives, and who have made a tidy bundle, cash in and rent, using that bundle to produce much higher returns in mutual funds, or even GICs!

4. Annuities

While I have yet to see a case where a RIF didn't do as good a job as an annuity for registered money, there are cases where it does make sense to purchase an annuity with non-registered funds. Since inflation continues near zero, an annuity can yield considerable real interest on top of capital returns. But before buying one, remember that most annuities are not commutable (i.e. they can not be cashed in for a residual value). Once purchased, you're usually stuck with the income stream for the contracted duration, regardless of whether interest rates subsequently go up or down. Here's a sampling of the more popular types of annuity:

Immediate Annuities: bought primarily for immediate income.

Deferred Annuity: purchased primarily to accumulate capital; seldom converted to an immediate annuity, they are usually cashed in or used to purchase a RIF. This is what all life company GICs are called.

Immediate annuities can be purchased in several flavours:

Guaranteed for life annuities: pay as long as you live, often with a minimum number of payments guaranteed in any event. For example, you may purchase an immediate life annuity with ten years' payments guaranteed, so that if you prematurely pass away, the life company will continue making payments until the end of the ten-year period.

Joint and Last Survivor: pays until <u>both</u> you and a partner (i.e. spouse) have died. Again, can be purchased with a guaranteed minimum number of payments.

Life Annuity with Cash Refund: pays for life with a cash refund guarantee that will make up to your beneficiary/estate the unused portion of your annuity if you haven't recovered your original investment before your demise.

Impaired Health Annuity: pays more per month because the annuitant is in poor health, with an impaired life expectancy.

Commutable Annuity: allows you to cash in your contract if you have an unexpected need for the money. But is expensive either in the amount of commuted value, or in the amount of monthly payments.

Prescribed Annuity: Because annuity payments are a blend of interest and capital, normally the income stream from an annuity would consist mostly of interest at the beginning, trending towards mostly capital at the end. This would make for difficult income tax planning. So Revenue Canada allows for something called a prescribed annuity where, for tax purposes, it is assumed that each payment consists of the same amount of interest and capital each month. See next article for more on prescribed annuities.

When purchased through life companies, all annuities, both deferred and immediate, can be made creditor proof and, when called for, residual payments are made directly to named beneficiaries bypassing probate time and cost.

5. Prescribed Annuities

If you're an older person looking for a no-risk way to reduce the tax bite on fixed-income investments, then consider a Prescribed Annuity. Their principle is simple: you lock away a given amount of capital on which you are paid an interest rate similar to that paid on GICs. However, because the interest and principal are repaid as blended payments, the tax on the total payment is less than that on the same amount of interest-only income. Unlike GICs, however, the capital invested in a PA is locked away forever. Once the income stream starts from a PA, it cannot be altered. So, while interest rates remain as low as they are right now, PAs are not attractive except to those who are planning a long-term GIC anyway. Such people will believe that today's low interest rates are here for the long term, in which case the lower income tax payable on PA income will be appealing. Note that interest rates on life annuities have not decreased anywhere near as much as rates on GICs with terms of no more than five years.

6. Life Insured Annuities

After a hike to about 9% early in 1995, medium- and long-term GIC interest rates have fallen back to near the record lows we were experiencing a year ago, of about 6%. For older folks, one way of increasing their GIC incomes is to purchase an annuity where the annuity capital is protected by the simultaneous purchase of life insurance.

Even though interest rates on GICs are now quite low, rates on lifetime annuities have not fallen nearly as far. Indeed, returns on life annuities are still quite attractive, especially given that a good chunk of non-registered annuity payments is not taxable.

Let us take a 75-year-old male as an example. A life annuity at that age for $100,000 of capital would pay an annual income of about $14,864, at today's annuity rates. This assumes an annuity whose income would stop on the owner's death (wait: I'll address your objection in a moment!). Of this $14,864 income, only 37% is taxable, or $5,518. The remaining annual income is considered by Revenue Canada to be a return of original capital and is hence not taxable (this is the concept known as 'prescribed annuities').

At a 55% tax bracket, this individual pays $3,035 in tax, leaving him $11,829 in after-tax income per year on his original capital of $100,000. Compare this with a 6% rate of return on a GIC, taxed at 55%. After tax, a 6% GIC pays only $2,700 per year.

Quite a comparison! After-tax income of $11,829 under the annuity versus only $2,700 under the GIC.

However, I'm not comparing apples to apples, which is why I said above: wait for your objection. Those knowledgeable about annuities will already have realized that the annuity described above ceases on death, with no return of any principal to the owner's beneficiaries. Well, for most folks, that simply is unacceptable. Here comes the solution and, hence, the moniker: 'insured annuity'.

With some of the annual income from the annuity, the owner purchases enough life insurance to provide a tax-free death benefit to his/her beneficiaries equivalent to the amount used originally to purchase the annuity.

In the case above, the 75-year-old would purchase a life insurance contract for $100,000 of tax-free death benefits with level annual premiums. If a non-smoker and in reasonable health, the annual premium would be $5,550.

After paying for the life insurance, the annual after-tax income from his annuity would now be $6,279, compared to the $2,700 of after-tax income from a 6% GIC. The after-tax income from the insured annuity is no less than 233% of the after-tax GIC income!

The only disadvantage to the above occurs when interest rates on GICs rise much above today's levels. For when that happens (and happen it inevitably will), then the annuitant is likely to feel trapped by his annuity, as indeed he is. All he needs to do is remember that he would be trapped by a GIC also, at least until 'the next renewal date'! At least with the annuity, his decision is made, and he'll never have to wonder or worry about what to do with those funds again. As long as he keeps up premium payments on his life insurance, then he knows his beneficiaries will receive the same amount of capital as if he had bought a GIC. Unlike GICs at banks and trust companies, his life insurance (or GICs purchased through life insurance companies) will be paid out within days of his demise to his named beneficiaries, with no messy and expensive probate. And his life insurance company assets can't be attacked by creditors, unlike his bank/trust company GICs.

In tabular form, here is how the above concept would look to individuals at various ages. All examples assume $100,000, and a reasonably healthy non-smoking male. The tax bracket of 55% assumes a retiree with an income of about $55,000, with no provision for OAS clawback.

	$100,000	**$100,000 Insured Annuity at age:**				
	GIC at 6%	55	60	65	70	75
Annual Income	6000	8540	9420	10703	12419	14864
% Taxable	100	52.6	48.9	45.7	41.7	37.1
Taxable Income	6000	4492	4612	4889	5173	5518
Tax at 55%	3300	2471	2537	2689	2845	3035
After-Tax Income	2700	6069	6883	8014	9574	11829
Less Cost of Insurance	nil	1544	2070	2792	3704	5550
Net Income	2700	4525	4813	5222	5970	6279
Improvement over GIC	—	68%	78%	93%	117%	133%

Annuity vs. GIC Returns

To summarize: Depending on the person's age and health, an insured annuity can provide, in times of low interest rates, from 68% to 133% <u>more</u> after-tax <u>income</u> than can a GIC of the same value. The primary reason for this is the unique tax advantage of prescribed annuities, where Revenue Canada taxes only that portion of each annuity payment that is estimated to be the average interest over the lifetime of the annuitant, and the balance is treated as a return of capital.

The reason why such a scheme is so safe, is that the life insurance replaces part or all of the original capital used to purchase the annuity when the annuitant subsequently dies (which is another way to further increase income as the annuitant gets older: cut back on the amount of coverage).

An insured annuity, therefore, particularly in times of low interest rates and low rates of inflation, can be a godsend to those on fixed incomes who are in reasonably good health.

Tip: To minimize any possibility of Revenue Canada treating both contracts as if they were one (for purposes of taxing income), the annuity and the life insurance contracts should be taken out separately, preferably with two different life companies. Because of the possibility of life insurance not being available (because of medical history), the life insurance contract should be arranged first.

7. Mutual Funds vs Individual Securities

Mutual funds have become big business in Canada. Over $200 billion is invested in them, up from only $2 billion 15 years ago. The average fund investor has about $15,000, There are over 500 funds to choose from, compared with 100 in 1982 and only 27 in 1962. Mutuals are attractive to those not happy with the returns on CSBs or other fixed-term and fixed-rate investments, such as treasury bills and GICs, but who don't want the risk of playing the stock- and bond-markets themselves. Mutual funds provide the ideal compromise since, once having chosen a fund, the investor need then only periodically check up on his/her fund investment. Mutual funds enable investors to spread their risks among a variety of securities while knowing the entire portfolio is being managed by professionals.

Mutual fund returns have been attractive for another reason: capital gains of up to $100,000 per individual have been income-tax free. Also, dividends from

Canadian Corporations, whether received through specific stock or mutuals, have had preferential income tax treatment compared to interest income. Mutual funds are easier to acquire than individual stock, and often less expensive to buy and sell. Rather than paying commissions to a broker based partly on the number of shares and partly on the value of the transaction, mutual fund investors generally pay a one-time load either on purchase and/or on sale. Many mutual funds have recently waived their front-end loads, which, for some funds, approach and even exceed 9% of the total purchase price. Yet other funds have been set up from the beginning with no loads at all. Mutual funds will usually do better for the small to medium investor than individual securities because:

- the mutual fund generally pays less in commissions than individuals to purchase and dispose of securities;
- the individual investor is usually less knowledgeable about investment cycles than professional fund managers;
- the individual investor is usually hard-pressed to find enough time to adequately manage a good-sized portfolio;
- the mutual fund manager has usually been able to diversify his/her portfolio sufficiently to minimize the impact of a swing, up or down, in one or more market segments;
- the mutual fund manager, unlike most individual investors, has been able to put together his/her portfolio over a long period of time, and has been able to average his/her purchase price per individual security at less than current market value (a technique known as dollar-cost-averaging. (See article below.)

8.   Segregated Funds

Segregated funds are life insurance company versions of mutual funds. They derive their name from a legal requirement that life insurance companies 'segregate' their investment assets from the pool of capital required to maintain their life insurance contracts, known as 'legal reserves'. Many Canadian segregated funds have performed as well as, or better than, the average mutual. Indeed the average segregated fund has had a better track record than the average mutual fund. Segregated funds are often less expensive to acquire and/or sell than many mutuals. Because they are administered by life insurance companies, most segregated funds have 'death benefit' and 'maturity value' guarantees which mutual funds don't offer.

The death benefit guarantee usually stipulates that the beneficiary will receive at least 100% of the net investment regardless of market conditions. The maturity value guarantee usually stipulates the client will receive a minimum of 75% of the net investment after ten years, regardless of market conditions at the time the investor decides to sell. These guarantees involve no additional charge to the client. The death benefit and maturity value guarantees are particularly attractive to older people concerned with either their retirement years or with ensuring that they leave something of minimum and guaranteed value to their heirs. In return, these investors have achieved higher returns than more traditional vehicles such as CSBs, term deposits, GICs, Treasury bills, and their generic equivalents, without the worry accompanying ownership of most individual securities.

Segregated fund contracts are also governed by the Uniform Life Insurance Act. On death, beneficiaries are protected from the creditors of the deceased. Beneficiary appointments avoid probate, probate fees, legal costs, and provide much quicker settlement outside the deceased's estate since probate often takes a year or more. By naming a beneficiary of the preferred class, e.g. child, spouse, parent, sibling, the contract owner is also protected from creditors while alive as well as when dead, even from Revenue Canada! Settlement options within segregated fund contracts also usually provide attractive arrangements not only at death, but also at retirement. For example, if the contract owner decides to annuitize, the insurance company usually will give a better rate ('inside money' rate) than it will to outside money.

9. Segregated Funds Have Tax Advantages

The traditional investments of GICs and CSBs generate income in the form of interest, which is fully taxable at the taxpayer's top marginal tax rate. Investment funds (i.e. segregated funds from life insurance companies, or mutual funds) earn dividend income and capital gains, as well as interest income. Dividend income and capital gains are taxed at lower rates than interest income. Therefore, investment funds such as segregated funds have substantial tax advantages over income from GICs and CSBs. Investment funds registered as RRSPs are not subject to tax as profits accrue within them, but withdrawals are fully taxed, with no distinction made between interest, dividends, capital gains, or return of capital. Non-registered funds, on the other hand, are taxed as contracts accumulate in value. Let's see how GICs and non-registered segregated funds compare from a tax standpoint.

GICs and CSBs: For purposes of illustration, let's assume you have purchased a $100,000 GIC earning 6%. At the end of the first full year, you will have earned $6,000 in interest. Let's further assume you are in a 55% tax bracket (with income of $55,000 or more; no OAS being clawed back). Your tax on this interest is as follows:

Interest Income:	$6,000
Tax Payable (at 55%):	3,300
Net Income After Tax:	2,700
Real Rate of Return:	2.7%

Investment Funds: Let's assume you invested the $100,000 instead in a segregated fund, and in a 'balanced portfolio'. Same tax bracket. At the end of the first full year, you would likely receive a T3 tax reporting slip that showed the following (based on the past ten years' performance history):

A gross profit of 10%, or $10,000, consisting of:

- $3,800 of dividend income; plus
- $2,400 of interest income; plus
- $3,800 of capital gains.

Because of the way dividends from Canadian corporations are taxed, the amount of dividends credited to your account are 'grossed up' by 25% to $4,750, on which tax is then calculated at 55% before then deducting a tax credit of 25% of the 'grossed-up' dividend amount. The tax picture on your investment fund is shown below.

Dividends (grossed-up):	$4,750
Tax (55%):	2,612
Less tax credit (25%):	1,187
Net dividend tax:	$1,425
+ Interest incl. tax at 55%	1,320
+ tax on 75% of capital gains:	1,567
Total taxes on $10,000	
of gross profits:	$4,312
Net after-tax income:	5,688
Real rate of return:	5.7%
Compared to	2.7%
or $2,700 for the GIC.	

10. Leveraging

'Leveraging' is where assets are purchased using other people's money to finance part or all of the transaction. The practice became widespread in the purchase of mutual funds, prior to the 1987 October Crash. The concept is best illustrated with an example: An individual buys $100,000 of mutual funds putting $10,000 down, borrowing the balance of $90,000 from a bank, at say, 10%. Let us assume the investor makes 20% profit on his mutual fund in the first year. The investor has made $20,000 profit on the investment before paying the bank $9,000 in interest, for a net profit of $11,000 on his original $10,000 investment. Or 110% in one year!

Leveraging in mutual funds or stocks is no different in concept than leveraging the purchase of a home through a mortgage. But that is where the similarity ends. Since most people know far less about stocks, bonds, and securities than they do about their principal residence, the leveraging of investments is a far riskier proposition for most than real estate. While long-term (ten years or longer) returns in mutual funds are far higher (12%) than real estate (7%), most individual investors will not do as well in stocks and bonds as they will in real estate or mutual funds. Having said that, leveraging stocks, bonds, and mutual funds became very widespread in the years leading up to October of 1987. The example above shows why. But when markets turn around, as they so dramatically did in 1987, a leveraged investor can be badly hurt. Consider the effect of a drop in the market value, in the above example, of say 20% in that first year. Our investor has lost $20,000 and owes the bank a further $9,000 in interest on his loan. His original investment of $10,000 has cost $29,000. He has not only lost his original $10,000, but owes an additional $19,000 on sale of the securities to the bank.

11. What Is a Mutual Fund Unit?

There are now so many people who have purchased mutual funds, it is not surprising that many people do not have an appreciation for the term 'mutual fund unit'. In its simplest concept, one can think of a mutual fund unit as being a share in the ownership of an investment fund or mutual fund. The same way one owns shares in Bell Telephone or IBM, one owns a certain number of shares, or units, in a mutual fund.

Instead of actually having possession of share certificates, as with Bell or IBM, investors own a number of units which is determined by dividing the amount invested by the unit value of the fund at time of purchase.

The value of a given fund's units is determined by dividing the number of units already purchased into the total value of the fund. If the fund is an equity fund, then the total value of the fund is determined by adding up the value of each equity component owned by the fund. These equity components are usually shares in corporations. So instead of owning a number of shares of Bell or IBM, a mutual fund investor has purchased a number of units in the fund which in turn itself would own so many shares of Bell, or of IBM, and of many hundreds of other stocks.

The reason why mutual funds are so attractive is that by investing in a mutual fund, an investor is leaving the picking of stocks (or bonds, or mortgages, or whatever that specific fund is designed for) and their subsequent sale to professional money managers. So, instead of putting all of one's eggs into just a few shares of a small number of corporations, the mutual fund investor has joined a pool of similarly minded investors, the contents of which are invested in many different stocks (or bonds, etc.) by a professional manager.

As time goes on, the mutual funds units gain (but occasionally lose) in value because the underlying investments appreciate in value. Some mutual funds allow their units to appreciate in value over time. Other mutual funds declare periodic dividends in the form of additional units. When mutual funds declare dividends, the number of units owned goes up, but the value of each unit goes down, such that the value of any particular investment is the same immediately after the dividend is declared compared to immediately prior the declaration of the dividend.

The number of mutual funds declaring dividends is a small fraction of all mutual funds since declaring dividends often causes confusion among owners of such funds. Indeed, I cannot think of a single reason why a mutual fund should declare dividends.

A mutual fund is usually started when a financial services company provides seed capital which is used to purchase the initial inventory of securities. The mutual fund units are then sold, by prospectus, usually at $10 per unit. The monies realized by the sale of the first batch of mutual funds goes back to the company which originally put up the seed capital. Once that seed capital has been repaid, additional units are issued and sold at a unit price determined by dividing the number of units outstanding into the total value of the investments owned by the fund.

The mutual fund usually has enough cash on hand to be able to purchase additional investments for the fund, and to honour redemption requests. When a mutual fund starts to run low on cash, it then liquidates enough of its investments to provide enough cash to meet redemption requests.

Most mutual funds are started with less than $1 million in seed capital. Over time, some funds can grow very large, in some cases to over $1 billion.

12. Funds Protected

Funds invested in Canadian mutual funds (or their equivalent offered by life companies, known as segregated funds) are protected against unscrupulous actions by the officers of the mutual fund companies, or by the brokers selling them. Traditional mutual funds are not covered against loss by the Canada Deposit Corporation insurance, while segregated fund death- and performance-guarantees are protected by CompCorp insurance coverage.

Traditional Canadian mutual funds must, under federal law, be administered by a trustee, such as a bank or trust company. Thus, scams are virtually impossible. But if a mutual fund did suffer losses caused by theft or other dishonesty caused by the trustee's staff, these losses would be covered by banking and trust laws. Similarly, investments in segregated funds offered by life companies must, under federal insurance laws, be kept separate from the life companies other funds (hence the term 'segregated funds') and, hence, investments are covered under federal insurance laws. Furthermore, any life company losses caused by malfeasance are covered by CompCorp.

Any losses suffered by unscrupulous brokers are covered by bonding for all types of traditional mutual funds, or segregated funds offered by life companies. Finally, several provinces, including British Columbia, Nova Scotia, Ontario and Quebec, have contingency funds to protect investors against losses through a mutual fund dealer (as opposed to broker or representative, covered by bonding) caused by fraud.

13.   Dollar-Cost Averaging

Dollar-cost averaging (DCA) and mutual funds are an ideal way to invest regular amounts of savings for long-term growth with minimum risk. This dynamic duo lets you take maximum advantage of a favourite maxim of many investors: it's better to be an owner than a loaner. What this means is that you'll profit more by investing in the ownership of companies through shares that trade on stock exchanges, than by lending money to corporations, governments or financial institutions in the form of bonds, deposits or other debt instruments. There's lots of historical evidence to support this theory — if it's applied over long periods of time. One study, for instance, tracked the performance of the shares of 500 American companies for the period 1926–1987. The net compound return for all 500 issues over the 62 year period, after inflation and with dividends re-invested, averaged 6.9% compared to 1.9% for corporate bonds, 1.3% for government bonds, and a mere 0.5% for Treasury bills. That clearly demonstrates how, over time, it is better to own than loan!

But the same study also showed that during shorter periods, stock markets are volatile. The best performances by the 500 stocks in any one year was a net gain of 59%, while the worst year showed a loss of 43%. Over year-year holding periods, returns ranged from +24% to −12%. For ten-year periods, performances ranged from +0.9% to +20%. And for 25-year periods, from +5.9% to +15%. There were no periods of ten years or longer in which investing in these 500 shares would have produced a loss. Clearly, if you want to reduce the risks of being an owner you should invest for at least ten years, and preferably longer. You can further reduce the risks of short-term fluctuations in mutual fund prices by using dollar-cost averaging to invest a fixed amount at regular intervals, usually monthly. With DCA you can buy shares or units for less than their average selling price during a given period, which helps flatten short-term fluctuations. If Fund A sells for $10 per unit in July and $5 in August, the average price during the two months would be $7.50. But if you invested $1,000 to buy 100 units in July, and a further $1,000 to buy 200 shares in August, your average price would be only $6.67. If you want to invest regularly, a mutual fund — based on the historical evidence — offers an ideal combination of investment safety and growth potential, as long as you stick with it for the long term.

14. Taxation of Mutual Funds

With ever-more people owning mutual funds (and segregated funds, the life company equivalent), we are often asked to interpret amounts that show up on taxpayers' T3 reporting slips. The following may answer some of those questions.

Most mutual funds are operated as trusts wherein a trustee manages monies invested by many people. During the course of a year, the trustee realizes profits or losses in such areas as dividends, capital gains, interest, and expenses. Each of these various items must be accounted for to the owners of the mutual funds as a group, since the manager makes his profit as a fee paid by the fund. Thus all profits, losses and expenses must be allocated to the fund owners, even where some owners may have had no transactions during the year. So it's easy for a mutual fund owner to get confused as to why amounts show up on reporting slips (usually T3s, sometimes T5s).

'Dividends' are not necessarily dividends as usually thought of by investors. They could be, but they could also be capital gains distributed to unit holders as dividends, or interest similarly distributed, or traditional dividends. In any case, the taxation of such dividends could end up being taxed at up to three different rates! A mutual fund owner can also have taxable capital gains even though the owner had no transactions during the year. This is because, even though the unit owner himself had no transactions, his/her funds were being used by the fund manager to buy individual securities which themselves may get sold when the manager feels the time is right. And whatever profit is realized must be allocated by the fund manager by T3s issued to unit owners. So you can have a tax bill even though you may not have seen the cash!

Note that if your T3 slip shows foreign income, the odds were that your mutual fund paid foreign income tax, which is claimable as a deduction on your Canadian tax return. This is an item often overlooked by taxpayers preparing their own returns who do not have access to sophisticated computer software.

Note that none of the above applies to mutual funds held as RSPs, since all types of income generated within the RSP is tax-free until withdrawn. At withdrawal time, all such income is treated as fully taxable earned income.

Note also that the above does not apply to funds operated in foreign countries. While many U.S.-based funds will send you an IRS tax reporting slip, most other foreign (i.e. 'off-shore') funds will not send you any transaction reporting slips except if you have bought or sold. This can be a significant tax planning advantage to those currently in high tax brackets who expect to fall back into a lower bracket, as for instance at retirement.

Confused? Join the crowd. Almost everyone is, including me. I have learned to accept that most mutual fund T3 slips are produced by computer, and information is rigidly scrutinized at source (i.e. at the mutual fund's office) by Revenue Canada. So, no matter how confusing T3s might be, we can rest assured amounts reported are equitably allocated to unit owners. If you wish additional details, invest $30 in a current copy of *Preparing Your Income Tax Return*, by Arthur Anderson and Co. Be prepared for a mind-boggling evening!

15. Asset Allocation

'Asset Allocation' is a buzz phrase that has caught vogue in the investment world
in recent years. This is a type of mutual fund where the fund manager decides
when to buy bonds versus equities and other types of assets, including real estate,
mortgages, and precious metals. In effect, the investor says to the fund manager:
do with my funds what you think best depending on economic conditions as those
conditions change. Asset Allocation has long been available to those who retain
an investment broker (such as Stevens Financial Services) to act as intermediary
in finding homes for their funds. However, in recent years, many banks and trust
companies have introduced funds whose stated purpose allows the fund manager to
move investments among several types of assets as the fund manager sees fit. While
many asset allocation funds have out-performed the average mutual fund, others have
done poorly. There are no figures available on how asset allocation funds have done
as a group, since the group has changed in size and makeup substantially recently.
However, it would appear the group has not done nearly as well as a competent
investment broker would have done during a comparable period of time.

16. Derivatives

During the past two to three years, a number of major organizations have come tum-
bling down because of huge financial losses suffered on what's called the 'derivatives'
market. Barings Bank in the U.K., and Orange County, California, are but two of
the better publicized victims of derivative trading gone bad. Others who have lost
hundreds of millions in derivative trading have included the B.C.C.I. (before it went
belly-up due to fraud), Proctor & Gamble, and Gibson Greetings, and France's Crédit
Lyonnais. Derivatives are a form of financial contract that, if used wisely, can help an
investor, usually a corporation, hedge bets against something adverse happening in
the future. Derivatives are so called because their value is derived from the value of
an underlying stock, bond, other financial instrument, or commodity. The two most
common types of derivative that individual market investors would be familiar with
are 'futures' and 'options'.

A future is an agreement to buy or sell a determined quantity of a specific mer-
chandise — it could be bonds, or commodities, or anything else possessing intrinsic
value — at a predetermined future date and price. Futures on bonds (and bankers'
acceptances, a type of liquid bond sold by banks) are used to hedge interest rate risk,
while futures on commodities are used to hedge against rising or falling prices on
commodities as widely disparate as pork bellies and newsprint.

An option gives the buyer the right, but not the obligation, to buy the underlying
product — stocks, bonds, bankers' acceptances — at a specified price within a given
time period. Options are used as hedges against market volatility and can be used
to ensure that any gains made on an investment are not lost or that any losses are
minimized.

Much of the world-wide market in futures and options is traded 'over the counter',
and usually custom tailored between the buyer and the seller, which is why derivatives
cannot be traded on the same markets as stocks and bonds. Derivatives markets have
exploded in recent years, and no one really knows the world-wide value. Some
estimates range from $12 to $35 trillion. Thanks to electronic transfer of funds and

electronic mail, billions of dollars can and do move across international boundaries in the blink of an eye, far more quickly and massively than can trading in stocks and bonds.

Who uses derivatives? Virtually any larger organization that trades internationally, either in products, currencies, or financial obligations. Banks use derivatives to hedge against swings in foreign currency rates. Insurance companies use derivatives to hedge against swings in interest rates. Auto manufacturers use derivatives to hedge against price swings of the raw supplies needed for the production of their autos, resulting in relatively stable prices for the buying public. Governments use derivatives to stabilize gyrations in their currencies when their currencies face attack from speculators. Speculators themselves trade derivatives in the hope their guesses will prove right at someone else's expense. Pension funds use derivatives to hedge against a fall in interest rates. Mutual funds use derivatives to hedge against steep declines in equity markets. Distilleries use derivatives to insure themselves against a collapse in spirit prices. Wheat farmers use derivatives to hedge against a fall in wheat prices during the next harvest.

Where derivatives have gotten a bad name in recent years is from the irresponsible trading by under-supervised wonderkinds for the pure purpose of profiting, as opposed to hedging risk. This is speculation in its purest form, and can lead to huge losses in very quick time. It is estimated Barings trader Leeson lost the bulk of the $1 billion he cost his bank in less than a month. He was able to do so from Singapore, 10,000 miles from London head office, because he had no effective supervision.

What do derivatives mean to you and I as investors in mutual funds or GICs? Well, few of us realize it, but Canadian financial institutions regularly use derivatives to lessen risk, or to enhance performance. Thus, a life insurance company which anticipates large volumes of GIC sales during the next 60 days will often buy a derivative that will then allow the insurer to 'guarantee' today's rates to a client even though the client won't deliver his/her funds to that life insurance company for perhaps another 45 days (as in, for example, a transfer of RSPs from another financial institution to the life insurance company). A mutual fund company will use derivatives to either minimize risk of devaluation of stocks, bonds, or currencies, or to enhance performance of its portfolios.

What can you and I do to take advantage of, or to minimize exposure to, derivatives? Ask, ask, ask!!!

Fortunately, the use of derivatives in Canada is extremely well regulated and tightly supervised internally within those organizations that use them. The chartered banks have, for example, tight controls on what their currency traders are allowed to do. And Canadian federal regulators keep a close eye on the principal derivative market, the Montreal Exchange.

While it is derivatives-based financial disasters that hit the press, there are success stories. One individual, well known among currency speculators, by the name of Soros, is believed to have made a $1 Billion profit two years ago almost overnight when he successfully bought derivatives betting against the British pound, which was devalued overnight by some 15%. The Rockefeller family made much of its many millions by buying and selling oil futures. McCains has become the world's largest seller of French Fried potatoes by being adept at hedging prices of raw potatoes and of currencies in countries where it sells fries, through aggressive and savvy use of derivatives. Indeed, were derivatives not available to lessen risk, it is doubtful that McCains would have even bothered to venture abroad.

17.   Investing — Post Referendum

The atmosphere on Canadian investment markets has been quite upbeat, following a very tight "no" victory in the October Quebec referendum. Canadian equities have been doing very well, beginning to catch up the 25%+ lag they had fallen behind American equities.

Interest rates and the Canadian dollar have been quite stable.

What's next?

The Canadian economy is steaming along. The economy is likely to stay healthy, returning record profits, for at least as long as interest rates stay low. Interest rates are likely to stay low as long as inflation remains at the current 2% or so, and the political situation remains relatively stable.

But that is where the rub is. The last referendum was so close that the governing Parti Québécois is acting as though they had won, promising another referendum sometime in 1997 following a provincial election, which could be held as early as this spring. My bet is that no appeasement by the other provinces and the feds will avert a "yes" victory next time, leading to the breakup of Canada as we have known it for over 125 years.

There is no question the breakup of Canada will be an emotional wrench that will take many Canadians a lifetime to get over. But, the logical fact is that it is Quebec that would suffer greatly economically, not the Rest Of Canada (ROC). True, it would take a couple of years for the ROC to adjust economically, but, in the long run, within no more than five years, Canada would end up being stronger economically without Quebec than with it.

At least until a provincial election is held (and not just called), interest rates will remain as low as they are now (with five-year GICs going for no more than 6.5%, and one-year deposits fetching only 5%).

Once the election is held, if the results confirm the Parti Québécois in their determination to hold a referendum in 1997, interest rates should rise, but by no more than 1%, if that. And as we get closer to the referendum, with the increased political instability that implies, rates might increase by up to 2% over present rates (remember that rates went up only 1% in the days immediately before the last referendum, when it looked like the "yes" side would win).

With the economy expected to continue doing well for at least the next two (and probably more like four) years, investments in Canadian equity mutual funds will continue returning much better profits than GICs.

For those with no stomach for any risk, then the only GICs to buy are those for a term of no more than 18 months, to ensure you can take advantage of the higher interest rates when the next referendum comes around.

As for those who wonder if they shouldn't invest in U.S. equities because of the tremendous gains in the Dow Jones (more than 30% last year), we would observe that Canadian equities should, having lagged behind U.S. equities for the past two years, over the next two years, do considerably better than U.S. equities.

For those who insist in investing in other than Canadian securities because of their concern over the safety of the Canadian dollar, they should seriously investigate a good insured and guaranteed off-shore fund, rather than investing in a U.S. equity fund offered by a Canadian distributor. This is because the Canadian distributor would have to convert your investment back into Canadian dollars when you wanted to be paid off, while an off-shore fund could pay you back in just about any currency of your choosing. If you pick the right off-shore fund, there are <u>no</u> taxes until you bring the profits back home!

That's how we see things, at least at the moment! But with those nationalists in Quebec City who are so good at avoiding logic in favour of emotion, anything's possible over the next 18 months.

Quebec's leaving Canada is not only a possibility, but, at this juncture, must be considered a likelihood.

1.   Have You Made a Will?

IS IT UP TO DATE?

SHOULD IT BE CHANGED?

IS IT IN A SAFE PLACE?

This article has been prepared by excerpting liberally, with permission to do so, from a booklet, "Have You Made A Will" by William MacKinnon, VP-Counsel, Metropolitan Life.

You just haven't got around to it, and anyway you haven't much to leave? Besides, you don't like to think about wills? And then it costs money to make one. Those are the most common excuses for not making one. But, despite them, you should make a will — if you do not have one — and it should be made before you put it off again. After your death it is too late to decide who will own your house, who will drive your car, who will wear your diamond. If you want to be sure your possessions are distributed the way you want them to be after your death, you must leave a sound, valid will. If your dependents are not adequately provided for, generally speaking, the court may make an order for their maintenance out of your estate.

Wills may be made by all persons who are not minors and who are otherwise competent. However, if you don't select your beneficiaries, the law will select them for you and decide what they will receive. The better off you are, the more important it is you have a will. If your widow(er) is going to have to count the pennies to pay the bills after your death, it is also important to see that your family gets whatever you have to leave, without large deductions or delays caused by legal red tape. In other words, make a will.

But if you say you're not married, you still need a will if you want anything to say about who gets your property. If you don't leave a will, the court will distribute your property in accordance with ironclad rules of descent and distribution that no one can tinker with. That cousin you haven't seen since you were 12 may become heir if there are no nearer relatives surviving. Wouldn't you rather decide yourself who is to enjoy your treasures? A will should state two things: how your property is to be distributed and who is to serve as executor. By naming one or more persons as executor, you know that your property will be distributed in accordance with the terms of your will. Naming your executor saves money, time and delay in providing for the welfare of your beneficiaries. In most cases the husband or wife is named as executor or executrix in the will. A close relative or friend may be named as executor. You should name an alternate executor in case the one named cannot serve.

In these days of complicated tax laws, it might be wise to name a lawyer or a trust company as executor along with, or instead of, your husband or wife. Except when the executor is also a solicitor, he will need the services of a lawyer. A corporate executor has the advantage of continuity. If you have minor children, you may wish, in those provinces that permit it, to make provisions for a suitable guardian in case both mother and father should die.

Competent legal advice is preferable for making a valid and adequate will. Select a good lawyer on the advice of family and friends. Before you engage him, ask him about his fees. The cost is generally reasonable, especially in view of the legal fees and frequent death or other taxes that it may save your estate. When you have selected your lawyer, give him/her all the facts as to your estate. Business dealings between lawyer and client are confidential. Your lawyer may also give you some further ideas on executor selection.

After the will has been drawn up, you will be required to sign it in the presence of two witnesses who must sign in the presence of each other and the testator (that's you). Do not allow anyone who is named in the will or his or her spouse to be a witness. Witnesses should be younger than the person making the will. This increases the possibility that they will outlive him and be available to testify to the carrying out of the will after his death. They should also be permanent residents of the country. In some provinces, including Ontario, wills are valid if made in the handwriting of the testator. Now that you have made your will, don't forget about it. Changes — birth, death, marriage, divorce, separation, higher living costs, major acquisitions of property — all have an effect on your will. Keep it up to date. The will you made when the children were small may not be what you want when the children are grown. If you were unmarried when you drew your will, your marriage may act to revoke it. Divorce or annulment may act to revoke part or all of your will. If you have moved from one province to another, the law of wills may be different in the jurisdiction to which you have moved and may require some change in the form of your will. A review of your will every year or two will assure your desires are clear and that your will is valid. Wills speak as of the time of death.

If you want to change your will, don't try to do it yourself. You can't cross out Mary's name and insert Louise's. After the will is signed there should be no alterations of any kind. However, you can make a new will or add a codicil at any time; but the codicil is subject to the same requirements as to the formalities of the will itself. It's good sense to make your will or change it when you are of sound mind and body. If you wait until you're critically ill or in a hospital, you may be inviting someone to contest a will made under such circumstances.

Making your will isn't enough. It's also important to make a list of business and legal papers for your executor. The list should include: where you have your insurance policies, the name of the company with whom you are insured, the amount of your policies and whether there are any loans against them; what securities you have and where they are; where your duplicate tax returns are; the deed to your house and the amount of your mortgage; where your chequeing account is, where your savings accounts are, and where the passbooks are kept; and where your jewellery, furs and other valuables may be stored. Some people consider it important that you leave instructions on how you want your funeral handled, whether you have paid for a cemetery lot, the description of the monument, and where you wish to be buried. Directions as to your interment may be put in your will as well.

Don't hide your will where it can't be found. Many have been lost. Others have been found in window shades, in old shoes, in almost every hiding place you can think of. You don't want your bereaved family to go on a scavenger hunt for your will. If it is never found, even the best will in the world is useless. You can store your will with your stock certificates and other important papers in a safety deposit box at your bank. You can file your will with your trust company or your lawyer, but be sure to tell your family where it is.

Some Words of Warning: Do not make your will without the advice of your lawyer (or notary in Quebec). Do not mention specific amounts where percentages will suffice. Do not name an executor solely for sentimental reasons. Do not forget to date your will. Do not wait any longer to make a will.

Now you've made your will, does your family know . . . :

- Where your will is?
- Where the key to your safety deposit box is?
- Where your safety deposit box is located?
- Where your securities are stored?
- Where your life insurance policies are?
- Where you have placed your duplicate tax returns?
- Where your bank accounts are located?
- Where your bank statements/passbooks are?
- Where the house deed is?
- Where the valuables and legal documents are?
- Name and address of your:
    - Executor
    - Accountant
    - Lawyer/notary
    - Life underwriter/broker
    - Financial advisor

<u>Write the answers to the above questions down, preferably today, as a guide for your executor. Tell your executor where your answers are located!</u>

2. Probate Fees

Probate fees, like fees for closing a house, are set by provincial regulations, and vary widely. In Ontario, probate costs $5/$1,000 for the first $50,000, and $15/$1,000 thereafter, with no maximum. Alberta charges progressive rates, starting at $25 for the first $5,000, increasing to a maximum of $1,000 for estates of $500,000 or more. B.C. charges a flat fee on the first $25,000, and $5/$1,000 thereafter with no maximum. Manitoba and New Brunswick charge $5/$1,000 with no maximum. Newfoundland charges a flat fee for the first $1,000 and $4/$1,000 thereafter. Nova Scotia also has progressive rates, starting at $75 for the first $10,000, increasing to $500 for the first $200,000 in an estate and $3/$1,000 thereafter, with no maximum. P.E.I. has a progressive system starting at $50 for the first $10,000 increasing to $400 for estates of $400,000 and $4/$1,000 thereafter. Saskatchewan has a flat fee for the first $1,000 and $6/$1,000 thereafter, with no maximum. In Quebec, there are no probate fees for notarial wills. However, they charge $45 for wills drawn in English!

As can be seen, there is a wide variance between the provinces as to amounts charged for probate. Ranging from nil in Quebec, the fees for an estate of $500,000 rise to a high in Ontario of $7,000. Note that the fees quoted above are court fees. These are not to be confused with other legal fees, nor fees to administer the estate while the estate is in probate. There are many steps individuals can take to minimize probate costs. See here in 'Minimizing Estate Costs'. Note also that the Province wherein an estate will be probated is not the province wherein the individual passed away, nor even for that matter the province where the individual last lived, but the province of domicile; i.e. the province that the deceased considered his permanent home.

3.   RSP/RIF Beneficiaries

Few owners of RSPs or RIFs are aware of what happens to their plans when they die. Hardly a month goes by that we don't run into someone who thinks they can leave their RSPs to a relative, tax-free. Here is a run-down of the regulations:

You can leave your RSPs and RIFs to someone tax-free only if the someone is: a spouse; or a disabled child/grandchild who is financially dependent on you; or to buy an annuity for a healthy child or grandchild with annuity payments ceasing when that child reaches age 18.

That's it! No, you can't leave some of your RSPs to a favourite aunt, or to the Humane Society, without triggering income tax. And if you leave your RSPs/RIFs to anyone outside the chosen group as defined above, the value of those registered monies is taxed in your hands as though you had cashed them in the day before you died. Only the proceeds after payment of income tax by you is available for distribution to the beneficiary(ies). So, if you have, say, $100,000 in registered plans, no spouse, and no children or grandchildren under age 18, and you were leaving these RSPs to your grown-up children, the $100,000 would be added to whatever other income you had in that year in which you died, and your estate would pay income tax on the total before any of your registered funds were paid out to your children. In some provinces, including Ontario, that could result in a tax rate of no less than 54%! That $100,000 now becomes only $46,000 after income tax, which if split between two children, results in each getting $23,000 !

What if you have $100,000 in registered plans and a further $100,000 in term deposits (i.e. GICs), and you want to leave the whole to your two 'of-age' children? Should you name one child as beneficiary of the GIC, with the other child as beneficiary to the registered funds? Or should you try to let your estate figure it out, pay the taxes, and make distributions from what's left over?

None of the above!! If you let your estate take care of taxes and distribution, your estate then must be probated. Any instructions you have left with the financial institutions holding your investments will be ignored in favour of what your will says, and in some provinces (especially Ontario), that will involve a lawyer and probate fees. On the other hand, if you leave all of your registered monies to one child, and your term deposits to the other, then the child who is to receive your registered funds will lose perhaps half the value in income tax while the other child will get virtually all of the proceeds from the term deposit.

The solution would be to name your children as equal beneficiaries with the financial institutions holding your funds, while leaving your estate with sufficient assets to pay whatever income tax liability resulting when the Taxman adds the value of your registered plans to whatever other income you had up to the date of your demise. Don't name minor children as beneficiaries. Should you die having named a minor as beneficiary of one or more of your investments, the financial institution will have no choice under the law but to pay the funds to that minor's legal guardian. If you have not named a legal guardian in your will, the province where you resided at the time of your demise will step in and name a guardian for that minor child.

We saw a situation several years ago where a wealthy widow left her assets to a 17-year-old son, who was attending university. The son turned 18 before the estate was wound up. But that did not prevent the widow's executor from transferring her registered funds to an RSP in the son's name, where it has been financing his higher education ever since.

4.   Lack of a Will

We have stressed the importance of a will in other articles herein if you want your assets divided according to your wishes on your demise (see above: 'Have You Made a Will?' and 'Probate'). But, what happens to your assets if you don't have a will? Obviously, you lose control of your assets when you die. What isn't so obvious is that you lose control to the provincial authorities in the province where you are domiciled at the time of your death. It is those authorities who decide what to do with your assets based on provincial laws that are very binding on those officials.

The Trust Companies Association of Canada recently commissioned a survey, in which it was found that approximately 50% of Canadian adults had not drawn a will. Yet, among those who haven't had a will prepared, approximately 75% think they know who will inherit their assets. See the table below for what happens if you die without a will. If minor children are involved, remember also that you lose control in naming a guardian. The province will appoint their guardian, who will have no leeway in providing additional amounts over and above the basic necessities for your children's care and upbringing. The survey also revealed that fully one third of Canadians who have made a will have not discussed it with the person(s) named as executor. Almost half also did not know that the executor could be held liable for mistakes while the estate was being probated. Furthermore, many people do not realize that a person named as executor can renounce the position. If provision is not made within a will for such an eventuality, the will would then be administered by provincial authorities acting on orders from the Surrogate Court. Your Executor must have full knowledge of the contents of your will while you are alive if you want your affairs settled the way you want them. Choosing your executor must be done very carefully, bearing in mind that your executor should have expertise in financial matters. If your spouse has no such expertise, avoid naming him/her to that post, even if you mistakenly believe that by doing so, you will save your estate large fees. You can easily find someone who will competently execute your last wishes for a negligible fee, if you avoid a lawyer (who is paid according to a schedule set by the Law Society and the Surrogate Court). If you do decide to name a family member as

Executor, remember that the Executor will be trying to follow your last wishes while he/she is still grieving!

What Happens If You Die Without A Will

	Survived By:			
Prov.	Spouse Only	Children Only	Spouse & one child	Spouse & children
Nfld	All to spouse	All to children	Split equally	1/3 to spouse; 2/3 to children
N.S.	All to spouse	All to children	1st $50,000 to spouse; rest split equally	1st $50,000 to spouse; 1/3 rest to spouse; 2/3 rest to children
P.E.I.	All to spouse	All to children	Split equally	1/3 to spouse; 2/3 to children
N.B.	All to spouse	All to children	Belongings to spouse; rest split equally	Belongings to spouse; 1/3 rest to spouse; 2/3 rest to children
Que.	All to spouse	All to children	1/3 to spouse; 2/3 to child	1/3 to spouse; 2/3 to children
Ont.	All to spouse	All to children	1st $75,000 to spouse; rest split equally	1st $75,000 to spouse; 1/3 rest to spouse; 2/3 rest to children
Man.	All to spouse	All to children	All to spouse	All to spouse
Sask.	All to spouse	All to children	1st $100,000 to spouse; rest split equally	1st $100,000 to spouse; 1/3 rest to spouse; 2/3 rest to children
Alta	All to spouse	All to children	1st $40,000 to spouse; rest split equally	1st $40,000 to spouse; 1/3 rest to spouse; 2/3 rest to children
B.C.	All to spouse	All to children	1st $65,000 to spouse; rest split equally	1st $65,000 to spouse; 1/3 rest to spouse; 2/3 rest to children

5. Power of Attorney

Every day, hundreds of Canadians lose their ability to manage and administer their financial affairs because of mental impairment or physical incapacity due to accident or illness. Many more are on holiday or business at a considerable distance from home. Many of these individuals then suffer hardship by not having set up their affairs whereby a trusted family member or other friend/advisor could make and execute decisions on their behalf. Reprinted herein, without permission, are excerpts from an excellent booklet published by the Self-Counsel Press folks, authored by M. Stephen Georgas, LL.B., entitled *Power of Attorney Kit*.

Should you be concerned about your financial affairs? You may be well organized, have all your financial papers filed and ready to access if something should suddenly happen to you. You may update your will regularly and rest assured that your family is well taken care of. But, what would happen if you suddenly became incapacitated overnight? How would your spouse or family access your bank account or take care of your affairs? You might want to grant a power of attorney to your child to provide for your care as you grow older. Or you might want someone to take care of your financial affairs while you take an extended vacation. In any case, a power of attorney is a useful document giving someone the authority to act on your behalf on certain matters.

5.1.   What is a power of attorney?

Simply stated, a power of attorney is a written document by which you grant to someone the authority to act on your behalf on various matters. A power of attorney can be a very useful device in the management of your affairs during your lifetime, particularly as you grow older. For example, you might grant a power of attorney to your child to enable him or her to provide for your care after a certain age. A power of attorney is different from a will, which provides for the orderly distribution of your estate <u>after</u> your death; in most situations, a power of attorney terminates on your death. The person who gives the authority is called the <u>principal,</u> or the donor; the person to whom the authority is given is called the <u>agent</u>, donee, or attorney. You can appoint your agent to carry out certain acts for you such as:

- negotiating cheques, bills of exchange, promissory notes;
- purchasing, selling, or dealing with stocks or bonds;
- collecting rents, profits, commissions;
- managing, buying, selling real estate; and
- conducting business operations.

5.2.   Agency

Because the law of agency applies to powers of attorney, it is helpful to understand some of the concepts of that law. The relationship between an agent and a principal is called an agency. An agency is created when one person, the agent, is given the authority to act on behalf of another person, the principal. An example of an agent that many people use is a real estate agent. Generally, a real estate agent is appointed to act for a principal on certain transactions dealing with real estate. The authority is given to the real estate agent in the listing agreement and in the agreement of purchase and sale. In those documents, the agent's terms of appointment, duties and remuneration are set out. An agent is <u>not</u> an employee or an independent contractor. Legally, an employee works under the direct control and supervision of an employer and is bound to perform within the employer's guidelines and directives; an independent contractor is free to perform work as he or she sees fit and is bound only to produce the result defined by a specific contract. On the other hand, although he or she is bound to perform duties according to the principal's instructions, an agent is not normally under direct supervision like an employee, but neither is he/she free to act like an independent contractor. An agent must be instructed and guided by the agency contract.

5.3. How is an agency created?

A contract of agency or power of attorney is created when two people formalize an agreement between them. Generally, this is done by signing and sealing a document in front of a witness and having the witness swear an affidavit he or she saw the document signed. (To 'seal' a document simply means to place a small red sticker or wafer next to the signatures of the people making the contract. This practice is a holdover from the days when wax impressions were used to record a person's seal of promise. Red wafers, or seals, are available in most stationery stores.) A power of attorney is created in the document when the principal gives authority to the agent to act in his/her name.

5.4. Who can be a principal or agent?

Generally, whatever you have the power to do yourself, you can do by means of an agent. Similarly, whatever you do not have the power to do yourself, cannot be done through an agent. If you can legally enter into a contract, you may grant a power of attorney. In most cases, only the following cannot grant a power of attorney or be a principal:

- an alien enemy;
- an infant (i.e., any individual under the age of majority, which age varies from province to province, subject to certain exceptions, the primary one being a married infant can delegate power of attorney);
- persons of unsound mind;
- corporations (unless permitted by a company's articles of incorporation, and appropriate legislation in its jurisdiction).

There are fewer limits on who can act as an agent. Anyone other than a mental incompetent can be an agent, including an infant.

5.5. What is *in* a power of attorney?

A power of attorney may be drafted to grant virtually any powers to an agent, except for certain limitations under law. For example, you could not grant someone the power to get married on your behalf.

Special and general powers of attorney: A power of attorney may be either general, which extends to all kinds of business, or special, which deals with specific duties only. An example of a general power would be a document stating 'to do on my behalf anything that I can lawfully do by an attorney'. An example of a special power is a document stating 'to enter into an agreement of purchase and sale, and sell my property known as 123 Main St. ... ' Another example of a special power is when a person grants another the power to perform banking matters. For example, elderly people, or people on vacation, may appoint someone to deposit cheques or pay bills on their behalf because it is difficult or inconvenient for them to personally attend to these matters. In these cases, rather than use a general power of attorney form, the banks usually use their own forms to be signed by the person granting the power of attorney. These forms are available at your local bank branch upon request and at no charge.

Power of attorney for Old Age Security and Canada Pension Plan: Just as a power of attorney may be signed by elderly people for banking purposes, a similar technique is available for administering benefits under the OAS Act or CPP. Recipients of cheques under these plans may be too old or ill to go to the bank and cash the cheques. In such situations, it is possible to name a trustee to receive cheques and administer affairs of the recipient. To do so, the agent must sign an Undertaking to Administer Benefits under OAS and/or CPP. As well, the principal must sign a Certificate of Incapability.

5.6. Duties of the agent

Whether or not the power is general or special, the wording in the agreement must be strictly construed and must not be interpreted in any way to extend the agent's authority beyond the agreement. If the agent does act beyond the authority in the agreement, the power of attorney becomes void. In addition to the duties specified in the power of attorney, the following duties of the agent are implied unless excluded by specific wording to the contrary:

- the duty to use reasonable care in the performance of acts done on behalf of the principal;
- the duty to be accountable to the principal;
- the duty not to make profits that the principal does not know about.

5.7. Signing the power of attorney

Once both principal and agent are satisfied with the power of attorney, it must be properly signed. When the principal signs, a red seal should be affixed opposite his/her name. Then the signature should be witnessed by someone other than the principal or agent. The witness should also swear an affidavit of subscribing witness.

5.8. Terminating a power of attorney

A power of attorney can be terminated in the following ways:

- by fulfilling a specific provision of the agreement, such as terminating on a specific date or occurrence of a specific event;
- by the principal revoking the power;
- by the agent renouncing the power;
- by the principal going bankrupt;
- by death or mental incompetency of the principal (with exceptions noted below).

Over the course of a lifetime, you may sign several powers of attorney, so the question may arise as to which agent has power to act in a particular situation. This potential situation may be overcome by including in the power a revocation of any previous powers of attorney. Many people have signed powers of attorney to look after their affairs during any subsequent mental incapacity and the legislation in some provinces, including Ontario, permits a power of attorney to survive a principal's mental incapacity if there is express wording to that effect, and if it is witnessed by someone other than the principal or agent. The power of attorney will, however, terminate if a committee is appointed for the principal in such provinces, including Ontario under that province's Mental Incompetency Act.

The above represents excerpts of the more important information contained in the booklet *Power of Attorney Kit*. The booklet contains other, more technical information, not germane to this article, which should be consulted by anyone contemplating a do-it-yourself Power of Attorney. As well, the booklet contains numerous examples of completed paperwork, as well as sample forms that require only filling in and signatures to be valid.

6. Ontario Powers of Attorney

Ontario's Bill 108, the Substitute Decisions Act was proclaimed into law on April 3, 1995. While Ontarions have the right to appoint someone to look after their property and financial affairs, the new law, for the first time, allows individuals to appoint someone to look after their personal care as well. The new law now allows Ontarions to specify what kind of care they are to receive while still alive, as well as what their attorney is to do with regard to their property and finances.

The government of Ontario has produced a kit explaining the new act, including forms you can use to appoint your attorney. It's free by calling 416-314-2989.

7. Disability

Disability strikes suddenly . . . anytime.

Accidents and illness don't advertise. They just happen. Their most crippling effect can be on a family's standard of living. They can also be devastating to a small business or proprietorship, a professional practice, a partnership, or a single person with a large income, particularly if that single person has a lifestyle to match. Everyone has some resources to help offset loss of income. But what would a long-term disability mean to you or your family's way of life? Think it can't happen to you? Here are the odds:

Between Ages:	% of people who will be disabled at least once for 90 days or more
25–65	75%
35–65	70%
45–65	55%
55–65	50%

Source: Commissioner's Disability Table.

It only has to happen once to happen too often!

This article is devoted to disability. It has been produced by virtually copying, with updated figures where necessary, the entire contents of a booklet entitled, 'Where will the money come from . . . if you're disabled?' This booklet is produced by the Information Centre of the Canadian Life and Health Insurance Association Inc.,

2500–20 Queen St. West, Toronto, M5H 3S2. Acknowledgement to use material herein is extended to Mr. Wayne E. Sinclair, Manager, The Information Centre. For further information on disability and how you can protect yourself and your loved ones from its economic ravages, call the Information Centre at their toll-free number, 1-800-268-8099, or talk to your professional advisor.

7.1. Introduction

Like most Canadians, you probably rely on income from your employment to cover your living expenses. But, what happens if you are unable to work because of illness or accident? To help replace salary or wages, a variety of government, employer, and individual plans are available. The challenge is to fit together these pieces of the income replacement puzzle so they can provide adequate income in case a disability prevents you from working. Anticipating possibilities such as premature death or disability is an important part of financial planning. Most bread-winners recognize the need to shield their families against financial disaster in case they die prematurely by purchasing life insurance policies. Yet, many of them have inadequate protection against loss of income if they become disabled, even though the average 30 year-old is almost seven times more likely to be ill or injured for 90 days or more than to die in the following year. If disability strikes you, where will the money come from to pay for food, housing, transportation and other basic expenses? Would it be enough? This booklet (sic) has been prepared to help you address these concerns. It will assist you in determining: a) your current protection; b) how much income replacement insurance you need; and c) what to do if you require additional coverage.

The plans offered through the government, employers and individual policies vary greatly, featuring different definitions of disability, benefit periods and elimi-nation periods. While some offer a wide range of coverage, others protect against loss of income from certain disabilities or causes. For example, employer plans may cover disabilities ranging from hockey injuries to heart disease, while car insurance will replace income lost only if you're hurt in a car accident. Benefits from the Canada/Quebec Pension Plans are available to most workers regardless of the cause of disability, while Workers' Compensation applies only to work-related conditions. Determining how much disability income replacement insurance you'll need to re-place your current earnings and the sources from which it is available need not be difficult, as we'll see . . .

7.2. What is disability income replacement insurance?

Disability income replacement insurance provides you with an income should you become sick and injured and unable to work. It can be the main buffer between financial well-being and catastrophe for you and your family, if you are unable to work even for short periods. These plans operate on the principle that many people pool their money to insure that if any of them become disabled, a portion of their income will be replaced until they can rejoin the workforce. Various forms of coverage are available, but they usually fall under two types: short-term disability or weekly indemnity plans and long-term disability plans. Frequently, these two main types of disability plans are coordinated so that payments from long-term plans begin immediately after payments end from short-term plans.

Plans are usually integrated to insure that the disabled person's benefits do not exceed the income that would normally be received from work. If benefits were set at very high levels, the individual's incentive to return to work could be destroyed and costs for other plan members would be pushed up. As well as providing regular monthly income replacement benefits, many plans assist disabled people in obtaining rehabilitation services which may enable them to return to work. The types of services which are appropriate vary widely from person to person depending on the type of disability, but may include pain therapy, physiotherapy, psychological counselling and vocational retraining. Other rehabilitation services include special assistance devices and renovations to homes or job sites.

7.3. Sources of income replacement insurance

It is important to understand the various sources of disability income replacement insurance and how they fit together. To find out how much coverage you already have you need to examine: a) government programs; b) coverage available through employment; and c) any individual plans you may have purchased. As you examine each of these sources, record the benefits available to you.

7.3.1. Government

The most common government income replacement programs are Workers' Compensation, UIC, and the Canada/Quebec Pension Plans.

Workers' Compensation: Employees of many industries are covered by provincial Workers' Compensation programs which pay benefits, based on earnings, for work-related accidents. Recently, some illnesses have been covered where evidence satisfactory to the Workers' Compensation Board has linked the illness to working conditions. Generally, payments under employer and individual plans are reduced by amounts received under Workers' Compensation programs. Alternatively, such plans may not cover work-related conditions. Benefits are not taxable.

Unemployment Insurance: Short-term disability benefits are provided under the UI Act, beginning two weeks after the disability commences and continuing for a maximum of fifteen weeks. These payments are 55% of weekly insurable earnings up to a maximum of $448 in 1995. Benefits are taxable. If employer plans provide benefits which meet certain criteria, they may be registered to substitute for these UI payments. Alternatively, benefits from employer plans may be payable only after UI benefits run out, or before UI benefits start. If both employer and UI benefits are payable simultaneously, UI benefits are reduced by the amount of the payments from the employer plan.

Canada/Quebec Pension Plans: Disability benefits under the C/QPP may be paid together with the employer and individual plan benefits for those with long-term disabilities. Generally, the C/QPP definition of disability is stricter than for employer and individual plans. The 1996 CPP maximum monthly benefit for a totally and permanently disabled person is $871 with an extra $161 a month for each eligible child. Under many plans, the total employer or individual plan benefit is reduced by any amount received initially from the C/QPP so that the total benefit is the same whether or not C/QPP benefits are payable. However, increases in the C/QPP as a result of changes in the cost of living index do not reduce payments from private plans in subsequent years. Benefits are taxable.

7.3.2. Your Employer

The next step in determining how much disability income coverage you have is to check with your employer, union or association representative. Some employers will continue your salary or wages for a specified number of days. These uninsured programs are generally called sick leave or salary continuation.

Group Disability Replacement Insurance: Many employers also provide protection for their employees through group disability income replacement insurance. Because these plans are intended to replace income which employees would be earning if they were not disabled, benefits are usually a certain percentage of normal earnings for a specified period, under certain circumstances. If the employer pays all or part of the premiums, these benefits are taxable. Because plans are usually integrated, payments from group disability income replacement insurance may be reduced if benefits are received from other sources such as government programs.

Short-Term Plans: Short-term group disability plans, often referred to as weekly indemnity plans, provide weekly payments; for example, 70% of normal weekly income. They often start the first day of a disability resulting from an accident and the fourth or eighth day when sickness is the cause. The maximum period during which the disabled person may receive benefits varies by plan, the most common being 15, 26, or 52 weeks.

Long-Term Plans: Long-term group disability plans normally provide between 50% and 80% of your normal income up to a stated maximum. Typically, they specify an elimination period of at least 90 days between the onset of the disability and the date of commencement of benefit payments. Benefits usually continue for up to two years if you are unable to resume your normal occupation and for a longer period, e.g. to age 65 or death if earlier, if you are unable to work at any occupation. When short- and long-term plans are coordinated, long-term benefits begin immediately after payments end from the short-term plan.

Plan Provisions: The provisions in a group disability plan depend on factors such as the size and composition of the group, whether protection is short- or long-term or both, the amount of coverage that is affordable, and the availability of other income replacement arrangements. For example, if work-related accidents are already covered by Workers' Compensation, the group plan may cover only other disabilities.

Questions to Ask About Your Group Coverage: Most of the answers should be found in a booklet outlining your employee benefits package. If not, ask your employer, union or association representative. Take a few minutes to record your answers . . .

1. What percentage of salary or flat rate benefit will be paid?
2. How long will benefits be paid?
3. How long will you have to wait (elimination period) before benefits begin?

4. Will the benefits continue if you return to your normal job on a trial or part-time basis? If so, for how much, under what conditions, and for how long?

5. Will the benefits continue if you can take another kind of job? If so, for how much, under what conditions, and for how long?

6. Are rehabilitation services available? If so, will benefits continue during rehabilitation?

7. Under what conditions could payments be reduced or stopped?

8. Does the coverage continue if you are on strike or on leave?

9. If you continue to work past normal retirement age, will coverage continue? For how long?

10. Will any benefits be taxable?

11. Does the coverage contain any exclusions or limitations?

12. Are there any special benefits, such as cost-of-living adjustments, offered in this contract?

13. Are there any differences in the definition of disability, elimination period and length of payments between accident claims and sickness claims?

I shall next review individual income replacement plans, and other sources of benefits during disability. Once you've found out what benefits you already have, you'll then be able to add them all up with other sources of income (e.g. investments) to see whether you'll have enough to support yourself and/or your family. We've seen how dangerous disability can be to one's financial situation and how government and employer plans help cushion the blow. We saw that an individual has at least a 50% chance of suffering a disability due to accident or sickness for ninety days or more before age 65. We also saw that those odds rise to 75% for 25-year-olds. We further saw what sources of disability income replacement were available from government and employer plans. Now I'll look at what other sources of disability income are available, including private plans, what kind of private plans are available, and what to look for when shopping for one. I'll then add it all up to see where we'd stand if we were to suffer a long-term disability tomorrow.

7.3.3. Individual plans

A disability income replacement plan that you buy as an individual can be an important means of bridging any gaps between your monthly living expenses if you're disabled and any benefits available to you from government and group plans. Like life insurance, it's an essential part of financial protection for you and your family. If you have group insurance, an individual policy can provide additional income in the event of a disability and can tailor financial protection to your individual needs. An individual plan is particularly important for people who are not protected by a group plan. Individual income replacement insurance can save self-employed people from bankruptcy if they're disabled. Business interruption insurance and other forms of coverage may also help pay the bills if your business is put on hold because of your disability. If you're self-employed you may be able to buy group income replacement coverage through a professional or business association. If so, compare the prices and features with individual plans. Like many Canadians, you may already own individual disability replacement policies. But, as with any other facet of financial planning, your coverage should be reviewed periodically to make sure it has kept pace with your present situation. For example, increases in family expenses in the past few years may require an increase in disability income protection.

Features of Individual Disability Income Replacement Plans: The value of an individual disability income replacement policy lies in the insurance company's promise to cushion you against loss of income resulting from sickness or an accident. You buy this promise with your payment or premium. The value of a company's promise to pay you benefits is measured by the answers to several questions:

How Much? The amount of benefits is specified in your policy. It is determined when the policy is issued, based on your salary or wages. Usually, benefits from all sources — government, employer and individual plans — cannot exceed 80 percent of your earned income. As with most types of insurance, the premium you pay is in direct proportion to the amount of the benefit yielded by the policy. Benefits under individual plans are not taxable (if the premium is payable by the assured. –author's note).

How Soon? You can choose a policy in which the benefit payments start anywhere from the first day to six months or even more after the onset of disability. The longer the elimination period, the lower your premium.

How Long? The benefit period specified in the policy determines how long benefits continue, which could be as little as one year or for a longer period such as for life. The shorter the benefit period, the lower the premium.

Under What Circumstances? Every disability income replacement plan contains its own definition of disability which determines what benefits will or won't be paid. The definition may vary by plan. For example, most provisions require that you be totally disabled before benefits begin. Benefits for partial disability are sometimes provided, but most often only if the partial disability follows a period of total disability for the same cause. Some plans pay only if you cannot perform your usual occupation. Before you buy a disability income replacement policy, ask to see a sample policy. Read it carefully, paying special attention to the way disability is defined. Also check whether a recurring disability would be treated as a continuation of the previous benefit period or a new benefit period. If you already own a disability income replacement policy, make sure you understand its definitions of disability and other important provisions.

Types of Individual Coverage: Three broad types of disability coverage are available for individuals: commercial, guaranteed renewable, and non-cancellable (or non-cancellable guaranteed renewable). In a commercial policy, the insurer can raise the premium rate on the policy anniversary to reflect claims experience or can decline to renew the policy. With guaranteed renewable policies, the insurance company must renew the policy, but premiums may be raised by class. This means that the increase applies to all policy owners; i.e. to a particular category rather than to one individual policy owner. Under a non-cancellable (or non-cancellable guaranteed renewable) policy, the insurance company can neither cancel coverage nor vary the premium rate specified in the contract. Policies specify at the time of purchase the length of time the coverage is non-cancellable and guaranteed renewable.

Questions to Ask About Your Individual Policy: Most of these questions should be answered in a brochure or policy summary from the insurance company. If not, ask your life insurance agent (or broker). Record the answers to your questions . . .

1. What monthly benefit will be paid?
2. How long will benefits be paid?
3. How long will you have to wait for benefits to begin?
4. Under what circumstances can benefits be reduced or terminated?
5. Under what circumstances can premiums or other provisions be changed?
6. Does the coverage contain any exclusions or limitations?
7. Is coverage provided for pre-existing conditions? If so, under what circumstances?
8. Are rehabilitation services available? If so, will benefits continue during rehabilitation?
9. Are there any special benefits such as cost-of-living adjustments offered in the policy?
10. Are there any differences in definitions of disability, elimination periods, and length of payments between accident claims and sickness claims?

7.4. Other benefit sources during disability

Extended Health Care Plans: Also called supplementary hospital or major medical plans, these insurance plans are most frequently offered on a group basis through work. They may pay for semi-private hospital accommodation, prescription drugs, paramedical services and other costs not covered by provincial health programs.

Automobile Insurance: These policies provide income benefits if you have been injured in an automobile accident. Payments may be integrated with other benefits.

Life Insurance: Disability waivers are available on many group and individual life insurance policies which enable you to stop premium payments if disabled for six months or longer while maintaining coverage. Disability income riders can also be arranged under some life insurance policies to replace a portion of income. Whole life policies build cash values which can be cashed in or used for policy loans. While this may be a safety valve during an emergency, consider your age and your family's protection. Consult your life insurance agent (or broker) before making any decision.

Credit Disability Insurance: Sometimes issued with a bank loan, car financing, and other debts, this insurance is designed to carry your payments if disabled.

Dismemberment Coverage: Available with many group and individual policies, this provides a lump sum if you lose a limb or your hearing or vision. A percentage of this amount may be paid for partial loss; for example, loss of one hand.

Employer Pensions: You may, in certain circumstances, be able to qualify for early retirement and start receiving benefits from a pension provided through work. However, as with other savings and investment plans, this could exhaust income you and your spouse or dependents will need later on.

Veterans' Income Replacement: If you have served in the Canadian Armed Forces, pensions are available if you become disabled as a result of your service. If you served in the armed forces of another country, check with the military authorities there.

Criminal Injuries Compensation Board: In most provinces, if your disability is a result of a criminal activity against you, you may ask this board to award you a lump sum, periodic payments, or a combination of the two in compensation.

7.5. Adding it up

Once you've found out what your benefits would be under these various income replacement programs, you'll have to add them to any other sources of income to see whether you'll have enough to support yourself and your family. With two-income households, the earnings from both spouses should be considered. Investment income should also be taken into account. You should look at income replacement from two points of view: whether you'll have enough money to tide you over while you recuperate and whether you'll have enough to get by if the disability continues. Just as life insurance is the responsible way to prepare for the worst, your decision about disability income replacement insurance should not stop at the chance of being disabled for only a few months. Don't forget, a disabled person may not need as much money for such items as transportation, food and clothing as he or she would if actively at work. On the other hand, expenses can soar for prescription drugs, paramedical care and other health products and services not covered by provincial programs, especially if you do not have extended health care coverage. Also, income needs may increase in future because of inflation or plans such as the educating of your children.

7.6. Charting your needs and benefits

Draw up a chart to help you determine whether you have enough income protection to see you and your dependents (and, if you're self-employed, your business) through a period of disability. You should list your monthly expenses and compare them to the income you can expect to receive under the total disability benefits you now have. You may have to draw up separate charts for different months, as payments and expenses may vary, or to determine your income level after any benefit period expires. Your life insurance agent (or broker) will be glad to help you itemize your benefits. When you're completing the chart . . . keep in mind that you probably won't qualify for benefits from all the programs listed. If you would be receiving benefits from more than one source, you'll have to calculate how integration of benefits would affect your income. On the basis of your calculations, would you and your family (and your business, if self-employed) have enough income to live on if you became disabled? If the answer is 'no', or if you have any further questions, get in touch with your life insurance agent (or broker, or your professional advisor). Show him or her the calculations you have made and ask for advice. And you should do it now, not some time in the future (when you might be disabled!).

7.7. Some final thoughts

As for most Canadians, an individual insurance program designed to meet your personal needs and circumstances is a necessity. As important as group and government programs are, chances are the coverage they provide would not replace a sufficient portion of your income should you become disabled, meet your family's income needs should you die, or provide you with a comfortable income when you retire. So, analyze your current coverage and needs and update your financial plans.

8. About Association Group Plans

This article will concern you if you belong to an association and have disability insurance through that association, or are thinking of acquiring such insurance. Many professionals, such as teachers, doctors, lawyers and nurses, subscribe to insurance from their professional associations to replace lost income in the event of a disability due to sickness or accident. If and when a disability strikes, the terms of the disability income contract govern the circumstances in which benefits are payable, and how much will be paid. A disabled professional needs income, not reasons why dollars are not forthcoming. Association Group Disability plans cost less than individual non-cancellable guaranteed renewable plans because they simply don't provide the same benefits and degree of financial security. Examine the terms of your disability coverage under your Association's plan and see how many of the following restrictions apply:

- The master policy governing the plan may be cancelled by the insurance company without any provision for continuing coverage upon employment termination. To an uninsurable individual, a cancellation could be disastrous.
- Premiums increase automatically but there is no guarantee that the present rate structure will be in effect when you reach various age bands.
- Benefits may be reduced automatically at higher ages.
- Usually, Association Group Plans do not recognize Professional Specialties and limit the benefit period if able to perform the duties of another specialty or another occupation. Thus, for example, a nurse trained for Critical Unit Care might find her benefits cut off if she was able to return to General Nursing care as she recuperated from a disability. Or an ophthalmologist might find benefits reduced or even cut off if he could do general practitioning as he got back on his feet after a disability.
- Total disability benefits are usually discontinued if engaged in your own occupation on a limited basis after a disability, or engaged in a different occupation being unable to return to the original occupation before disability.
- Partial disability benefits, if available, are usually limited to three months.
- Benefits may be reduced if insurance coverage exceeds 100% of earned income at the time of the claim.
- Usually, no benefits are payable in the event of disability resulting from an attempted suicide, whether sane or not.
- Aviation restrictions may apply if flying as crew member or as a passenger on a non-scheduled airline (i.e. charter).
- Benefits may not be payable in the event of a disability resulting from alcoholism or drug addiction.
- Regular membership dues in the Association must be maintained at all times to maintain coverage.

- Some contracts are restrictive if disabled while a resident, or even a visitor, outside North America.
- Waiver of premium benefits are usually available after 180 days, but there is no provision for refund of premiums during the first 180 days of disability.
- No provision for automatic increases in coverage to take into account higher incomes, or increases in the cost of living.
- No benefits available in the event of riot, civil commotion or insurrection.
- Disputed claims may have to be resolved by referral to an arbitration committee.

These are some of the pitfalls that may be present in your Association Group Disability Insurance Plan. Worried? Then take out that plan, and read it over again carefully. Call your insurance advisor if you still have qualms.

9. Life Insurance

Life insurance is one of the cornerstones to family financial security. The life insurance industry is one of the pillars of the Canadian economy. Life insurance has saved countless families from financial ruin upon the premature death of a breadwinner and has provided additional financial resources for even more Canadians as they approach retirement years.

How important is life insurance in Canada and Ontario? A look at some facts and figures published by the Canadian Life and Health Insurance Association places the question into some perspective. Through life and health insurance policies and annuities, over six million Ontario residents have guaranteed themselves and their families a measure of financial security. The activities of life and health insurance companies and their branch offices provide thousands of people in Ontario with work, either directly at home offices, branch offices and agencies/brokerages, or indirectly through investments in the economy of the province. The people of Ontario now own over $300 billion of life insurance while Canadian ownership approaches $1 trillion. In Ontario, the average amount of life insurance per household is just under $100,000, about 5% more than the national average. About 60% of all life insurance in force is of the group variety, with the remainder being individually owned personal policies. Life insurance premiums in Ontario are now $2 billion per year, while annuity purchases run a further $4 billion. About $4 billion are now being paid out each year in Ontario alone in the form of death benefits and annuity payments. Of each dollar paid out, about $0.20 is in the form of death benefits to beneficiaries, while $0.80 go to living policy owners in the form of annuity or retirement benefits, dividends on participating policies, matured endowments, or disability benefits. The safety record of life and health insurance throughout Canada is remarkable. No policyholder or beneficiary in a Canadian legal reserve life company has ever lost a dollar through non-payment of amounts guaranteed in policies on death or maturity. The industry is now 150 years old in Canada, where it had its origins in southwestern Ontario.

Perhaps the most important by-product of the life insurance industry is the accumulation of the savings of over 15 million Canadians, which are then channelled into productive investments. These help keep down the cost of insurance, pay for future benefits to policyholders and beneficiaries, and provide the capital required for the stability and growth of the economy. Nationally, about 175 life and health companies employ almost 70,000 people, directly. Over 100 of these companies have their head offices in Ontario. About 10,000 agents and brokers serve the people of Ontario, while a further 35,000 are employed directly by life and health insurance companies in Ontario. Many thousands of additional jobs are the direct result of life company investments in the province.

9.1. 'How much life insurance do I need?'

'I'm insurance poor!' is a comment frequently heard. Seldom, however, does the widow complain the cheque was too large! Just how much and what type of insurance should an individual own? The answer depends on what would happen to the individual's loved ones and business in the event of his/her premature death. An orphaned hermit, living off the desert, certainly doesn't need life insurance (he likely wouldn't qualify for disability insurance either!). There are many other people, usually single and without dependents, whose need for life insurance is, at most, small. Most adults, especially those of child-bearing/rearing age, do have dependents and loved ones where life insurance is a must for protection against severe economic hardship in the event of premature death. As well, many business owners have very legitimate uses for life insurance to protect the business, its owners, and/or its creditors, from the loss that would occur to the business in the event of the loss of one or more key employees and/or owners.

There are many ways of calculating how much coverage is required. Many life insurance agents will be only too happy to spend time with you doing research of the resources you would leave behind at your death, the additional capital your family would need to maintain a standard of living, and the government benefits that would, or might not, be available at some future unknown date when you're no longer here. Such research becomes dated, though, when there is a subsequent change in the family/business situation or when there is a change in government benefits. Marriage, birth, promotion, pay raise, new home, new car, education, a bequest from a rich aunt, new business partner; all of these change the resources available at a subsequent death. Clearly, the determination of how much life insurance will be needed at some point in the future needs periodic review and update. On the question: how much life insurance do I need?, the Canadian Life and Health Insurance Association has this to say: the most important factor to consider is the income-producing value of your insurance. A $25,000 policy sounds like a tidy sum until your widow tries to raise a family on it. Your dependents will be well protected if you use the following conservative calculations.

1. Add up the other sources of income that would be available at your death, e.g. savings, survivor benefits from a group insurance policy at your work, Canada/Quebec pension plan benefits.
2. Estimate your dependents' living expenses.
3. Subtract 1 from 2. This is the monthly income that should be available from investing a lump sum settlement. Let's assume this amount is $1,000.
4. Now decide how long your family will need this income. Presumably, when children are grown, and the mortgage paid off, the same income would not be

needed. Let's suppose you conclude your family would need income for 15 years.

5. Finally, let's suppose your spouse or dependent invests the lump sum from insurance at 5% net of inflation and income tax.

6. Using the following table, we can calculate what the value of the policy should be:

Monthly income for:	Multiplier:
10 years	94
15 "	126
20 "	152
25 "	171
30 "	186

Therefore, the amount you need is $1,000 × 126, or $126,000. To this, add your debts if you wish these to be discharged upon your demise. Include your mortgage if you wish to leave your family in a debt-free home after you're gone. The above shows a policy of $126,000 would yield an income of $1,000 per month for 15 years if the capital were invested at a net 5% after income tax and inflation. In fact, your beneficiary might not be able to invest in today's market for as high a yield since interest rates are about 6%, while inflation is at not much more than 1%. However, it should be remembered that income tax is payable on the interest, at the recipient's top marginal tax rate. The proceeds of life insurance, in this case $126,000, is of course tax-free.

9.2.   What type of insurance?

Unless you're self-employed, or employed in a job that doesn't carry normal employee benefits, think of your group life insurance as a key element of your insurance plan. This is usually the type of insurance provided in your employee benefit package. Group life insurance is the cheapest life insurance available because insuring a group of people means less work for the insurance company and because your employer may contribute to premiums. Check whether your policy provides a lump sum and/or monthly income to your beneficiary. You can take over your plan if you leave your employer, albeit at higher cost. Your benefit plan administrator will have details about this conversion option, which, under a uniform law applicable in all provinces, must be extended to you for 30 days after your last effective day as an employee. Group life insurance is often limited to an amount of one or two times your annual salary. If you decide you need additional coverage, or if there is any possibility you might change to an occupation or employment where there likely wouldn't be any group life insurance, you will want to consider personal life insurance.

With your first purchase of individual life insurance, you may, for a very small additional premium, include a 'guaranteed insurability clause' or rider which gives you the right to buy more life insurance at regular intervals and at standard rates without evidence of good health. This rider is particularly important for young people who know their responsibilities will increase in future years. In today's market for personally owned life insurance, the two basic types of plans are term and whole life insurance. Many interesting variations and combinations on these two basic forms are available.

Term Insurance: simply provides protection in the event of death within a stated term of years — one, five, ten or 20 years; or to a specified age, usually not beyond age 65 or 70. If you die within the stated term, your beneficiary receives a lump sum or monthly income payments. If you don't die, you get nothing back for your premiums except the peace of mind that goes with knowing you had coverage. Term insurance is the least costly private insurance coverage you can buy for a short and known period of exposure. It provides a high level of protection for a crucial period, such as the years when your children are growing up. For a nominal extra premium, term insurance can include convertibility to whole life without evidence of insurability.

Whole Life: is also called cash value insurance or permanent insurance. Unless you allow it to lapse, it remains in force until your death, so there is always a death benefit for your beneficiary. This is because, unlike term insurance, whole life builds up cash value. You can borrow against this cash surrender value, either from a bank or directly from the insurance company, usually at preferred rates. If you discontinue the policy, you can withdraw the accrued value in cash. If you live until the policy matures, you can get back the accumulated savings. You can also stop paying premiums and the insurance coverage will continue until the cash value is used up.

Term and whole life are generically related, whole life simply being term insurance carried to the end of life — usually assumed to be age 100 at the latest — with the premium risk costs averaged to produce a level annual premium cost. In a very real sense, then, whole life is simply a level premium term to age 100 plan. Those two basic types of insurance plans are, therefore, complementary. Their selection in a sound personal insurance plan should be based on the lower initial costs of term insurance weighed against the practical options whole life will provide when approaching retirement. Variations and combinations of term and whole life plans add further dimensions to this selection process. In today's market, the buyer can consider combinations of whole life and term in any proportions:

- whole life participating insurance, where dividends are accumulated with the possibility the dividend fund will carry the policy without further premium payments after, say, 12 or 15 years;

- whole life participating insurance where dividends are used to buy additional term insurance coverage;

- interest sensitive policies (both whole life and term) where premiums are based on current interest rate levels that are adjusted periodically, usually every five years;

- universal life where, in fact, the coverage is term insurance with part of the premium invested in a separate fund, the combination permitting the coverage to stay in force for life;

- and policies called 'term to 100' where premiums are reduced by restricting some of the options normally available under a whole life plan.

10.   Life Insurance Really "Lifestyle Insurance"

It is really *Lifestyle insurance*. That's the key point in deciding how much is enough. Enough so your family or other dependants can maintain their current standard of living. That means enough to replace your pay cheque, cover your debts, and pay the bill your investments will be subject to under the capital gains tax.

Do you own a sunbelt condo or American investments? When you die, they will attract U.S. estate tax plus Canadian tax. Many people buy insurance to cover that.

How much is enough? Unfortunately, there is no simple answer. It depends entirely on your situation. If you are married with a growing family, you likely have the greatest need. Your family will probably require 60 to 80 percent of todays after-tax income. Don't forget special needs such as funding university education or supporting aging parents. If you are a single parent, where would your support payments come from if the contributor dies?

If you are single, do you expect to have a family or support any relatives? A life insurance agent can help quantify your situation. A three-step method is often used:

Step One: Determine the value of your estate

Add up all investments and estimate the market value of cars or other assets that could be sold without hurting your family's lifestyle. Include your RRSP only if it would be cashed in. Remember, the RRSP can be rolled into your spouse's plan tax-free. Otherwise it is added to your final year's income and fully taxed. Add the lump sum death benefit from Canada/Quebec Pension Plan plus existing life insurance, such as group coverage at work. Now, list your debts. Don't forget funeral expenses and any taxes due to death. Are your mortgage, car loan or credit card balances insured separately? If so, exclude them. Subtract your debts from your assets. The result represents a pile of money your family can invest for monthly income.

Step Two: Estimate your family's expected monthly income

First, find out what Canada/Quebec Pension Plan will pay. If you have a pension plan at work, it may also pay monthly benefits. Assess your spouse's job prospects. How much can he or she earn and when? Would a return to work require new training? Subtract daycare and house-keeping costs. Some people believe stay-at-home mothers should not be insured since they earn no income. But that woman's death would probably create the need for housekeeping and childcare.

Next, convert the cash pool from Step One into monthly income. Consult a life insurance agent or other financial adviser about assumptions for investment returns and inflation.

Time is a key factor. The longer the money must last, the less that can be paid out each month. Who will depend on you the longest: a newborn who needs 21 years of support or your spouse who lacks a pension and will need help in retirement?

Step Three: Measure the "Income Gap"

You should now have an estimate of how much money your survivors will need and how much is already available. Subtract the money arranged from the money needed. The difference is your family's income gap. A life insurance agent can easily determine how much insurance you need to cover the gap. If you have small children, the amount may seem high; it is not uncommon for a breadwinner with a growing family to need $500,000 of coverage.

But various types of policies are priced at different levels. Also, the unit price falls as the policy amount goes up, so full protection may not cost much more.

11.   Recession Takes More Than Jobs

The Recession takes more than jobs. Thousands of Canadians have also lost their life and disability insurance. These people relied on group coverage at work. While group coverage is very easy to get and reasonably priced, it is tied to the job. That is a potential problem many don't see until they get dismissed or resign.

11.1. Security of coverage

A well-selected individual policy lets you increase coverage without a new medical exam. That way, you buy minimal coverage while in the group plan and boost it if you leave. Insurance pricing is based largely on health and age. Lock in rates at their lowest by obtaining coverage when you are healthy and, ideally, young. If you buy term life insurance, make sure renewal is guaranteed without evidence of insurability. Also look for policies that guarantee the schedule of renewal rates.

Group plans normally let departing members convert to individual life insurance policies, but rates are often high and coverage may be limited. For example, one group plan insures active members for up to $1.1 million but caps conversions at $200,000. That's not a lot if you have small children. Note that while group life insurance is convertible, group disability coverage is not — and you are more likely to be disabled than to die prematurely.

11.2. Extent of coverage

Group life plans tend to pay out a multiple of salary — perhaps three times your pay. That is good since coverage rises as salary goes up; life insurance is meant to replace income. But that under-insures young people who start families and careers around the same time.

Term insurance — often sold for five or ten years at a time — provides a low cost way for families to buy full coverage. Individually-owned disability policies can be tailored to fill gaps in group plans.

For example, your group plan might pay benefits only if you cannot do any job for which you are trained — a tighter definition than "own-occ" coverage which pays benefits if you cannot do your own job.

Your group plan may have an own-occ provision but pay those benefits for only two years, after which you face a tighter definition of disability.

Group disability benefit levels are based on your salary and don't protect earnings from supplementary incomes or a sideline business. They are also usually not indexed for inflation, and may be capped at a dollar level well below the percentage of income you need to maintain your family's lifestyle.

Your group plan may cut back life insurance coverage when you retire, or when you turn 65 if you keep working. It is felt seniors don't need as much life insurance because the kids are grown and the house is paid off.

But many do as part of their estate and retirement planning. For example, the recent federal budget effectively removed future gains on cottages from the $100,000 lifetime capital gains exemption. That means many Canadians will leave heirs a hefty tax bill with the family retreat.

Some cottages might even have to be sold to pay off Revenue Canada. That can be avoided to cover the expected bill. If you are in a pension plan, having adequate life insurance can boost your retirement income.

12.   Mortgage Life Insurance

Skip this if you don't have a mortgage, or if insuring your mortgage is not important to you. Many people, upon assuming a mortgage, end up believing they have taken some life insurance offered by the mortgage lender. Don't confuse life insurance on a mortgage with mortgage cancellation insurance. The latter, prevalent on new housing, especially housing with high-ratio mortgages under the National Housing Act (i.e. CMHC), is designed to protect the lender from the borrower's default. This type of insurance is paid for by the borrower typically by a charge against the original mortgage proceeds. It usually amounts to about 1% of the proceeds. Mortgage life insurance, on the other hand, when obtained through the mortgage lender, is designed to liquidate the mortgage so that the deceased can leave a mortgage free property to his/her beneficiaries. This type of insurance, when obtained from the lender, is almost always charged for separately, usually monthly. It is designed, when obtained from the lender, to liquidate only the balance of the principal outstanding at the time of the borrower's death.

Is the mortgage lender the best place to obtain mortgage life insurance? Not necessarily. Many in today's mobile society change mortgages quite frequently. It's not unusual to see younger people go through half a dozen mortgages before they retire. Each time they do, they have to re-apply for mortgage life insurance, which means they have to pass a medical. Which means they might not be able to get life insurance on their next mortgage. But, there are other reasons to consider obtaining mortgage life insurance directly from a life insurance company, as opposed to from a mortgage lender. Some of these would include:

- Payment on death goes to the mortgage holder's designated beneficiaries, as opposed to directly to the mortgage lender. A beneficiary then can use the funds whatever way suits him/her best. It may indeed be to the beneficiary's advantage to not pay down the mortgage, particularly if the mortgage interest rate is lower than re-investment interest rates at time of death.
- The beneficiary may want to sell the property, in which case the sale may be facilitated with a mortgage, versus without.
- Personally owned life insurance policies usually don't have a decreasing face amount of life insurance coverage, unlike that obtained through the mortgage lender. Thus, a personally owned policy has a fixed and known death benefit payout.
- A personally owned policy can provide for second mortgages that can later be reduced as the mortgage is paid off.

- Personally owned policies can have a waiver of premium benefit upon the borrower's disability.
- Personally owned life insurance can almost always be later converted to a plan of whole life or permanent insurance which the policy owner can keep after the mortgage is paid off, or until, and indeed after, retirement.
- Personally owned life insurance to cover a mortgage can be tailored with level premiums. Insurance through a mortgage lender almost always has premium increases every five years.
- With a personally owned plan, both spouses can be covered. Insurance through a mortgage lender usually covers only the parties to the mortgage, often excluding one of the spouses.
- And if you already have personal life insurance, consider adding more to cover the mortgage. Such term insurance is almost always less expensive than insurance from the lender.

Remember: If you think you're covered at present under a lender's plan, double-check soon to make sure the coverage really is for life insurance. Also, verify just what the terms, conditions, and costs really are.

13. Life Insurance Loan Taxes

In recent years, many owners of whole life (i.e. permanent) insurance contracts have taken advantage of their right to borrow from their policies at fixed rates of interest that typically were from 5 to 6% on older policies. Some of these contract owners discovered belatedly, and too late, that they had a tax liability for the year in which they took out the loan.

In the mid 1980s, thanks to the then Liberal Finance Minister, Marc Lalonde, the tax rules were changed on whole life insurance contracts. Effectively, the rule change states that profits accumulated within a life contract will be taxed when they exceed the accumulated premiums paid since the contract started. For example, let us assume a policy with a $100 annual premium that has had ever increasing dividends which have accumulated to $4,000 after 30 years in force. If the dividends have been paid as declared, then there will have been a profit of $1,000 in recent years, on which the owner would have received annual profit statements from the insurer.

However, if the dividends have been used to buy additional insurance, then the dividend profit tax will have been deferred until either the contract is cashed, or a loan is taken out. If the loan is less than the total of premiums paid, then there is no imputed taxable gain. But, if the loan exceeds the premiums paid, then there is a taxable gain reportable in the year the loan is taken out equivalent to the excess above the accumulated premiums.

A problem has frequently occurred with such loans when the policy owner discovers, too late, that he/she has tax to pay the following February when he/she receives a tax-reporting slip from the insurer. We have often seen such a move bump the taxpayer into a higher tax bracket, and owing lots of money in tax on what the client regarded as a simple loan.

Fortunately, the damage can be reversed as soon as the loan is paid down below the total of accumulated premiums. Indeed, we have seen several savvy taxpayers use their loan availability as a tax-planning tool. Since the judicious balancing of policy loans can raise or lower taxable income, we have seen several taxpayers use their borrowing ability to level their taxable income from one year to the next when they are receiving varying amounts of other taxable income. Since the ownership of a life contract can be assigned to a close family member with no tax attribution or reporting, we have also seen many cases where one taxpayer in a high bracket will transfer ownership to another family member, who then triggers a reportable taxable gain either through a loan, or by cashing in accumulated dividends.

Many permanent life contracts of 30 years or more of age have very substantial build-ups of cash in the form of dividends. This cash build-up can attract sizable tax if not handled properly. On the other hand, such cash build-ups can be used to reduce tax liability when used creatively with some planning. I would be happy to provide assistance to any reader who is wondering what to do with his/her whole life policy accumulations.

Since interest rates have fallen so far in the past two years, the attractiveness of low-interest life contract loans has also fallen. If only for that reason, many loans are being repaid.

14.   Critical Illness Insurance

We all know something about life insurance. Indeed, most of us know something about disability insurance to replace lost income in the event of disability caused by accident or illness. Now comes a new form of insurance designed to protect us against the cost of critical illnesses.

The need for critical illness insurance has increased due to medical advances. Premature deaths have been significantly reduced. However, statistics show an almost 55% increase in disability from heart disease, hypertension, cerebrovascular disease and diabetes. It has touched all our lives.

In the United Kingdom, where critical illness insurance was first introduced, critical illness insurance sales have grown at unprecedented rates since 1987, unlike the limited growth in individual life insurance sales. In the almost ten years in which such coverage has been available in the U.K., sales have gone from zero to some tens of thousands of contracts yearly.

Why?

Statistics show that half of all Canadians over the age of 40 will suffer a heart attack, cancer and/or stroke before the age of 75. Within the smoking community, that rate increases to no less than two thirds!

Statistics also show that, because of increasing improvements in medical science, and general awareness of symptoms within the overall population, the chances of someone surviving such a critical illness is actually increasing.

Over the past 25 years, higher levels of stress in our daily lives have contributed to an increase of almost 55% in disability resulting from heart disease, hypertension, stroke and diabetes. But premature deaths from these ailments have decreased significantly. What this means is that more and more people as a percentage of the population will suffer from one or more of these ailments. Yet, at the same time, more and more of those struck down will survive, and survive longer.

Here are some other disturbing statistics:

- one in four Canadians will contract heart disease;
- 75,000 Canadians suffer heart attacks each year;
- one in four Canadians currently suffers from cardiovascular disease, whether they know it or not;
- 60% of the 60,000 stroke victims each year are women;
- 75% of stroke victims survive the initial event;
- one in 20 Canadians run the risk of stroke before age 70;
- there are between 200,000 and 300,000 stroke survivors in Canada today;
- there has been a 50% decrease in the death rate from heart disease and stroke over the past 40 years;
- one in three Canadians will develop some form of life threatening cancer;
- 125,000 new cancer cases are reported each year;
- one in four Canadians will suffer from kidney disease;
- 85% of kidney transplants are successful;
- at least 50,000 Canadians have Multiple Sclerosis, and 30,000 or more suffer from paralysis of two or more limbs.

What would happen if you woke up in the hospital tomorrow after experiencing a mild heart attack? Your doctor might simply recommend a change of diet and more frequent exercise. But, what if you were required to modify your lifestyle even further? What if you were forced into an early retirement or to trade in your old job for one that is less stressful and less productive?

That's where critical illness insurance comes into play. If you do suffer one of the critical illnesses covered, the insurance company pays you the face amount. We foresee this becoming the largest growing segment in the life and health insurance industry in Canada very quickly.

15. Supreme Court Decides on Creditor Proofing

The Supreme Court has issued a definitive ruling regarding the ability of creditors to gain access to Registered Retirement Savings Plans and Registered Retirement Income Funds, when held with a life insurance company.

In a case we have written about previously, a Saskatchewan doctor went bankrupt two years after having transferred his RSP with a bank over into an RIF with a life insurance company, naming his wife as beneficiary.

Another bank went after the RIF in bankruptcy court, claiming the RIF was properly available for seizure as an asset to cover debts owed that bank by the doctor.

The Supreme Court ruled unanimously that the RIF was immune from seizure by creditors because, in the absence of fraud, the doctor had transferred the asset while solvent into an exempt contract with a life insurance company. Therefore, the creditor bank could not now claim access to the asset just because of the doctor's insolvency.

In other words, since the doctor was solvent when the assets were transferred from a non-exempt bank contract, to an exempt life company contract, and since fraud against the doctor was not an issue, the doctor's creditors could not now claim the right of seizure just because the doctor had gone bankrupt.

The doctor's assets with the life insurance company were exempt from seizure both before and after insolvency, by virtue of the fact the doctor had invested with a life insurance company, and had named a close relative as his beneficiary.

To summarize, any and all investments held with a life insurance company, in which contract a close relative (spouse, child, parent) is named as beneficiary is protected from seizure by any creditor.

16. Minimizing Estate Costs

One of our elderly clients passed away, leaving her husband as sole beneficiary of her estate. This client left a good-sized estate, comprising real estate worth $300,000, bank accounts of $15,000, GICs of $80,000, CSBs of $10,000, with an aggregate value, excluding chattels, of better than $400,000. Working with both spouses, we were able to make a number of suggestions before the client passed away that allowed the client's estate to be wound up without probate, at a cost of $200, in less than six weeks. Most of the cost was to have the client's will notarized. An estate of the size of our client's normally takes at least a year to wind up in the Ottawa area and costs at least $10,000, more probably $20,000, in legal and admin costs while the will is probated. During that time, the beneficiary is cash short.

How did I accomplish the quick settlement and at such low cost? First, I made sure that all real estate was jointly owned by both spouses. Under the law of survivorship, any survivor(s) from the death of any owner(s) becomes automatically the new owner(s) of any real estate without the need for probate. Only proof of death must be furnished to the Registry Office to have the deceased's name removed from title. Next,Ie made sure all bank accounts were jointly owned. When my client passed away, the surviving spouse only had to close the accounts, and transfer the client's funds to his own accounts. Then, I persuaded the client that a much better home for her GIC investments was with a life insurance company. Not only was I able to get her higher rates than at her bank and co-op, but by naming her husband as beneficiary, I ensured the funds would be paid to him within days of her demise.

I never did do anything before the client's demise regarding her CSBs. Since she was earning 10.75% on those, and since the husband had power of attorney while she was alive, we decided to leave those as is, even though our client was the sole owner. After her demise, we applied to the Bank of Canada with a funeral director's statement, a notarized copy of our client's will (that was what cost most of the $200!) and the bonds. The Bank of Canada issued a cheque to the husband in less than two weeks.

Because my client had named her three children as co-executors along with her husband, I became, with all four approving, the administrator of the estate. This not only allowed the estate to speak with one voice, it reduced considerably the written approvals required, and was a contributing factor to the settling of the estate within six weeks.

17. Beneficiary Designations and RIF/RSP Deposit Insurance

In its July 12, 1993 edition, the *Ottawa Citizen* carried an article by one of its correspondents with which I take exception. I reprint here the verbatim reply I made to the *Citizen*, since it affects many readers:

The Editor/*Ottawa Citizen*:

This is to take exception with a business section column written by Ms Ricarda Smith in your edition of July 12. Therein, in response to a readers question, Ms Smith implies that naming a beneficiary with a financial institution other than a life company for an RSP or RIF will result in the beneficiary receiving the funds directly, without going through the estate and, hence, probate. The problem I have is with the writer's frequent use of the phrase 'should be able to', implying that that is what will happen under law. Quite the contrary occurs both under law and practice, and her phraseology is hence very misleading!

While many financial institutions will pay a named beneficiary directly, they will do so <u>only</u> after they have ascertained there are no conflicts in any last will and testament. They will (and must) protect themselves from potential conflicts by demanding, as a matter of course, a notarized copy of the last will, wherein they will expect a letter from the notary/lawyer that the will is the <u>last</u> known will, not likely to be contested. They will then satisfy themselves there are <u>no</u> potential conflicts between the will and the named beneficiary. Thus, if the deceased has left everything to his/her spouse in the will, but has named Aunt Jenny as beneficiary of the RSP, they will <u>not</u> pay Aunt Jenny! They will wait until the will <u>has</u> been probated, and a letters probate issued by the Surrogate Court directing them to pay the RSP to whomever the Surrogate Court determines is the valid beneficiary. I have seen many estates where we have acted as administrator, trustee, executor or advisor, where <u>every</u> financial institution, save life companies, will pay a beneficiary directly <u>only</u> when they are absolutely sure there are no conflicts within the last will. While this technically <u>should</u> avoid probate, it does not necessarily follow. Nor will the lawyer or other professional handling the estate waive their fees for handling the paperwork necessary to satisfy <u>any</u> financial institution (excepting, again, a life company) that the beneficiary is the only one with a valid claim on the RSP, RIF or, for that matter, any other investment.

To sum up: in most provinces, including Ontario where most of your readers presumably reside, naming a beneficiary will avoid probate <u>only</u> with a life company investment contract. As a bonus, the life company will almost always pay the beneficiary within days of proof of death, compared to many months required with most other financial institutions.

Ms Smith also states that CompCorp insurance <u>should</u> protect owners of life company RSPs and RIFs, implying that it sometimes does not. She further states that CDIC will cover up to $60,000 for <u>any</u> RSP and/or RIF with a bank or trust. In fact, CDIC insures <u>only</u> term deposits of five years or less duration, and not other investments. On the other hand, CompCorp insures <u>any</u> investment, regardless of type or term. As well, CompCorp coverage applies on any capital amount which produces up to $2,000 per month of benefit with A RIF. With today's interest rates of approximately 8% available from life companies with long-term RIFs (compared to less than 7% from traditional banks and trustcos on their insurable deposits of 5 years maximum term), up to $300,000 of capital is thus insured under CompCorp compared to the maximum $60,000 under CDIC.

Note I am <u>not</u> picking on Ms Smith per se. I am finally writing since this is just one of many such articles written by your correspondents in recent years that do <u>not</u> clarify the situation, but instead provide very misleading advice. You would do your readers well to correct these false impressions caused by your writers by printing the facts. And you might circulate this letter among your correspondents. I have seen too many estates where the deceased was under the impression that naming a beneficiary with a bank or trustco would preclude probate and result in a speedy payment to the beneficiary. In practice, there are few things legal further from the truth! Sincerely,

Geoff Stevens, President, Stevens Financial Services Inc.

18.   Settling An Estate Yourself

If you are named as an executor in a will, you should know that you can do most of the work, if not all, on your own, saving hundreds, if not thousands of dollars in legal and para-legal costs. Be prepared for a long process of red tape thrown up at you by lawyers, financial institutions and bureaucrats. The process can be frustrating, but also informative and interesting to those with a bent in that direction.

Trust companies will normally tell you that as an executor, you are responsible for any mistakes you make along the way, suggesting that if you give them the task, you will have one less legal ramification to worry about. But if the estate you are named as executor for is relatively straight forward, and if the deceased was relatively well organized, you should have few situations that would cause grief as far as legal liability is concerned.

If it's a family member who has passed on, it can be quite satisfying to act as executor where the contribution of your time and effort goes into cleanly settling their estate in accordance with your loved one's final wishes.

If more than one person has been named as co-executor, then you should try and reach a consensus as to which one of you will act for the others. A tremendous amount of time and nervous energy can be spent simply keeping each other informed and obtaining consent if there is more than one executor actively doing the work. Far better to have all but one executor renounce their obligations in favour of the one who most clearly seems equipped, both professionally and time-wise, to handle the job. This renouncing does not relieve the remaining executor of any requirements under law to provide the beneficiaries and the Surrogate Court with an accounting of how he/she has handled the job as executor.

Your first reaction, as executor, may be to try to get the job done as quickly as possible. It's difficult, however, to speed up the process because you're dealing with government and financial institution bureaucracies. In other words, be prepared to spend a lot of time waiting for someone else to do his/her job.

You can't do much until you receive copies of the Death Certificate (usually from a funeral director). So start there. While waiting for the copies of the Death Certificate, you can deal with some of the minor matters, such as cancelling credit cards, transferring auto ownership, and locating assets. You'll need copies of the Death Certificate for almost every transaction, so make sure you obtain many copies (at least one copy for each financial institution the deceased dealt with at death, plus four or five more).

The Death Certificate will also give you access to the deceased's safety-deposit box, where you'll probably find the will and other important papers (we usually recommend a valid copy of the will be given to the executor by the willmaker at the time the will is drawn up, and/or subsequently modified, so that the executor can get a handle on what will be required while the deceased is still alive!).

Although the Death Certificate will give you access to the safety-deposit box, you won't be able to remove anything until the will is probated, unless you were able to persuade the deceased to name you as joint safety-deposit box owner while the deceased was still alive.

Probate is simply the process of having the will recognized by the provincial government, through Surrogate Court, as being the last valid will drawn up and executed by the deceased. Fees range widely for this service, and are highest in Ontario and lowest in Quebec. Fees are a function of what assets are to be 'probated'.

Assets that are not probated do not go through Surrogate Court, and are, therefore, not 'taxed'. Such assets would include assets with life insurance companies where one or more beneficiaries are named, whereby the life companies pay directly to the named beneficiaries (once adequate proof of death is furnished). You will not need the original insurance company contracts, despite widespread belief to the contrary. Every insurance company in Canada now is satisfied with a proper proof of death certificate, and adequate proof that the claimant is the rightful beneficiary.

It often takes as long as six weeks for the Surrogate Court to complete the probate of a will, and only then can distribution of assets that have been probated take place (probate of a complicated will and/or assets can take up to six months or longer).

As well as insurance company contracts that name a beneficiary, company pension plans are another asset that doesn't usually require probate, and you can busy yourself with that task while waiting for Surrogate Court to complete probate. You can also contact the Canada Pension Plan to turn off any monthly CPP benefits, and to claim the lump-sum Death Benefit. Similarly, you can also contact the Old Age Security people to turn off that monthly cheque, if the deceased was over the age of 65.

Except for very small deposits, most financial institutions will also require a 'notarized' copy of the probated will, along with the Surrogate Court's probate order. So, you should arm yourself with enough copies of both of these documents, along with the Funeral Directors Proof of Death Certificate, before approaching any financial institution for distribution of such assets to the named beneficiaries.

Real estate assets, stocks and other property can also be transferred to beneficiaries at this time. The same holds true with Canada Savings Bonds, except here you'll have to deal with the bureaucracy at the Bank of Canada. One quirk with the Bank of Canada is that the executor's signature will usually have to be guaranteed by 'an approved financial institution', which means you'll have to make another trip to another financial institution even before the Bank of Canada will distribute the deceased's CSBs to beneficiaries that may not even include you!

Here's a check list of things you may wish to consult if acting as executor:

- Get lots of copies of the Death Certificate; seems just about anyone you'll be dealing with will want one.

- Take at least one notarized copy of the will along, if you're dealing in person, since many financial institutions will at least want to see it, if not keep a copy for their own protection against lawsuits after they've paid out to the beneficiaries named in the will.

- If you think you need a lawyer to get you over the tough spots, find one you trust, <u>and</u> who knows his/her way around the business of estates. Some financial institutions give more weight to a lawyer's letter than they would to a letter from you.

- Don't forget to apply for the CPP/QPP Death Benefit. It can be a healthy sum.

- Keep a list of the deceased's more important biographical data, including date and place of birth, date and place of death, SI number, address, phone number, and bank account numbers with you at all times. You'll be constantly asked for this information as you visit various financial institutions, stock transfer agents, lawyers, and others.

- Make a check list of the many smaller things that have to be done, and when you did them, such as changing car registration, cancelling car insurance, cancelling or changing house insurance, cancelling credit cards, redirecting mail, cancelling subscriptions and getting refunds where appropriate, and paying funeral and other last expenses.

- Don't forget that as executor, you will likely be required to complete and file the deceased's last income tax return, unless the deceased has made provisions for having this done by someone else within the will. If you are to be responsible for the final tax return, but don't have much expertise, then turn over the task to whoever the deceased had been using in the past.

- As well as the deceased's final income tax return, you may also be responsible for completing any late returns the deceased had not yet filed, as well as a return for the 'estate' (unless the estate was wound up quickly) and for 'rights and things', which is where the deceased was owed certain amounts at the time of death, but which had not yet been paid (i.e. corporate dividends).

- If the deceased is still alive when you find out you've been named as executor, attempt whatever is needed to review with the person naming you as executor that person's assets <u>before</u> death, if only to allow you to know what the person intends. And if you find that many of the person's assets will have to be probated after death, attempt to find out if the person would be amenable to shifting to similar assets that would <u>not</u> require probate.

19. Estate Settlement Checklist

I am indebted to Mr. David Darwin, of Ottawa, for submitting the following checklist in answer to a challenge I issued earlier this year for ideas for articles for *GASletter*. Mr. Darwin wins a whole lot of postage for his efforts. Thank you, Mr. Darwin!

The following is meant as a checklist to be used by a family member who is appointed or becomes the de facto representative of a just-deceased relative. The checklist could also be used by someone discovering that he/she had been named as the trustee of an estate.

While written for someone domiciled in Ontario at date of death, the points itemized below apply to all provinces.

1. Arrange a meeting with family, executor(s), and beneficiaries, to address:
   - Reading of the will
   - Confirmation of executor(s) and agreement on roles and responsibilities
   - Access to legal advisor
   - Allocation of tasks required for settling of the estate (if more than one executor, or if family members wish to help out)

   (**Note**: Consider setting up a notebook for making notes of decisions during the meetings for future reference and to record actions taken, contact names, advice received.)

2. Get an overview of documents of the estate, including
   - Insurance policies (life, medical, employment, house, car)
   - Memberships
   - Investments (real estate, stocks, bonds, GICs, CSBs, mutual funds, ...)
   - Bank accounts (pass books, statements)
   - Safety deposit box location, number, and key
   - Deeds
   - Pension account number (CPP, OAS)

3. Actions required to settle estate (priority is indicated in brackets)
   - Record biographical information on the deceased and spouse (immediate):
     - Address
     - Date and place of birth
     - Date and place of death
     - SIN (also for beneficiaries)
     - Names and birth places of parents
     - Marriage certificate
     - Birth certificate
   - Process the will (immediate)
     - If probate not required (i.e. insignificant estate, single beneficiary, contesting of will not anticipated): get original will and one or two notarized copies.
     - If probate required:
       * Notarized copy of will
       * Names and addresses of all heirs
       * Location of all assets, valuable personal or household effects
       * Place and date of filing last income tax return
       * Birth and marriage certificates of surviving spouse
       * List of any significant gifts made in the last five years

  * Obtain forms from Surrogate Court and file (allow several months for processing)
- Notifying financial institutions (high)
  - Notification of banks and trust companies. Each will want a copy of the death certificate and will want to at least see a copy of the will if not also keep a notarized copy for their files.
  - For joint accounts: apply for release of all funds to surviving party
  - For sole accounts: apply for release of funds (depends on whether or not probate is to occur). Forms and procedures vary by financial institution.
- Cancellation of credit cards
  - Visa/Mastercard/AmEx
  - Department stores
  - Others
- Disposition of other investments with a named beneficiary entails contacting the institution and requesting information on forms and procedures. Copy of the death certificate will be required for each institution.
- Transfer or redemption of Canada Savings Bonds requires a phone call to their nearest office to obtain appropriate form. Will be required to submit death certificate and other documents (e.g. notarized copy of the will) depending on circumstances.
- Establishment of an account for the estate at a financial institution (some will not establish the account until a deposit [cheque] in the name of the estate is in hand).
- Cancellation of/changes to social security payments (Human Resources Canada; check for office nearest you). Complete required forms in advance (usually provided by the funeral home) and take along a copy of the death certificate and the will for verification by the intake clerk. Benefits for the month of death which are payable:
  - Canada Pension Plan
  - Old Age Security
  - CPP Death Benefit (payable in about three months; amount is six times the monthly benefit)

If surviving spouse or children, survivor's/orphan's benefits (must be applied for within one year of death of the contributing spouse/parent)
- Apply for benefits (high)
  - Insurance policies
    * Call for claim settlement
    * Select option for payment of the benefits (note tax implications)
      · Interest only (paid periodically by the insurance company)
      · Life income or annuity (fixed sums at specific dates)
      · Fixed instalments
      · Lump sum (for reinvestment, purchase of an annuity, payment of debts)
    * Complete forms and submit with copy of death certificate and the original policies (if available)
  - Health coverage (medical, drugs, hospitalization, out-of-country travel, ambulance)
    * Call insurance provider to notify them of death of subscriber and determine if survivor's benefits available (if applicable)
    * Complete required forms and submit

- House (medium)
  - Arrange for title transfer in accordance with the provisions of the will (legal assistance may be required as the forms and the filing process are not easily understood by the uninitiated).
  - Obtain Form 4 — Document General (from stationery store) for submission to the Land Registry Office. This is used to file a copy of the death certificate.
  - Obtain Form 1 — Land Transfer for submission to the Land Registry Office. This is used to register the ownership change and indicate the value of the transaction for tax purposes.
  - Change insurance policy by contacting the company about the process to follow.

- Car (medium)
  - At the local Ministry of Transportation licence centre:
    * Cancel driver's licence
    * Transfer ownership
  - Change insurance policy by contacting the company about the process to follow.

- Payment of outstanding debts (medium)
  - Funeral home
  - Cemetery
  - Credit cards
  - Securities

- File final income tax return(s) (low)
  - Get estate information package and special forms (from local or district Taxation Office)
  - Assemble documentation, slips
  - Check for any roll-back provisions, terms
  - Get advice and guidance — research on tax minimization
  - Prepare the tax return for year(s) prior to death
  - Prepare tax return(s) for the year of death

- Arrange disposition of personal effects (low)
  - Clothing
  - Personal items
  - Special equipment

- Prepare and send thank-you cards/notices (medium)
  - Friends and relatives
  - Hospital
  - Funeral home
  - Pastor

- Notification — Others (low)
  - General practitioner's office
  - Offices of specialists
  - Dentist
  - Pharmacy
  - Any scheduled appointments

4. Future Planning
   - Amend surviving spouse's will
   - Financial and tax planning by surviving spouse
   - Joint ownership of assets to avoid taxes and speed up transfer (especially the house, car and investments)
   - Establishing trusts
   - Investment strategies
   - Establish joint ownership of accounts, safety deposit box, . . .

5. Update or arrange for power of attorney
6. Plan for asset management (especially for a surviving spouse)
7. Maintaining the house and property
8. Security of house and important papers
9. Review insurance requirements.

6

Of General Interest

1. Perils to Financial Health

The following remarks were made by Geoff Stevens at the Celebration of Aging Conference, Ottawa Congress Centre, 1990, again at Financial Forum in 1991, and updated 1996:

Welcome! Hope you're enjoying the Conference as much as we are! I'm going to speak on 'Perils to Financial Health'. This talk will be of interest to anyone already retired, or contemplating retirement. There will also be a number of suggestions made this afternoon that will be applicable to anyone concerned about <u>money</u>. But first, a few words to qualify me as a speaker at this Conference.

I operate an investment brokerage business and I'm independent of any financial institution. My clients all have income tax problems that require expertise in that area, as well. Hence, through a wholly owned company called GASletter Inc., I offer a tax consulting service and a monthly newsletter on financial matters in general, and income tax in particular. I'll handle about $8 million in new investment funds on behalf of my clients this year. The value of the portfolio I manage now exceeds $35 million. The majority of my clients are over age 60. We are now the largest independent investment broker in Ottawa concentrating on the 'over 50' market, dealing exclusively with life insurance companies.

My topic this afternoon is 'Perils to Financial Health'. We're all here to celebrate aging. Such a celebration does not require money, but having it sure helps. Statistics Canada reminds us periodically that a substantial percentage of the older population is living in poverty. There probably aren't too many poor people here today, if only because of the admission charge! But I suspect there are a number of you who feel poor from time to time! And there are probably even more of you who are genuinely worried about poverty in the future, if only because you're now living on fixed incomes, augmented by dipping into your life savings from time to time. I see the principal perils to financial health as being:

- Inflation
- Income Taxes
- Death Taxes
- Not Paying Attention to Investment Yields
- Dealing with the Wrong Financial Institutions
- Probate and Estate Fees
- Disability
- Not Having a Good Financial Advisor

For the entire twentieth century, beginning with the world-wide recessions of the early 1900s, <u>inflation</u> has been the scourge of those living on fixed incomes. You

123

can't see it, feel it, smell it, but the effects of inflation on disposable incomes is just as real as death and taxes. You notice it when shoes you bought last week were a dollar less at Christmas. That lettuce costing five cents more than it did last winter is another reminder. Inflation is the biggest threat to purchasing power for those on fixed incomes. The value of the dollar drops by half in just 12 years at an inflation of 6%. At 7%, you'd be able to buy only half of what you could today only ten years from now. There frankly isn't much you and I can do as individuals to fight inflation itself, except to support the Bank of Canada Governor's attempts at capping inflation by his interest rate policy. You can directly influence your ability to keep ahead of inflation by ensuring your investment yields reflect interest rates. While high interest rates are a curse to people who have to borrow to finance their purchases, such as young people buying their first home, or business people financing plant expansions, there is no doubt that higher rates are of benefit to those with savings.

Income taxes this year will rob everyone of more income. While the Finance Minister claimed he was introducing no new taxes in his last budget, he didn't have to. Measures introduced in previous budgets ensure that everyone will be paying at least one full percentage point more in tax this year. Meanwhile, for those with income of $53,000 receiving Old Age Security, the infamous Clawback tax will add 15% to tax rates this year.

What can be done? Politically, make sure you're supporting a Member of Parliament who is fiscally responsible. More practically speaking, there are a number of things you can, and should, be doing. If your income is such that you're in a higher or lower marginal tax bracket than your spouse or close family member over 18, then income split with that family member. This is the single most important, yet overlooked, strategy for reducing income taxes among older people. The disposable income of a couple where only one individual declares a total income of $60,000 is over $5,000 less than the same couple would have if each declared $30,000. For such a couple, getting an extra $5,000 in disposable income is the same as getting a raise in pension of $10,000 per year, before tax! Even though the Department of Finance has closed many of the income splitting loopholes that were being abused, there are still many remaining, all quite legal. If you're not familiar with them, you owe it to yourself to find out about them.

Most people believe death taxes disappeared a decade ago. Not so. They are just called something else now. Capital Gains and RRSPs are the largest sources of death taxes, and they represent much more to the federal treasury than succession duties ever did. Yes, capital gains taxes on that cottage you've owned for the past 30 years are payable immediately upon your demise. Such taxes could easily amount to 70% of the profit you've made on that cottage, even though such profits are only on paper. And that pile of RRSPs you've been building is also taxable immediately upon your demise, at the highest marginal tax rate, quite possibly at 70%, if you leave it to anyone but your spouse or to a minor and financially dependent child! There are a number of techniques for minimizing such death taxes, including selling capital gains assets while you're still alive to take advantage of the temporary $100,000 capital gains exemption. As for RRSPs, there are a number of ways you can ensure that pile doesn't grow too large including subscribing to spousal RRSPs. You can minimize the effects of taxation on the remaining RRSPs you own through life insurance designed to be paid when the last of you and your spouse passes away.

Your investment yields during 1996 should have been a minimum of 8% on your total portfolio of safe assets. In other words, the total of your savings-type accounts, CSBs, GICs, and term deposit RRSPs should have grown by a minimum of 8%. Your risk type assets, i.e. stock, mutual funds, and long bonds, should have yielded at least 10% in 1996. If your investments didn't do as well, you're not paying attention to your portfolio. One of the best ways of getting better yields is to reduce large daily interest balances in favour of longer term, but cashable, GICs, or in insured and guaranteed mutual funds. Another is to abandon those Canada Savings Bonds you've been religiously buying, also in favour of longer-term GICs. There hasn't been a single CSB issued during the last decade that has performed as well as a balanced portfolio of GICs. Regarding yields, don't look to real estate per se as a hedge against inflation, unless you're contemplating a rental property for income tax loss purposes, or unless you're looking at a real estate tax shelter, what used to be known as MURBs.

Most people, particularly older individuals, are dealing with the wrong financial institutions. I don't mean to imply there is anything risky about the Royal Bank or Canada Trust. But your investments are, indeed, at risk if they are anywhere but with a life insurance company. Bank and trust GICs, RRSPs and RIFs are almost always locked in. On the other hand, most GICs with life companies can be cashed in early, albeit with a small penalty. If you're worried about becoming disabled, and the drain this may cause on the family treasury, stay away from Banks and Trusts.

When you die, anything you have at Banks and Trusts will be frozen until your will is probated. Then the lawyers get their share of your assets, usually at least 5% and sometimes as much as 10%, before your beneficiary gets any of your money, usually at least a year after your demise. So, don't leave more than a month's living costs at a bank or trust, and in any event, certainly no more than $5,000. This includes your RRSPs and RIFs and annuities. All such investments at banks or trusts are subject to probate and the loss of value such probate entails, even if you have named a beneficiary. All such investments, when with a life insurance company, are paid directly to your beneficiaries without probate, usually within days of your demise. Many life companies offer rates more competitive than leading banks and trusts.

Finally, I've saved perhaps the most important advice until last. If much of what I've said this afternoon is gobbledygook, or if you're just having too much fun celebrating aging to devote enough time to your financial affairs the way you'd like, then get yourself a good financial advisor you can trust and have faith in. Not just someone who'll help you in the short term, but most importantly, someone who'll be around for the long-haul; who'll be there to help your loved ones when you're no longer around. Look for someone like me!

Thanks for listening. I hope you've each and every one gotten at least one good idea this afternoon.

2.   Leaving Town?

Many Canadians leave town, some for extended periods. If you are one of those, here are some personal planning tips culled from a list by Royal Trust.

Get a medical exam. If you're not in tip-top shape, consider buying private health insurance, if you're not covered by your employer's plan, to pay the difference between foreign medical costs and the much lower provincial medicare limits. Most private medical insurance plans cover only unexpected or emergency type conditions, not pre-existing ones. That's one of the reasons for the medical. Another is that if you're in good medical shape and have a good history, the cost of a private plan may not be worth the minimal risk. Check your credit card company plan availability. Some issuers provide such coverage at no charge for limited periods.

Check your prescription supply. Stock up before leaving if you're covered by a provincial drug plan, or by a plan through your employer. On the other hand, if you're travelling to a foreign country other than the U.S., you may discover many drugs requiring a prescription in Canada are available at a fraction of the price over the counter. For example, practically any drug requiring a prescription in Canada is available at any farmacia in Mexico over the counter, at not much more than 10% of the price back home. Yes, that reads 10%! (I am aware of readers who pay for an annual trip to such a country as Mexico just from savings on prescriptions.)

Review your home insurance. Are you covered for damage from ice build-up, water seepage and sewer backup? If not, and many policies don't cover for such events, ask your agent to add the cover by means of an inexpensive rider or floater. Consider also upgrading your policy to provide replacement cost coverage, rather than the more traditional depreciated cost method of claim handling. Make sure you have the premises checked as often as your policy calls for, otherwise you won't be able to collect in the event of a heating system failure and resulting water damage from burst pipes.

Review your car insurance liability limits. Liability limits in many U.S. states are frighteningly low. U.S. damage awards tend to be much higher than in Canada.

Renting a car while you're away? Your credit card issuer may already offer collision coverage, which tends to be rather expensive when obtained through the rental company. If your credit card doesn't offer such coverage, check with your agent to see if he/she can temporarily transfer such coverage from your own vehicle to another while you're away. Careful: only one vehicle can be insured at a time; so while the rental vehicle is being covered, your auto back home isn't.

Income tax instalments? Make arrangements to pay these on time. Otherwise overdue interest, compounded daily, is charged.

With just a little planning before leaving, your trip will be that much more enjoyable. Bon Voyage!

3.   Should I Incorporate?

Many people are in business for themselves, either drawing commissions as agents/ brokers, or in the professions, or operating a business out of their homes, or owners of businesses with employees. These folks often ask: Should I incorporate? Let's start with a review of the ways of doing business as an owner. There are essentially three: sole proprietorship; partnership; and limited or incorporated company. A limited company is the same as an incorporated company. Three other ways include joint ventures, limited partnerships, and co-operatives. These latter are seldom used, and are hence not discussed herein.

Sole Proprietorships: This is a business owned by only one person. The owner is responsible for any debts or legal obligations. A proprietorship does <u>not</u> have to have its name registered. The owner can use a name other than his/her own, but runs the risk of using someone else's name, and the legal problems this might entail. A simple solution is to have a name search performed by a firm specializing in doing so. A search, costing about $50, will examine the provincial name data base to see if anyone else is using a similar name. If not, the proprietor can then register his choice with the proper authority (in Ontario: Ministry of Consumer and Commercial Relations; name registration fee: $50).

Unless the proprietor is concerned about contravening bylaws, the municipality does not have to be informed. If the business sells products or services that normally carry sales tax, registration with the appropriate tax authority <u>is</u> required, including the federal GST people, if the annual non-exempt gross of the business will be greater than $30,000.

Proprietorship need not involve any paperwork. For all intents and purposes, a proprietorship is an extension of the individual running and owning it. Because there are no formal requirements in setting one up, proprietorships are the most common form of business venture. In Ontario alone, there were, as of the end of 1987, over 400,000 small businesses, 70% of which were <u>un</u>-incorporated. There were over 100,000 new business starts in Ontario in that year!

Because a proprietorship is an extension of an individual, there are no tax advantages to a proprietorship versus a limited company. Profits are considered salary; no dividends can be declared. Profits must be declared on a personal tax return in the same year as earned. Finally, perhaps most importantly, proprietorship does not remove liability for mistakes, injuries, negligence, or debt.

Partnership: In this form of venture, two or more individuals agree to operate a business jointly. As with proprietorship, there is no protection from legal liability. Each partner is wholly and severally responsible for the obligations of the entire partnership. This means if one partner cannot meet his/her share of liabilities or responsibilities, the others becomes liable. A partnership <u>should</u> (but doesn't have to) be operated under a written agreement between the partners. Included in an agreement would be such matters as which partner is responsible for what functions, how the partnership is to be capitalized, how earnings are to be shared, what will happen when a partner wants out, or dies, or becomes disabled.

Perhaps the most important element of a partnership agreement is a method or formula as to how the partnership will be valued at any subsequent point in time. Since it will be apparent a partnership cannot operate indefinitely, as can a limited company, each of the partners will have a vested interest in knowing ahead of time that his/her share can be fairly valued upon any eventuality causing the partnership to cease. A partnership ceases to operate immediately upon the death of any one of the partners. A partnership does <u>not</u> automatically cease upon disability of a partner. These are reasons enough for a written valuation formula. While most people think of a partnership as being an equal proposition for each of the partners, it does not have to be so. For example, in exchange for capitalization, one partner might have a 30% share of profits, while the other, who does all of the work, might be entitled to 70%.

Like a proprietorship, a partnership does not have to be registered. If there is a possibility that a unique name is already being used by another, a search should be performed and the name registered with the appropriate authority. While a written agreement between the partners is highly recommended, most partnerships don't have one. Of the three forms of business ventures discussed here-in, partnerships will almost always benefit most from legal advice, if only in the drawing up of a partnership agreement.

Limited/Incorporated Company: Such a business is considered a separate legal entity from its owners, almost as a separate human being. Shareholders have limited liability for the company's debts or other legal obligations. All they can lose is the value of their shares. A company must be set up under either federal or provincial laws, following prescribed procedures and paperwork. Unless a company plans nationwide operation, provincial incorporation is usually sufficient. Being incorporated in one province does not restrict operation of the business in any other province, for most types of trade and service. Provincial incorporation will mean the company's head office must be located at an address in the province of incorporation. Provincial incorporation is less expensive, and involves less red tape, than a federal one. No municipal licences are required for a company, unless municipal bylaws are involved. While a lawyer should be employed in setting up a company, one is not strictly needed. Paperwork is relatively simple and straightforward (at least in Ontario!). Cost of a do-it-yourself incorporation can be less than $400 including name search, registration, and corporate stamp/seal.

Many people think of companies as owned by many shareholders. Quite the contrary. In Ontario, over half of all companies are owned by only one individual. Two thirds are owned by three people or less, who are often related to each other by birth or marriage.

The main advantage to incorporation is limited liability. It's possible to have only one shareowner, and it's possible for that one owner to have bought the only share issued for $0.01. But that's all the owner personally loses if the company is bankrupted by a successful suit for malpractice, negligence, breach of contract, or bad debt. Speaking of malpractice or negligence, certain professionals, including doctors, cannot incorporate their practices for that very reason. If they were able to incorporate, they would be able to avoid personal responsibility for their mistakes or omissions. Many professionals still own their own limited companies to provide ancillary services to their practices in such areas as accounting, real estate, furniture, equipment and staff. Revenue Canada has clamped down on the tax advantages available to such 'personal services' corporations. There are thus few such companies being set up these days.

It is possible for one individual to be the sole owner, the sole director, and the sole officer of a limited company. But it's not advisable. If the major shareholder wants to see his/her company flourish and expand, he would do well to have a number of different directors <u>and</u> officers, in order to bring expertise and experience into the business.

Companies can pay their owners salary, bonuses, commissions, dividends, retiring allowances, or combinations thereof. This allows for optimum return of profits to the owner from an income tax standpoint. A company may also lend money to the owner, with or without interest. A company may have a different year-end than a calendar year, and indeed, many do. A closely held company could have a year-end of January 31, for example, and make considerable payments to the owner in January, which the owner would not declare until his/her tax return was filed 15 months later. Thus, revenue to the owner might not be taxed for over two years from the date it was first received by the corporation.

Depending on where a company is incorporated, there can be significant short-term tax savings. Most provinces have a reduced tax rate for new companies. Indeed, up until 1988, Ontario had a three-year tax holiday for new companies. Most new companies qualify for a reduced federal tax rate as well. A corporation, unlike an individual, can retain earnings from one year to the next, with no tax implications to the owner until actually paid out. If the owner of a company is also working for it, the owner can structure company-paid perks not normally available from a proprietorship, such as group life and disability insurances, social club memberships, group RRSPs, and deferred profit sharing plans. It should be noted that tax considerations are not normally sufficient in themselves to justify incorporation. Revenue Canada takes a jaundiced view of those who incorporate primarily to benefit from lower tax rates. Under Tax Reform, Revenue Canada now has the authority to consider a business transaction null and void if the main purpose was to otherwise pay less tax. An individual thinking about incorporation so he/she can pay less tax on his investment portfolio had better think again!

Directors of limited companies also have limited liability over a company's debts or legal obligations, which liability is not as limited as the shareowners. Directors can be held accountable in some circumstances for back pay or damages suffered by an employee terminated without cause. Directors can also be liable for remittances due for CPP and UIC on behalf of employees. Directors have a legal obligation to pay attention and blow the whistle if an officer is behaving illegally. Ignorance is insufficient excuse for a director who should have known that his/her company was acting illegally. While it's possible to secure director's liability insurance, few companies have it because of the expensive premiums. The best protection for a director against liability is to make sure he/she knows the officers and key employees, as well as the other directors, as to character.

Another myth needs demolishing: that incorporation suddenly provides all sorts of tax deductions not normally available to proprietorships and/or partnerships. There are very few deductible expenses available to a company that are not also available to proprietorships or partnerships. While the primary justification for incorporation will usually be limited legal liability, there are a number of tax-related considerations flowing automatically from incorporation. The more important include:

- Retained earnings may be stored until the owner finds himself in a lower marginal tax bracket.
- There may be a provincial tax holiday.
- There may be a lower federal tax rate.
- Up to $400,000 of tax-free capital gains is available to each owner of qualified small businesses upon disposition of their shares.

- The owner has a choice of income from the business as salary, commissions, bonuses, dividends, retiring allowances, perks, or a combination thereof. He/she may borrow from the company, with or without interest. Tax planning is thereby much simplified and optimized.

- Estate planning and family involvement are more readily accommodated with a company than with proprietorship or partnership.

For more information on incorporation, the Counsel Self-Help folks have an excellent title, *Business Methods and Incorporation (For the Province of . . .*), less than $15.

4. Insurance Companies Self-Insured

Most life insurance companies operating in Canada have joined a pool that insures all policyholders against financial failure of any of the members of the pool. Not only life insurance contracts are covered by the pool, but disability insurance (income replacement) contracts, and investment/ savings/ retirement products as well. The pool, known as CompCorp (the Canadian Life and Health Insurance Compensation Corporation) is designed to protect consumers against loss of benefits in the event a life insurance company becomes insolvent.

What's covered by CompCorp? To quote from their press release:

> In the event a member company is declared insolvent, CompCorp will guarantee payment under covered policies up to certain specified limits for policyholders of that company. This means annuity and disability income payments continue, claims under life and health insurance policies will be paid, and requests for cash surrender will be honoured. Policy-holders receiving income from annuities and disability insurance are guaranteed payments up to $2,000 per month. Death claims under covered life insurance policies are protected up to $200,000. Health insurance benefits up to a total of $60,000 are protected.

For money accumulation products, CompCorp's limits are similar to those of the Canada Deposit Insurance Corporation (CDIC). Plans registered under the Tax Act (such as RRSPs and RRIFs) are protected up to $60,000 per person. In addition, non-registered plans, and the cash surrender value in life insurance policies are protected up to $60,000 per person.

A consumer information brochure is available. Should you wish a copy, or have any questions, contact the Canadian Life and Health Insurance Association Info Centre at their toll-free number, 1-800-268-8099. Everything else being equal, investments with life insurance companies are far more secure than with banks or trust companies. This infers not so much that banks and trusts are not safe, but, on the other hand, that consumer protection laws governing assets held by life companies make life company investments far more secure from creditors, and far more available to beneficiaries, and at no cost.

Recently, the Canada Deposit Insurance Corp waged a vigorous advertising campaign to inform Canadians about what kind of deposits, and their limits, were insured with member companies of the CDIC. These members are mainly banks and trusts, although credit unions and caisses populaires also qualify to belong. Deposits with life insurance companies are insured by CompCorp, that offers, in all cases, equal coverage. In some cases, CompCorp coverage is better than CDIC. Deposits insured by CDIC cannot have a term longer than five years. With CompCorp, the term can be any length of time.

When deposits are converted to income products, as with RRIFs, CDIC members are covered only to $60,000 of total income contracts per client, and with terms not exceeding five years. With CompCorp, on the other hand, such income products are covered to $2,000 per month, with no limit on term. Such contracts, as annuities, could be worth more than $200,000 before conversion, depending on the insured's age and sex. With equity based products, such as mutual funds and/or bonds and mortgages, CDIC offers no coverage. If equivalent life company funds are guaranteed by the issuer, these (known as segregated funds) are also covered by CompCorp in the event of the issuer's financial insolvency. CompCorp coverage is clearly at least as good as that provided by CDIC. For older people contemplating retirement products, the coverage provided by CompCorp is definitely superior.

5. Buying U.S. Real Estate

Over the years, many people have asked my advice on buying real estate south of the border. My replies have always been that it depends on the specific investment, coupled with general advice on taxes, which are considerably different than taxes in Canada. My advice usually is to older people thinking of retirement property. These are the very people who should beware more than younger people, if only because older people have a higher chance of passing away before they can recoup their investment.

As a rough rule of thumb, an investor in American real estate should be prepared to remain with the investment for at least five and preferably ten years in order to ensure a profit. If profit is not a consideration, then the investor should at least be aware of other pitfalls. These include rental cost versus outright purchase, ongoing taxes and taxes at death ('estate' or death duties) applicable in the States that are different from, and in addition to, those in Canada. Renting a property simply means shelling out monthly amounts for rent, insurance, and travel. However, purchase involves not only mortgages, but also state and local taxes, and an estate tax that can amount to from 18% to 55% of the net value of all U.S. property that exceeds the first $60,000.

Then, there are differing real estate appreciation experiences, depending on the location of the property. Just because real estate in Ontario may have grown over a given period does not mean that the vacation home you are looking at in Florida will have done the same. Or vice versa! While real estate in Canada has taken a beating during the just-ending recession, real estate in some parts of Florida, despite the U.S. recession, has appreciated significantly during the past 12 to 18 months.

Those who buy while still earning a living in Canada, and who then rent the property out until they retire, must file a U.S. income tax return as well as a Canadian one.

In all fairness, ownership does have some advantages. Over a long enough period of time, the property will realize a profit on sale. As well, for those who plan to spend at least several months a year residing in their American property, there are the advantages of eliminating rental fee hikes, yearly moves, and the hassle of packing. Older people, especially, like predictability, and for some, it's important for them to feel a part of the community. For those who choose Florida, the savings on food and gas compared to Canada more than make up for the hassles and expense of ownership.

6.   Algonquin Business Management Program

I am committed to carrying information of use to entrepreneurs, as a glance at other articles herein will attest. Here are excerpts from a brochure published by Algonquin College. The needs of small business are practical. People want a straight-line approach to learn how to establish a new business. Existing firms require clear-cut and simple advice on how to increase their profits and reduce work-load and stress. This program is Algonquin's response to the public need for advice on start-up or profit improvement. The instructors are experienced in small business and eager to respond to your specific needs. The program of study includes:

- Starting Out — Look Before You Leap
- Profit Through Planning
- Management of Small Business
- Tax and Small Business
- Franchising
- Management — The Business Plan
- Business Economics and Finance
- Accounting/Bookkeeping
- Computers in Business
- Street Smart Marketing — Retail/Service
- English — The Business Plan
- Import/Export and Small Business
- Sales/Advertising
- Home-Based Business

You can register for any Continuing Education course by phone, mail or in person. Contact Algonquin at 1385 Woodroffe Ave., Room C-101, Nepean, K2G 1V8, or call Mr. Ron Knowles, the dynamic head of the business program at 727-7667.

7.   Directors Are Liable

Are you a director of a club, or organization such as a business? If yes, you may be financially liable for certain responsibilities that you may not be aware of. Directors are ultimately responsible for the behaviour of a company. When things don't go well, and a company starts to fail, directors can be liable for government claims, employee claims, and other corporate actions. Major liabilities occur in:

Employee Claims: Under the Ontario Business Corporations Act and the Canada Business Corporations Act, directors are responsible for wage arrears for a period of up to six months. Directors can be sued for these amounts for up to two years after ceasing to be directors. There is no limit to the number of employees who can come after you under this heading.

Government Claims: Directors are liable under the Income Tax Act if the company does not pay source deductions, taxes for non-residents, the employee portion of UIC and CPP contributions. The government can also come after you for shortages in OHIP premium remittances and mishandled pension plan payments.

Corporate Finance Liabilities: Directors are liable where improper financial assistance has been given by the company of which they are director to shareholders, directors, officers, employees or affiliated companies. A director will also be liable if he/she supports a resolution to pay dividends when there are reasonable grounds to assume there are insufficient retained earnings to do so.

As a director, there are a number of ways of protecting yourself:

- Diligently attend board meetings;
- Obtain background material/agendas in advance and carefully understand the issues;
- Ensure the board has sufficient legal, accounting and other professional advice before embarking on complex tasks;
- Carefully review minutes to ensure accuracy;
- Obtain periodic confirmation in writing from management that tax obligations are on time;
- Similarly ensure employee pay is not in arrears, along with source deductions and remittances;
- If available for your organization, insist on liability insurance.

Being a director can be challenging, rewarding, and satisfying. With proper care and diligence, it need not turn into a financial nightmare.

8. Government Aid to Businesses

Many operate their own business. Many more plan to. Here is a precis of government aid available to small businesses. Federal aid is available to any company anywhere in Canada, while provincial and local help mentioned below is oriented towards National Capital area Ontario businesses. Most provinces operate assistance plans similar to Ontario's. Consult your provincial government for more information. What kind of help is available? Governments at federal, provincial and municipal levels have a variety of programs designed to assist new or existing small businesses. The problem most small business owners face is identifying which government programs might help their particular business. So, the first level of assistance consists of information offices and publications which can facilitate the process of sorting through the maze and identifying applicable programs.

New businesses should examine the Ontario government's New Ventures Loan guarantee program. This program is administered through the chartered banks, and will guarantee a loan of up to $15,000 in Eastern Ontario, if the applicant makes a cash equity contribution of half the loan amount applied for. For example, a $7,500 cash equity contribution would be required to obtain a $15,000 loan. Interest is calculated at prime plus one percent, and principal repayment does not begin until the second year of the loan. For younger entrepreneurs, there are two loan guarantee programs administered by the Ontario Ministry of Skills Development which are similar in scope to the New Ventures program. The Youth Venture Capital loan program is designed for those under the age of 25, or up to 29, if they have been out of school for less than one year. It follows the same rules as the New Venture program, but the maximum loan is $7,500, and the equity contribution can be made in cash or assets. This loan is interest free for the first year, with principal and interest repayment at prime plus one percent beginning in the second year.

The Student Venture Capital loan is available to students wishing to start a summer business. They must be over the age of 15 and returning to full time school in the fall. A maximum of $3,000 is available as an interest-free loan, but must be repaid in full by October 1.

Administered through the chartered banks is the Business Improvement Loan Guarantee Program, which falls under the federal Small Business Loans Act. A guarantee of 80 to 90 percent may be obtained on loans of up to $100,000 for the purchase of land, equipment or leasehold improvements, at an interest rate of one percent over prime. The Federal Business Development Bank may also provide loans, loan guarantees or equity financing to businesses unable to secure adequate capital at reasonable terms from traditional sources. There are programs to assist the entrepreneur seeking equity financing from the private sector. Provincial legislation allows investors in Small Business Development Corporations that invest in eligible Eastern Ontario businesses a 30 percent tax-free cash grant or tax credit for corporate investors.

Many government programs provide counselling on management or marketing, and skills training. Inexpensive counselling may be obtained through the FBDBs Counselling Assistance to Small Enterprise (CASE) program, which uses retired business people to advise on almost any area of business management or planning. The Department of Regional Industrial Expansion and MITT can provide marketing assistance, which may include grants for feasibility studies, particularly for manufacturing, export or high technology industries. The Kanata Enterprise Centre offers the Small Business Owner Development Program, subsidized by the Ontario Ministry of Skills and Development, which includes both a half day of individual advisory services and a seminar each month for one year. The Ontario Ministry of Skills and Development and Employment and Immigration Canada have programs which may assist with employee training costs, or even provide wage subsidies during the training period.

The programs described here comprise a small selection of the variety of government assistance available. The small business owner who takes the initiative to inquire is likely to identify additional programs which may be useful to his or her business. The common thread that unites the objectives of all government programs is a desire to help entrepreneurs help themselves.

When in doubt, you can call:

- The Small Business Loans Act: (613) 954-5539
- The Federal Business Development Bank: (613) 995-0234
- Ontario's Small Business Start-Up Hotline: 1-800-387-0070
- Ontario's New Ventures Loans program: 1-800-387-0070

- Ontario's Student Venture Capital Loans: 1-800-387-0777
- Innovation Ontario Corp: (416) 963-5717
- Small Business Development Corporations: 1-800-263-7965
- Canada Opportunities Investment Network: 1-800-387-8943

Algonquin C.A.A.T. has a wide range of very useful courses/workshops on starting a small business, emphasizing in particular the need for, and preparation of, a business plan. Call their School of Business at 727-7667. One of our Federal MPs, Mac Harb, Ottawa Centre, is very accessible. Contact him at 996-5322. Before election as MP, Mr. Harb was a long-time City of Ottawa Alderman.

9.   Mortgage Renewal

I am being frequently asked: Should I renew my mortgage early, and now, given the steep decline in interest rates. The answer will depend on many variables, not least of which will be what rate you are paying now, how long until the normal renewal date, and what financial institution you're with. For those with mortgages of more than 13% and only a year or two to normal renewal, the penalty to renew early may indeed make economic sense. However, if the penalty seems high to you, you might wish to wait a little longer, since, if anything, mortgage rates will go down some more, before they start going back up. Our current estimate is that mortgage rates won't start rising again until after the next federal election.

If the area of mortgages is confusing you, then consult, and perhaps retain, a mortgage broker. The better ones are well worth their minimal fees. As borrower rather than as lender, you have nothing to be concerned about as to the solvency of mortgage brokers despite the collapse of several of them in the Ottawa area in the past three years. I would be pleased to recommend a mortgage broker I have been sending my clients to for several years, with nothing but praise for his knowledge and service, not to mention the better deals he has come up with for those clients.

10.   Saving vs Investing

According to the Investment Funds Institute of Canada, there's a difference between 'savings' and 'investments'. Saving is actually a loan activity, while investing in- volves the purchase of assets.

If you save, you:

- have a specific use for the amount put aside;
- have a short-term goal or objective;
- loan your money to a financial institution or government for an agreed interest rate; and,
- accept the prevailing rate of return offered.

If you invest, you:

- build assets with growth potential for your future financial welfare;
- have long-term financial goals;
- own assets which you expect will appreciate in value;

- are concerned with maximizing your rate of return; and,
- are actively involved in the ongoing management of your assets.

Working towards meeting your goals, the Institute recommends you consider:

Time: To meet your long-term security goals you should think of the value of your capital in five, ten or 20 years' time, not six months. Investment is a long-term process in which time, depending on your age, is usually on your side.

Risk: Every financial undertaking involves some element of risk. The point about risk is to recognize that it exists and to learn how to manage it.

Inflation: Inflation is more than just higher prices; it eventually erodes the value of the money you accumulate. Investing your accumulated assets protects the real value of your capital. Owning a share in a mutual fund, for instance, allows you to participate in its growth as well as sharing in its profits. The best defence against inflation is to own assets which increase in value, offsetting the decrease in purchasing power caused by inflation.

Liquidity: One of the most important facets of asset accumulation is that you have access to your funds when you need them.

11.   Off-Shore Investing

Over the years, quite a few of our readers have inquired about establishing investments outside Canada. Most of these have been of the 'retirement home in the U.S. sunbelt' variety, but not a few have been investments abroad in the form of GICs and mutual funds. Motives have ranged from a desire to obtain higher yields, escaping or reducing income tax, diversifying portfolios and establishing funds in a potential post-retirement country of domicile. Recently, such inquiries have increased because of Canada's ever increasing income tax rates, and because interest rates have dropped quickly since 1991. Such investments may very well make sense for some Canadians, and here is a round-up of some considerations that apply.

Yields: Yields on GICs in other parts of the world are still at 12% or better. Contrast that with no better than 7% in Canada at present.

Safety of Capital: While most GICs carry insurance in Canada against the borrower defaulting, such insurance is still quite rare outside North America.

Income Taxes: While there usually will be no income tax due to the country where the off-shore investment will be placed, as a Canadian taxpayer, the investor is still legally required to declare all income world-wide. Even though there is little risk of ever being caught not reporting such income, penalties when caught make this kind of non-reporting potentially quite expensive. A Canadian ceases to have a legal liability for Canadian income tax when no longer deemed a resident of Canada. This has nothing to do with citizenship. Even those who renounce or lose their Canadian citizenship are still liable for Canadian income tax if they have not severed properly their Canadian residency. One key component of severing residency is that the individual spend no more than 182 days per year in Canada. Another is that the individual no longer own property that could be considered a principal residence.

Diversification: Some investors, worried about the impact of a potential division of Canada into two or more regions, want to diversify their holdings to protect against currency devaluations relative to foreign currency. This makes sense only if such a person intends leaving Canada to reside permanently elsewhere. In that case, an investor can buy most foreign currencies ahead of time through a Canadian financial institution and have the funds invested in Canada paying Canadian yields, without having to resort to dealing with a foreign financial institution.

I have travelled extensively in recent years accumulating a file of good-quality foreign investments. These consist mostly of GICs and mutual funds offered by major European financial institutions. I would be pleased to lend this file to anyone wishing to borrow it.

I continue to see significant interest in Canadians investing off-shore. If anything, this is manifesting itself in the fastest growing segment of our product line. Reasons are many, including portfolio diversification, currency hedging, potential for better returns. Perhaps the most significant reason is, I suspect, to be able to hide chunks of capital from the Canadian taxman, and the profits thereof, until the owner of the investment is in a lower tax bracket here at home, or has left the country for a more favourable tax climate.

I believe this flight of capital is becoming a worrisome problem to the officials at the Department of Finance, and may become as crucial a problem as the so-called 'under-ground' economy, the latter driven by barter transactions, or transactions strictly for cash, in attempts to avoid income tax and sales taxes (not least of which: the GST).

As Canada's politicians demolish universality in social program delivery, and as they tackle the ever-mounting national debt, requiring further belt tightening <u>and</u> higher taxes, more and more affluent Canadians and their capital will continue leaving the country for lower-tax jurisdictions. As Canadians become better educated as to what can be done legally, more and more Canadians will ship their capital to tax havens ahead of their own bodies, if only to 'hide' the capital and resultant investment profits until they can join their capital and profits in a comfortable and amenable retirement overseas.

It will take a re-drafting of our tax laws to bring them more into line with the American system before we see capital flight slow down. The alternative is currency controls, which are usually resorted to only by banana republics.

A House of Commons committee recently studied a measure whereby an amendment to the Citizenship Act would automatically revoke Canadian citizenship to any adult who voluntarily and formally, except through marriage or adoption, acquires any other nationality. Many observers, at the time, felt this proposed legislation was aimed at Quebecers, many of whom believe that even with succession, they could continue retaining their Canadian citizenship.

I see something more sinister: that this legislation is also aimed at those who take up a second citizenship, while retaining Canadian citizenship, for purposes of avoiding paying <u>any</u> and <u>all</u> taxes in Canada (and, if they have chosen their new home with some care, no taxes there either!).

Of course, it is not necessary to take out citizenship in most tax havens in order to cease paying Canadian taxes; only residency is presently a consideration. However, this proposed legislation would fit in nicely down the road with any plans to force Canadian citizens to either file tax returns regardless of where they were domiciled, or to forfeit their Canadian citizenship if they formally became citizens of another country. By forfeiting Canadian citizenship, of course, a former Canadian would have to join the end of any lengthy queue of those waiting to emigrate to Canada if they subsequently changed their minds and wanted back in.

I have recently come into possession of an excellent book on off-shore investing and banking, called *Behind Closed Doors; Unlock the Secret to Offshore Banking*. I'd be delighted to lend it to anyone requesting a loan.

12.   Home-Based Businesses

Many people operate businesses out of their homes. The following article describes an association that may be of interest to such readers. The Canadian Association for Home-Based Business (CAHBB) is a non profit association originally founded in 1986 as A-Line, and federally incorporated in 1988. CAHBB's mission is to:

- Create and maintain a public awareness of home-based business;
- Foster the spirit of entrepreneurship;
- Provide educational/information services and support opportunities, for operators of home-based business and to other interested parties, through communications, member participation and member resources.

Objectives of the Association are to:

- Educate the public, government, and industry on the contribution of home-based businesses to the Canadian economy;
- Educate members on methods of improving their businesses and lifestyles;
- Create start-up procedures for home-based activities;
- Provide guidelines and standards to encourage the ethical operation of home-based businesses;
- Develop statistics on the numbers and types of home-based businesses; and
- Provide a starting point for member networking, with a view to sharing resources (e.g. equipment, contacts, experience) and marketing our services and products to each other, when feasible.

CAHBB holds an annual conference where members of CAHBB and the general public can come together to attend seminars on matters of relevance to entrepreneurs. The conference is an ideal opportunity for members to network. CAHBB meetings are held on a regular basis, usually monthly, to focus on issues affecting home-based business. Meetings are open to the public. A Business Services Table is available for the distribution of information by attenders of the meeting. CAHBB's newsletter is published six times a year. It contains practical articles on running a business, relevant news, and classified ads. All members receive the newsletter as part of the membership package. Non-members may subscribe for $12 annually. The Association publishes a directory of members once per year. Membership dues are $40 per year, tax-deductible if the member operates a business. For additional information, please contact the Canadian Association for Home-Based Business at 1200E Prince of Wales Dr., Ottawa, K2C 1M9, (613) 723-7233.

13.   Lawyer Referral Service

You may need legal advice (or think you do), but don't know how to find a lawyer. The Lawyer Referral Service can help! Just call the Lawyer Referral Service and when the operator answers, briefly explain the type of problem you have and where you're calling from. The operator will give you the name of a lawyer in your area who participates in the Service and can deal with your problem. Then, call the lawyer and make an appointment. Be sure to tell the lawyer you have been referred through the Lawyer Referral Service. You will not be charged for up to one half hour with the lawyer. After that, the lawyer's regular rates apply. In metro Toronto: 947-3330; outside Toronto: 1-800-268-8326. Lawyer Referral Service/Dial-A-Law are public services of Ontario's lawyers through the Law Society of Upper Canada.

14.   Back at School?

Many Canadians are returning to school. If you or a family member are attending a post-secondary institution, you should be aware of the Ontario Student Assistance Program (OSAP), administered by the Provincial Ministry of Colleges and Universities. Even if the student doesn't <u>need</u> supplemental government financial help in paying tuition and other costs, government generosity should still be investigated. Major programs available to Ontario residents and/or students include:

- Canada student loans
- Ontario study grants
- Ontario student loans

Loans and grants are available to university and community college students. Students studying agricultural technology, nursing assistance, hairstyling, chiropractic, horticulture, art (at Ontario College of Music) and students at Royal Military College, Ryerson, Toronto Institute of Medical Technology and approved registered private post secondary Ontario institutions also qualify for loans and/or grants. For information, call the Financial Aid Department of your nearest university or community college or the Ministry of Colleges and Universities at 1-800-465-3013.

15.   Expenses Moving to University

Do you have a son or daughter who moved away to attend university? If the move brought your child at least 40 kilometers closer to school than where your child lived before, then your child may be able to claim moving expenses as a tax deduction. Even if the deduction does not directly lower your child's taxes, it may reduce his/her taxable income enough to allow you to claim some of his tuition expenses. To whatever extent moving expenses reduce the student's net income, the amount of refundable tax credits (such as the quarterly GST rebate and Ontario Tax Credits) will be increased accordingly.

Many students and their parents don't consider this. Even if it's only a plane ride to Toronto, or $50 to ship their bicycle, it may be worth using the expenses at tax time. Expenses that can be claimed by students are identical to others moving for purely job related reasons, and include transport costs, room and board while moving and apartment hunting, and U-haul rentals. Expenses are deductible only from income earned in the new location, but can be carried forward to a year when there is enough income at the new locations.

If you'd like more information, pick up a copy of Revenue Canada's brochure on moving expenses or give us a call, and we'll send you one.

16.   Students and Financial Help

Many of our readers have children and/or grandchildren at university, who often wonder if their child is getting the best possible financial advice and assistance while away at post-secondary school. This article attempts to lay down some guidelines and pointers as to where to go.

University education, particularly where the student is living away from the parents' home, can cost upwards of $10,000 annually for tuition, books, supplies, computers, travel, and room and board. Even where a student has student loans, some money saved up from a summer job, some parental assistance, and some ongoing revenue from a part-time job during school term, making ends meet for most students is still a painful exercise, especially so for those who have led a caseated life at their parental home before leaving for the big U.

While parents, and especially grandparents, can provide guidance, most students are not adequately prepared, especially during that first semester away from home.

Most university campuses now operate student financial advice centres, which provide students with assistance in planning budgets, preparing expense reports, and managing their financial resources through individual counselling. Such on-campus organizations will also routinely aid students in identifying which aid programs are available from provincial and federal coffers, as well as providing students with the proper application forms, and advice on how to fill them in.

In most on-campus student advice centres, the emphasis is also on preparing students to avoid a debt bomb after graduation by counselling students on how and when they should be able to pay off their student loans after graduation, given the course of studies enrolled in and the likely income projections from job placement after graduation.

Off-campus bank branches, especially those within walking distance of campus, are also good places to go to for advice of a financial planning nature. Both the Bank of Montreal and the Bank of Nova Scotia have produced easy-to-read books offering information on loans and other financial aid, budgeting, banking, credit use, and income tax. Indeed, Bank of Montreal's U-Choose even has sections on food shopping, economical transportation alternatives, computer buying, and interior design (?).

The Royal Bank offers free computer software containing a spreadsheet to help students with budgeting. The Toronto Dominion Bank has a number of student money-management articles available on (you guessed it) the Internet!

Most of the big banks have service packages tailored to post-secondary students, where, for a set monthly fee, the student is entitled to low- or no-charge services, such as ATM withdrawals, over-the-counter cheques, direct (debit card) purchase payments, and credit cards.

17.   Saving for University

Income attribution rules, introduced some ten years ago during 'Tax Reform', make it difficult for parents to save any meaningful amounts for a child without profits on those savings being taxed in the hands of the donor parents. One exception is the so-called Registered Education Savings programs, where a child can have up to $1,500 per year donated by others with the profits therein sheltered from tax until the funds are needed later for education.

Another exception is the investing of the Child Support credit (that which replaced the 'Baby Bonus' a couple of years ago), however, most readers earn too much to qualify as recipients. Another is to open a life insurance contract for the child, whereby profits are not taxed under the government's 'exempt life policy' rules.

Yet another is to open an investment account, disguised as a 'deferred annuity' for the child, in trust, by the parent, whereby profits would be taxed in the child's name when the child was ready to cash in part or all of the investment for education, at which time, presumably, the child would have little other income, and hence, pay no tax on the investment's profits.

To get around the attribution rules, however, we're seeing more and more parents opening investment accounts for their children with a grandparent as owner, and contributor, in trust for the child. Another increasingly popular way to build future educational savings is by investing off-shore, and not reporting any profits until the child is ready for university.

18.   U.S. $ Accounts

Does it make sense to hold U.S. dollars? Herein, I'll give my rationale for not holding any, even though I spend five figures annually travelling abroad, and am continually changing Canadian dollars into a host of foreign, including American, currencies.

The principle reasons why some people like to have an American currency denominated account, either in Canada or in the U.S., include: a) avoiding paying currency conversion costs twice too often; b) as a hedge against a drop in value of the Canadian dollar relative to the U.S. dollar; and, c) as a mechanism for paying bills in the U.S. while living there. In my opinion, none of these makes enough sense to justify holding more than a few hundred dollars in an American account because of the spread of interest rates between Canadian dollar and American dollar accounts.

Whether your funds are in an account south or north of the border, the interest rate you will get on your funds, regardless of how invested, will be a minimum of 3%, and up to 5%, higher on Canadian dollars than on American. That has been the historical spread in rates for at least a decade. There is no reason to suspect the monetary authorities of either country are about to change that economic fact of life.

Even if the Canadian dollar were to be drastically revalued downward relative to the American dollar because of, say, a breakup of the present confederation, there would still be a four to six percent spread in interest rates. Therefore, the rationale for keeping American dollars only makes sense if the short-term objective for holding such funds comes true. For example, if you have several hundred U.S. dollars left over after a trip, and you plan on going back there in a few more weeks, then it doesn't make sense to convert back to Canadian for those few weeks before then converting back to U.S.

Similarly, if you expect the Canadian dollar to drop four or five cents in the next few months, then it would make sense to convert your Canadian funds to U.S. How likely is that, though? The Canadian dollar has been falling fairly steadily for the past year, having dropped about a dime from its highest value three years ago. If you had bought U.S. dollars three years ago, they would now be worth about 12% more in Canadian dollars today. But, you would have lost at least 4% interest, compounded for each of those three years, or at least 15%. So, while you would have 12% more Canadian dollars by having bought U.S. dollars three years ago (assuming you converted back to Canadian today), you would actually have had 3% more Canadian dollars if you had left them in Canadian currency to begin with. For those who like to pay their American bills from a U.S. chequing account while they are living in the U.S., this makes sense only if you are living in the U.S. at least six months out of each year. If you are down there for only a few weeks or months each year, you would again be further ahead financially to convert whatever you need into U.S. money orders through your Canadian bank and mailed to whomever you owe in the States from Canada. This is something easily accomplished now that FAX machines are so widely available.

Finally, the biggest reason for holding U.S. dollars is the potential for significant depreciation of the Canadian dollar in the event of a break-up of the country. For those individuals seriously concerned about this eventuality, keeping hundreds, or even a few thousand U.S. dollars isn't going to save or make you very much money. If you have significant equity in Canada, as in a home, you would be much further ahead to borrow heavily against those assets and invest them off-shore. Not in U.S. dollars, which are paying less than comparable Canadian investments, but in something like English pounds, or European ECUs, which are paying 4% more than Canadian accounts. Better yet, invest in an international mutual fund through a Canadian life company and benefit from the performance guarantees in case your hunch proves wrong!

Despite my heavy expenditures in overseas travel, I simply do not find it makes any sense to carry U.S. dollars, either cash or travellers cheques; I go with about half our funds in Canadian dollar travellers cheques, and the rest in Canadian currency. If I have any Canadian travellers cheques left on my return, I cash them in unless I know I'm going back out of the country within a few weeks. The interest I make by depositing those funds in a Canadian account more than offsets the cost of buying the travellers cheques in the first place. I find that, next to American currency, Canadian is the most widely accepted world-wide, ahead even of Swiss, British, or Hong Kong currencies.

19.   Getting Cash While Abroad

Running short of cash while travelling can be a serious problem, even if you do have credit cards. In many countries, especially outside North America or Western Europe, no credit cards are routinely accepted, and local banking networks may not accept the brand of travellers cheques you're carrying. What to do? Don't wait until you are almost out of cash to arrange a back-up. Despite the best laid plans, transfer of cash or credit to a foreign country is not instantaneous, and can take several days. Here are the more popular ways to get cash from home.

The best alternative to cash or travellers cheques (American Express is the most widely recognized followed by cheques bearing the VISA symbol, such as those issued by Barclays), is a letter of introduction from your bank guaranteeing a line of credit up to a specific amount. If your local bank manager is not familiar with such an instrument, go to their regional office. Usually free, it will be issued speedily if you've banked there for some time. This letter will allow your personal cheque to be cashed by a foreign bank, with a guarantee by your own bank that there will be no NSF (non-sufficient funds).

The next best method of getting cash outside Canada is to carry an automated teller machine (ATM) card allowing access to either the CIRRUS or PLUS worldwide banking networks. About 50,000 ATMs in 17 countries are plugged into PLUS while another 60,000 in 21 countries are serviced by CIRRUS. Check with your bank to see which network is honored by your card, if not already indicated on the card. This allows access to cash in local currency up to your card's daily limit, usually $200. This limit can be increased by talking to your bank. The transaction fee is about $1 and the foreign exchange rate is better than you can get in a foreign bank.

With a VISA card, you can access a cash advance at any of 330,000 affiliated members worldwide. Mastercard is also accepted worldwide, but not as widely. Advances are treated as loans, subject to interest of about 20%, with exchange rates somewhere between the inter-bank rate on ATM cards, and the rate on cash or travellers cheques. Don't bother getting a special VISA or Mastercard (such as VISA Gold) just for getting cash abroad.

The American Express card will allow you cheque cashing privileges in hotels and some 1,500 Amex offices in 120 countries world-wide. However, only more expensive hotels will cash cheques and will apply the cash to their own bills, before paying you the balance. Amex will cash personal cheques up to about $1,000 CDN in any seven-day period in the U.S. or 14 days elsewhere. Most of the 'cash' will be travellers cheques.

If none of the above are appropriate for your needs, you'll have to make arrangements with someone back home to send you cash. These arrangements should be made before you leave, so if you are caught short, a simple telephone call can set the transfer in motion. While it's possible to send a money order through the mail, such are rarely sent because of the uncertainty as to when it will arrive. A Western Union money transfer will get you up to $10,000 just about anywhere in the world in 15 minutes, but it's not cheap. Between 5 and 10% of the amount being sent is charged! An American Express Moneygram will accomplish the same thing, but it's even more expensive. Getting money wired by a Canadian bank usually takes one business day, and is relatively inexpensive. For example, Royal Bank charges an $8 wire charge, plus a $2 phone charge to wire $1,000 to the bank of your choice plus the cost of your phone call back home. Courier delivery of bank drafts or other negotiable instruments is not recommended outside continental North America for the same reason the postal service is not recommended: uncertainty of arrival date/time.

If you are caught critically short of cash, and must make arrangements to return home immediately, any Canadian Embassy abroad will make a cash advance to any Canadian upon proof of citizenship and address (i.e. passport and driver's licence). Done by cashing a personal cheque out of petty cash. If you'd like to share some of your own experiences in getting cash while travelling abroad, or wish more details on any topic above, we'd be delighted to hear from you!

20.   OHIP and Travellers

OHIP (the Ontario Health Insurance Plan) has announced a ceiling on payments for care abroad of $400 per day for hospital stays. Previously, there were no ceilings. Ontario joins all other provinces in limiting the amount it pays for care rendered outside Canada. There are no changes to what OHIP pays within Canada, i.e. no limit. Those planning extended stays out of the country, especially those in poor health, will be well advised to purchase supplementary coverage from such a medical plan as Blue Cross to ensure they will not be economically crippled by expensive hospital stays while abroad. Supplementary coverage cost will increase substantially as insurers gain experience with the new OHIP coverage limits. Those with pre-existing conditions may even be unable to get coverage.

Snowbirds and others who spend much time outside Ontario, beware: OHIP announces a rule change: anyone spending six or more months outside Ontario in any 12 months loses medical coverage, if caught! So, someone who spends just under six months wintering in Florida, and then goes on a short camping trip to the Gatineaus and breaks a leg, could find he/she isn't covered by OHIP. Of course, OHIP would have to know how long that person had spent outside Ontario, something not easily accomplished except in a police state. Nonetheless, this is a potentially dangerous rule change for those who do spend a lot of time outside the province. The former rule limited out-of-province stays to eight months total in any 12. In fairness to OHIP, most other provinces have a six-month residency rule.

I know of one client, visiting an ailing relative, with a claim for a foreign hospital stay, who was questioned about when she left Ontario. Fortunately, her claim occurred just under the six month limit, and she has been reimbursed by OHIP. This person is still out of the country, and a new medical claim would likely be refused.

This kind of rule change has got the Snowbirds in Florida organizing. The Canadian Snowbirds' Association hopes to address issues relating to retirement living and travelling outside Canada. Membership information available by writing Box 4430, Seminole, Fl, 34642.

21.   Travel Abroad

Do you travel much outside North America? If you are like me, you may occasionally worry about what kind of medical care is available in some of the outlying boonies. Also like me, you may occasionally worry about what kinds of bugs you might encounter while abroad, and what you could do here at home before you leave in order to minimize the potential impact of those bugs. Until recently, I have consulted an M.D. in Ottawa who is plugged into tropical medicine, and who is also an advisor to the World Health Organization. However, his advice and medicines, are not covered by OHIP (nor do I expect they should be).

So, it was with delight that I recently discovered the existence of the International Association for Medical Assistance to Travellers (IAMAT), a little-known outfit headquartered in Guelph, who've been around apparently for decades. They have more American members than Canadian, which speaks volumes about how little advertising they do here in Canada. Membership is free, but donations are gratefully accepted. By joining, here's what you get:

1. a membership card, for use in introduction to medical personnel while abroad;
2. a world immunization chart;
3. a clinical record form;
4. a world malaria risk chart and protection guide;
5. a world schistosomiasis chart;
6. a world directory of IAMAT affiliated doctors;
7. a chagas disease risk chart and protection guide;
8. donor members also receive 24 world climate charts.

Working with the World Health Organization, IAMAT has an international board of physicians from various countries. Travellers to over 125 countries can use the medical directory to seek medical help from physicians who speak English and whose medical qualifications are up to IAMAT standards. This means that all IAMAT-certified physicians have been trained in Europe or North America.

Furthermore, doctors listed in the IAMAT directory have agreed to make house or hotel calls at maximum fees, currently $US45 for office consults, $US55 for house or hotel calls, or $US65 for night calls.

Founded in 1960, they are located in Guelph, and in Toronto at 1287 St. Clair Ave. West, M6E 1B8; 416-652-0137.

22. Assets in Marriage

Several of my clients have gotten married recently for the second, or subsequent time. I have been asked by several people what they should be doing to protect themselves financially in the unfortunate event of another marriage breakdown. Family property laws across the country have changed radically during the past decade, with the Family Law Act of Ontario as the change most often cited. Similar laws to Ontario's have been passed in most of the common-law provinces as well as Quebec.

Generally speaking, upon marriage breakdown, if the parties are unable to arrive at their own amicable settlement, the Court will impose a settlement according to law. That law usually lumps all assets at time of separation, then makes allowances for what each partner brought into the marriage, as well as inherited or won by way of lottery, and then divides the pool into equal halves. Adjustments are sometimes, but increasingly rarely, made for such conditions or eventualities as one of the partners being disabled or unable to fend for themselves in the job market, or for unusual contributions to the other partner's business or education.

One area that many marriage bound partners fail to give due thought to is when one or both of the partners is bringing a home into the marriage. This is a common occurrence for those getting married a second time, and can be a financial trap for the unwary. The 'equalization' principle mentioned above on marriage breakdown will usually include a home brought into a marriage by one of the partners when that home is used subsequently as the matrimonial home. To many people getting married a second time, their home often represents their largest single equity asset. For the unwary, half the value of that home would automatically be given to the other spouse upon marriage breakdown.

Let's take a sample case at its simplest, but most common occurrence. Say both you and your intended each own homes worth $300,000, and each home is clear of debt. Your intended sells his/her home before marriage. At marriage, you both move into your own home. You split ten years later when your home has doubled in value, and your spouse's $300,000 in cash from the sale of his/her home has also doubled to $600,000. Ready for the shock?

In Ontario, because your spouse's $300,000 cash was brought into the marriage, the original $300,000 is excluded from equalization. Only the $300,000 profit goes into the pot. But all of your $600,000 home value goes into the same pot, so that you will each wind up with $450,000 after the Court divides the pot. So your spouse is left with $750,000 and you with $450,000, only 75% of the present value of your own home, which is probably now far too big for you since your spouse has left, and your kids too!

The solution to the above potential nightmare is a thorough review of your respective financial situations before you tie that knot, and, if appropriate, arranging a low-cost pre-nuptial agreement with a trusted lawyer. If you don't like the unemotional nature of a pre-nuptial agreement, another solution is to heavily mortgage the home in which you will both live, preferably at 100% of its value, just before the marriage. Then pay off the mortgage immediately after the wedding. But make sure you keep all of the relevant financial documentation for later proof to the Court, if, like so many others, your second marriage falls apart too!

Co-habitation in lieu of a wedding ceremony will not solve the problem described above since, in most provinces, people co-habitating for a minimum of one year (in some provinces, two years), enjoy the same rights, privileges and obligations of otherwise legally married spouses!

Here are some other observations and pointers.

Knowing you're divorced should be easy. You get a court document so indicating. But what about separation? In Ontario, at least, legal separation starts when one party leaves the other with no intention of returning. Living apart even for as little as one day could mean you are legally separated. From that point on, each partner has the right to claim equalization and support, though not necessarily divorce, immediately. Rights to equalization claims last, in Ontario, for up to six years after the start of separation, or two years after divorce, whichever comes first. Support claims may be filed up to two years after separation. With divorce, there's no time limit.

Support of a spouse with minor children can make a big difference on remarriage, since such support orders become nil and void. Thus, a partner receiving large support payments from an ex-spouse in respect of very young children is at significant financial risk in a second marriage, since the second marriage will terminate the support payments, even if the second marriage ends up being very brief. The new spouse in the second marriage is also at financial risk since, if he treats the children of his new spouse as his own, he will be considered by the Court as having the same financial obligation as the natural parent!

Determining who owns what at marriage termination can also be quite tricky. If one spouse puts property into the name of the other spouse, the second spouse may have a legal claim on equalization, unless the original owner is careful to document why and under what circumstances the property is being placed in the other's name. This applies not only to real estate, but to automobiles, jewelry, art, cash investments, even the favorite family pet!

If all of the above scares you when contemplating a second, or even a first marriage, here is some further advice:

- Assemble a net worth statement and supporting documentation as of the date of marriage, for each spouse. In the event of a later breakup, you'll need such documentation anyway, unless you are in one of the rare marriage breakdowns that results in an amicable property settlement.

- Check how your province's equalization rules apply. They are not all the same as Ontario's, described above.

- Determine if an estate freeze is beneficial to protect the children from your first marriage, before your second wedding.

- Separation does not automatically revoke a will. So a spouse you hate could end up with a slice of your estate. Divorce doesn't revoke a will either, but references to your former spouse will be read in probate court as though he or she died before you did. Remarriage <u>does</u> automatically revoke that will, unless it was drafted with that remarriage in mind. But then, until you execute a new will, you are considered to have no will, on death. Make sure any will drawn after remarriage is coordinated with your former spouse's separation agreement or divorce decree. Make sure the will clearly covers any ongoing support obligations to the members of your previous family after your death. Note that while property may be transferred tax-free to a current spouse, such a roll-over to a former spouse will trigger capital gains, which may be taxable. So be sure your estate will have enough cash to pay Revenue Canada, since the recipient of such property after your death will <u>not</u> be responsible for any income taxes due.

23. Don't Forget Taxman in Divorce

When splitting up, most partners are in a hurry to get it over with. Quite understandable, but also potentially very expensive to both parties if they overlook the taxman. The problem with most couples breaking up is that they don't have a good written settlement agreement. Every year, at tax time particularly, we see former spouses lose out, sometimes many thousands of dollars, to the taxman because they had not spent sufficient time, and a few extra bucks in legal expenses, in planning and drawing up the 'least-tax' separation and maintenance agreement.

Rarely do couples break up where there is no income tax consequence, especially if the partnership has lasted years, and/or there are children involved. And when there is a business interest, and/or young children, and/or large debts, the taxman's influence can become quite perfidious.

The biggest objective should not be to see which of the two partners can get the bigger piece of the pie, but rather to see how the former partners can ensure the taxman's share of the pie is not only the smallest but, if possible, an even smaller share than when the partners were living together. While the notion of co-operating with someone you no longer love may be repellant, failing to communicate on material and monetary matters at break-up can cost both of you, not to mention costing your children.

Professional help, while costing some money, is usually worth it. Just as representing yourself in court is usually not a bright idea, same with looking after your own financial planning while you're in the middle of an emotional divorce. And, if one party will be paying monthly support, or if there is a business involved, the legal costs are tax deductible!

Here are some Income Tax Act traps to avoid when negotiating a separation/support agreement between two ex-partners:

Amount of support payments: Who is responsible for paying income tax on support payments is up in the air pending an appeal by Revenue Canada to the Supreme Court, not expected to be heard until Fall of 1995, at the earliest. So, parties to an agreement should stipulate <u>after-tax</u> amounts.

Include Life Insurance: If you are counting on support payments, insist life insurance on your ex-spouse be part of the divorce agreement. Otherwise, the death of your ex-spouse could throw you in the poorhouse. Make sure that whatever life insurance you end up getting is owned by you, even if your ex-spouse is responsible for the payments. That way, you know the contract won't lapse, and you know the beneficiary will remain you, unless you change either yourself. We've seen many a life insurance contract taken out by one spouse to protect the other, only to have the insured change the beneficiary to a new 'beau'!

Don't forget your will if you have one. If you don't change it after splitting up, the law presumes your ex-spouse no longer exists. That may indeed be what you want, but what about your kids? Maybe you <u>do</u> want your ex-spouse to receive some portion of your estate, if only in trust to maintain your children. On the other hand, if you don't have a will, and separate, your ex-spouse will inherit all of your estate if you die before divorce proceedings have been completed. Since years can (and do) go by between many separations and final divorce decrees, this can be a large exposure if you don't have a will, or don't change it after separation.

Principal Residence Claim: If the two of you own both a house and a cottage, plan carefully to decide who will get which and who will get to claim either as principal residence (on which there is no income tax payable when subsequently disposing of same for profit). Otherwise, you may get a nasty surprise when you sell your own property only to discover that some time earlier your spouse claimed principal residence status on his/her property!

No need to sell immediately: If market conditions are poor, or you need further time for reflection, there is no hurry to sell an asset, such as a family home. Agreeing to dispose of an asset at a later date between two

24. Bankruptcy

The recession has caused many people and businesses to go bankrupt. While none of our clients has experienced that calamity, it seems as if we all know at least one person who has done so. Last year, the federal bankruptcy laws underwent change. Here are the more important provisions.

When a person can no longer meet his/her debts, and either starts a bankruptcy proceeding on his own, or is forced to by one of his creditors, a bankruptcy trustee takes over to make sure the bankrupt gets what's coming to him under law, and that creditors get what's coming to them. The trustee is also responsible to ensure the Bankruptcy Act is adhered to by all parties, many of whom do not have a working knowledge of that Act.

To qualify for bankruptcy, a person must have at least $1,000 in debts, have no ability to pay bills, have ceased paying them, and have no assets to pay them. The potential bankrupt discloses all pertinent information required by the Act to the trustee in a set of legal documents which, if and when accepted by Consumer and Corporate Affairs, forms the basis of the actual bankruptcy. That's when the fun, er pain, begins. The bankrupt is still not discharged. All of his assets are in effect seized and sold, with the exception of up to $4,000 worth of furniture, a home worth up to $40,000, an auto worth up to $8,000, but only if the auto is required for work, and all assets with life insurance companies (including RSPs) where a beneficiary of the preferred class (i.e. close relative) is named within the contract(s).

If the bankrupt is single, half of what he makes over $1,240 per month goes into the bankruptcy pot along with the proceeds from the forced sale of his assets described above. If married, half of all income over $1,800 goes into the pot, less an extra $340 per month per child.

After a minimum three months and before 12 months, the bankrupt must apply for discharge. The trustee notifies the creditors and places ads in newspapers saying the application for discharge has been made. If unopposed, the matter is dealt with by a master in chambers of the bankruptcy court. If it is opposed, the matter goes to trial at the Court of Queen's Bench.

Once discharged, the bankrupt owes nothing and can start all over again, albeit with a credit rating of zilch for a minimum of seven years. It costs $795 to file a bankruptcy, plus GST. The trustee will probably want cash, up front!

25.   Are You Fit Financially?

Year-end is a great time to do financial planning, although it is a bit late to do tax planning! Nonetheless, for all those who procrastinate about financial planning, here is a checklist to help you determine just how financially fit you are (courtesy of Kates Peat Marwick):

- Have you sat down and determined your lifestyle goals within the past two years?
- Have you determined if your financial resources can meet those goals?
- Are you satisfied with the amount of money you are saving?
- Have you reviewed and updated these documents within the past two years:
  – your will? – your net worth statement? – your disability income insurance?
- Do you have a power of attorney?
- Have you determined if your insurance (life, health, car, home, business) coverage is sufficient or too much?
- Do you contribute the maximum to an RSP each year?

- Do you make that RSP contribution at the beginning of the year, or near February 28 of the following year?
- Are you satisfied with the performance of your investments?
- Have you determined your short- and long-term investment strategies?
- If you have children, have you determined a strategy to ensure they will have enough funds to go on to university?
- Have you established an emergency fund, or personal line of credit?
- Do you take advantage of all of the income tax deductions available to you?
- Is the interest on your loans tax deductible?
- Have you done all you can to shelter your income from income tax?
- Did you use up all of your capital gains exemption?
- If not, have you recently reviewed whether it makes sense to claim a deduction against the exemption, even at this late date?
- If you know of a large future income tax liability, have you figured out how you're going to pay it?
- Did you know how much you will owe Revenue Canada next April?
- Are you a member of a company pension plan?
- If you are a member of a company pension plan, have you reviewed their latest annual statement, and are you familiar with all of the terms therein?
- Are you maintaining a retirement fund outside the company pension plan, and outside of RSPs?
- Have you determined how much income you can expect on retirement?
- Have you determined if your income expectations at retirement are sufficient to meet your projected lifestyle needs after retirement?
- Do you feel in control of your financial future?

According to Kates, Peat, Marwick, if you answered at least 17 of the above 25 questions 'yes', then congratulations! You're in great financial shape.

If you answered 'yes' to between nine and 16 questions, you need to do some homework. Talk to someone who can help you put your affairs into better shape.

If you answered 'yes' to fewer than nine of the above questions, you're in serious trouble! Put this newsletter away, and start with some basics, at either your local library or bookstore. Attend some courses at your community college, ask for literature at your favourite financial institution, watch several of the many excellent introductory programs on financial matters on community and public broadcasting television.

Then, once you think you now know some of the basics, meet with a qualified financial counsellor to develop a plan for getting into financial shape!

But start, now!!

26. Educating Yourself

So the previous article has scared you into wanting to do something to improve your financial planning skills! You think you need a professional advisor because you lack the expertise to do it yourself. Yet you need a certain amount of expertise to know whether the financial advisor is snowing you.

What do you do?

Well, if you were all-trusting, and hired the ideal financial planner, that planner would have to draw from many different skills, including: accounting; insurance; stockbrokering; legal; trust; corporate; investing; and income tax. By rolling these skills into one person, the financial planning industry hopes to provide financial planners less expensively than if you were to obtain each of these skills individually. But the down side is that many financial planners are not as knowledgeable as the experts in the above named specialties that they wish to replace.

When it comes to investing (considered with income tax as the most important element of financial planning), you have to understand what you are buying, and how its value will be affected by interest rates, and the economic cycle. When it comes to financial planning, an educated consumer is the best consumer.

A consumer should understand, for example, that if he/she invests in bonds and/or mortgages, and interest rates rise subsequently, there will have been a paper loss on capital. Yield, which is why the consumer bought in the first place, won't have changed if rates rise, but if the bond or montage is sold when interest rates are higher than at original purchase date, there will definitely be a loss, and a potentially large one at that.

Too often, people are unwilling to spend the time and effort needed to learn the basic principles of investing. For example, many people will have spent countless hours buying this year's Christmas gifts, shopping around for the best values and the best products. Come January or February, however, these same people will take half an hour or so to invest even more money, perhaps $2,000 or $3,000, in RSPs without having done any homework or shopping.

There is no shortage of courses, seminars and books on the subject, some more or less objective, but many designed to predispose the consumer to buy what a company or the industry is selling.

If you're thinking of hiring a financial planner, you may first want to take the Personal Financial Planning correspondence course offered by the Canadian Institute of Financial Planning (sponsored by the mutual funds industry). The tax-deductible course, which costs $150 plus a $40 registration fee, covers such topics as saving and borrowing money, basic income tax planning, investments, life insurance, simple wills and RSPs.

After four written assignments and a final exam, you will have learned to assess your current financial position, set goals, decide whether you have enough insurance, arrange your income taxes to your best advantage, assess your pension plan, and be able to tell the difference between a stock and a bond mutual fund. For course information, contact the institute at 151 Yonge St., Suite 503, Toronto, M5C 2W7, or call 416-865-1237.

If you want to know more about investing than what's on offer by the Financial Planning Institute, then you may want to look at the various tax-deductible courses and seminars offered by the Canadian Securities Institute. The CSI is the educational arm of the investment industry. Among their most popular products are the CSI's Intelligent Investing Seminars, offered twice yearly in the spring and fall.

So far, seminars are limited to major cities, but the institute hopes to take the seminars onto the road soon. The six session course costs $165 and is designed to help novice investors communicate better with their investment advisors.

People who want an even more complete understanding of investments should consider taking the Canadian Securities Course, which comes in three- and six-month versions, and costs $415 for non-industry students.

Graduates of the above course can move on to the Canadian Investment Management course, which is divided into two parts, each costing $380, which will equip the student to manage his/her own portfolio.

In addition, the CSI offers books and booklets, among them, *How to Invest in Canadian Securities*, $25 plus GST.

Contact the CSI at 121 King St. West, Suite 1550, Toronto, M5H 3T9, or call them at 416-364-9130.

The CSI also has offices in Montreal, Calgary and Vancouver (the other locations, along with Toronto, that have operating stock exchanges!).

27.   Financial Planning Mistakes

Here's a list of the more common mistakes I see among people who say they are good at their financial planning:

- Failure to determine and set a goal objective. Unless you know what you are striving for, raising enough motivation to set and achieve a financial plan may be difficult, if not impossible.
- Procrastination.
- Not having a holistic approach to the plan. For example: a person may be looking at investments for security, but may be forgetting about the impact of taxation.
- Impatience. Many tend to lose sight of the eventual long-term payback when their plans suffer temporary short-term setbacks.
- Not being able to delegate. This is particularly serious when coupled with impatience, and is the single biggest reason for breakdowns in communication between a client and a financial planner.
- Having too many advisors. As with lawyers, dentists, and other professionals, consulting too many financial experts can be time consuming and confusing.
- Fear and greed.
- Going along with the crowd.
- Not reviewing your financial plan from time to time.
- Too much debt.
- Not taking maximum advantage of employer provided benefits.
- Not having a clear enough idea of where the paycheck is currently going.
- Not communicating with your spouse.

28. Financial Planners

Many folks out there are passing themselves off as Financial Planners. I thought I'd devote a little space herein describing what types of financial advice can be obtained from various sources, as well as providing some information on the Canadian Association of Financial Planners.

The table 'Financial Advisors' (next two pages) shows what kind of advice you can expect from what kind of individual. I myself offer many of the services shown across the spectrum, but concentrate on helping more affluent investment clients. Those who are having heavy financial difficulties may also wish to consult, for free, the 'Credit Counselling' people in their home city. These folks also have lots of free literature. Before retaining any financial planner, however, make sure you know what he/she can provide, and at what cost. Here is some material I have 'borrowed' from the CAFP.

The Canadian Association of Financial Planners is an independent national association that represents and acts as a unified voice of Financial Planners, encourages professionalism, the promotion of high quality financial advice, adherence to its code of ethics and provides its membership with ongoing professional development and other benefits. CAFP is dedicated to raising the standards of financial planning services and promoting its membership as the most qualified and credible financial planners in Canada. Founded in 1981, CAFP now has over 1,200 members nationwide. A national board oversees a number of local chapters. Members can apply for, and after taking requisite courses and complying satisfactorily with other criteria, the designation Registered Financial Planner (RFP). Their national office is at 1111-120 Eglinton E., Toronto, M4P 1E2; Tel 416-481-1225; FAX 416-481-6904.

29. Moving Reimbursements

A recent and obscure Tax Court case may be of interest to those readers moving to a higher-cost city who are able to persuade their employers to reimburse for additional one-time costs. Some years ago, the Canadian National Railways moved some employees from Moncton to Winnipeg, where the cost of replacement housing was somewhat higher. The union representing the affected employees negotiated a one-time payment to each employee by the CNR of $10,000, to cover the higher housing cost. The employees took the position that the payment was not taxable. Revenue Canada took the opposite view. Several years later, the Federal Court, Trial Division, has decided in the employees' favour, ruling that the employees did not get an economic benefit from the payments; indeed, for many employees, the payment was only a partial re-imbursement of the higher costs of acquiring comparable accommodations in the new city.

The Judge's decision said, in part: 'Employees ... facing this kind of transfer decison are entitled to be financially restored to similar circumstances related to their previous residence without it being considered a taxable benefit'. One interesting aspect to this case is that the Court did not set any kind of limit to what might have been a tax-free re-imbursement of additional expenses resulting from moving to a new work site.

The implication for my readers is that if you are moved by your employer to a

Financial Advisors

	Financial Planner	Bank Manager	Chartered Accountant	Investment Counsellor	Stockbroker	Insurance Agent
Primary Services	– comprehensive computerized plan – counselling re estate, tax and insurance planning – preparation of tax return – referral services to specialists – sale of investment products (e.g. insurance, mutual funds)	– advice pertaining to banking – advice on budgeting – broad money-management counselling – referral to loans officer	– specialized tax planning – preparation of personal income-tax return – some retirement and estate planning; some investment knowledge – accounting advice for big and small businesses – audits	– portfolio management on a discretionary basis (has client's permission to make trades) – buying and selling stocks, bonds, GICs, CSBs, T-bills and occasionally mutual funds and options; management of RRSPs – financial counselling regarding investments; technical analysis – in some cases, preparation of tax returns; paying client's personal bills	– buying and selling of stocks, bonds, mutual funds, T-bills, RRSPs, CSBs, GICs, tax shelters, stripped coupons, RRIFs, etc. – allocation of assets within portfolio (building proportion of growth, fixed income, cash) – investment recommendations (not applicable to discount brokers) – periodic summary of holdings	– sale of whole-, term- and universal-life policies; sale of RRIFs, annuities & products comparable to and competitive with GICs and mutual funds – counselling re insurance needs & related financial planning
Who would Benefit	– people needing a financial coach, and/or with family income of $75,000+; assets of $250,000+ – anyone within 10 yrs of retirement who hasn't made provisions	– those who cannot afford other financial advisors (e.g. younger people starting work or buying 1st home; families on a budget; retirees on ltd income) – those needing loan/credit line	– anyone requiring counselling on minimizing taxes, assistance on tax return – the self-employed – small-business owners	– those with $250,000+ to invest	– anyone wishing to buy investment products	– individuals in need of insurance coverage (e.g. those with dependants) – individuals who want to know how insurance should fit into their plans

Fee	– $80–125/hour; average $2,500/year ($6,000 for best plans); + Commissions which vary by product sold 3–9% negotiable with planner.	– varies depending on degree of specialization, reputation – basic advice $60 an hour, up to $300 an hour for international tax advice	– % of invested capital in portfolio (e.g. 1–4% of accounts of $1 million, % declining thereafter) or – % of invested capital plus commission on sale of securities	– full-service broker: commission-based, generally one to three percent of trade (higher for mutual funds), but declines for accounts in excess of $100,000 – discount broker: varies, generally 0.5 to 2.5 percent of trade	– commission, depends on product: from 1.5–65% (the latter for first year of life-insurance policy) – financial planning: $75+/hour
Risks/ Weak-nesses	– risk of bias toward own investment or insurance products – cannot buy or sell stocks or bonds	– limited investment and insurance advice – cannot sell investment or insurance products or draft legal documents	– risk of mismanaging portfolio – cannot sell insurance products – cannot give legal advice	– cannot provide legal, estate- or tax-planning services, limited retirement planning – risk of "churning" (unnecessary trades for the purpose of generating commissions)	– bias to own institution's products – cannot sell stocks, bonds – limited tax planning
Qualifica-tions to look for	– at least a CFP; preferably an RFP	– CA – CFP and/or RFP	– investment counsellor designation – in addition, CFA or some CFA courses	– Registered Rep designation from the Canadian Securities Institute – employment with member of the IDA – CFA	– CLU – CFP and/or RFP – ChFC
Where to complain	– CAFP – Securities commission – Insurance regulators	– provincial branch of CICA	– provincial securities commission	– branch manager of investment dealer – Securities commission – IDA	– LUAC

more expensive living location (i.e. from anywhere to either Toronto or Vancouver), you should attempt to negotiate a one-time payment in reimbursement of higher accommodations costs, which will end up being tax-free. This applies, presumably, just as importantly to the self-employed, where such people should be able to pay themselves a tax-free one-time allowance to reflect higher accommodation purchase costs, while at the same time treat the payment as a tax-deductible business expense!

30.   Seniors' Financial Perils

There are many scam artists and confidence tricksters only too ready to prey on those of us who are gullible and inexperienced. It seems that such criminals prey especially on at-home seniors, usually those living alone, and often widows. Indeed, a recent Manitoba survey showed that scamming seniors was the crime most frequently committed against this age group. The survey found that widows, who used to rely on their husbands to take care of the family finances, are the most vulnerable, especially those widows who are trusting in nature. Here are the most common documented scams used on seniors:

- The bogus bank inspector, who calls to ask for help in catching a dishonest bank employee. If the senior falls for the initial pitch, the 'inspector' asks the senior to withdraw cash from his/her account and to give the cash to a 'bank official' for use in investigation. The bogus 'employees' then disappear with the cash, often a life's savings.

- A con artist will meet with a senior and offer to share a 'found' sum of money if the senior makes a show of faith by first contributing a small amount to the 'pot'.

- Someone claiming to represent a bank will call a senior supposedly to help clear up a credit card mixup, with the aim of getting the senior's credit card number and expiry date.

- A fake contractor will attempt to sell a senior home repairs requiring up-front cash down payment. If the work is even done at all, it will be over-priced and shoddy.

The Royal Bank recently published a list of tips on how seniors can protect themselves from these and other scams. As the list states, a bank will never ask someone to withdraw funds over the phone, nor will a bank ever ask for your PIN, your Personal Identification Number. The Royal further advises being suspicious of anyone making unsolicited sales pitches by phone or in person at the door. Check on callers by getting an address or phone number, and verifying who they are by following up. Be doubly cautious also of dubious and unnecessary 'financial and/or investment advice'. If you'd like some financial advice, ask friends or relatives for referrals, or consult your local association of financial planners.

Here are some further tips published by the Manitoba Seniors Directorate:

1. Keep large amounts of money in the bank, never at home.
2. Keep blank cheques secure; never sign a blank cheque.
3. Never leave identification, credit cards, cheques or passports unattended in a vehicle.

4. Sign new credit cards immediately and cut up the old ones.

5. Make sure incorrect credit card slips are torn up; rip up the carbon copies as well.

6. After using a credit card, make sure you get it back, and that the card you get back is indeed yours.

7. Have pension and other regular periodic cheques deposited directly to your bank account if you cannot get to the bank in person often enough to avoid having cheques accumulate at home.

8. Don't change your will without the advice of more than one person.

9. Be especially careful when granting someone power of attorney over your affairs. Pick someone trustworthy, and consult a lawyer if you aren't sure what powers you want to grant. Make sure the person you choose understands you want regular and full accounting of all transactions initiated on your behalf.

31. Seniors Rely More on Pensions

Statistics Canada recently published the results of a survey showing that seniors are relying more and more on their pension incomes, as their investment incomes drop. In 1993, pensions represented about one third of the overall income of families where at least one individual was over the age of 55, an increase over the previous year. At the same time, income from investments in that year fell to 11% of total income, a drop from 13% in the previous year.

Decreases in investment income for those age 75 and over was even higher, for which pension income represented more than half of their family incomes.

What this survey shows is what people have known for some time: that reliance on short-term fixed-rate investments, such as Canada Savings Bonds, or short-term GICs, has dealt the retired community a serious blow as interest rates have fallen over the past three years.

Unfortunately, reliance by seniors on low rate investments will likely cause further hardship, since interest rates are likely to remain low for at least the next three years, and because the federal government is about to overhaul the government pension schemes (Canada Pension Plan and Old Age Security).

As time marches on, more and more people will have retired leaving the financial burden on fewer and fewer workers, whose resentment against those they are financially supporting in retirement grows. Hence, more and more organizations will be under increasing pressures to trim back the pensions they are already paying their retired workers, especially to those who may have retired decades ago.

What many seniors are discovering as interest rates stay low is that short-term investments carry substantial risk: not risk of losing capital, but risk of not keeping up with their former living standards because those seniors have remained too conservative in their investment outlooks, and their tolerance for risk. Paradoxically, those seniors who have avoided all risk by staying with short-term GICs and CSBs have suffered the risk of losing ground in their living standards. Such individuals will have to learn to tolerate some risk if only to be able to restore the investment yields they were used to up to the early 1990s.

32.   Low GIC Rates Spur Fund Sales

As the above article notes, seniors will have to adjust their tolerance to risk if they are to gain back their traditional rates of investment returns. Another survey, this one by Toronto consultants Marketing Solutions, has found that 80% of the general investment population will avoid GICs paying only 7% in favour of mutual funds. But when GIC rates hit 9%, over one-half of the survey respondents would buy a GIC in favour of mutual funds.

At present, GIC rates range from 4% to 6.75%, depending on term. At that level, GIC sales have fallen off dramatically in recent months, in favour of substantial sales of new mutual funds.

The survey referred to above found that at 5%, 88% of the survey respondents would favour mutual funds over GICs.

A spokesman for Marketing Solutions compared the re-education taking place by investors with first-time and frequent-airplane fliers. The first time flier, when encountering turbulence for the first time, would immediately jump out of the aircraft if parachutes were available. But the seasoned traveller would just buckle up his/her seat belt and ride it out, knowing that flying was the safest way to get from A to B.

Similarly, first-time buyers of investments that contain some risk must remember that, over the long haul, they'll do much better with professionally managed equity mutual funds than they would with more traditional, but low yielding, GICs.

33.   Minimizing Bank Charges

Bank service charges are a nuisance at best, and down-right upsetting at worst. Most of us assume there is little we can do about them, except complain. Actually, there are a number of ways we can reduce that amount that appears at the bottom of our monthly statements. Here are a few, as provided by one of the big chartered banks:

Choose the right account: Pick the account (or combination of accounts) best designed for your kind of banking. Having a chequing account if you only write two or three cheques a month makes less sense than having a savings account with chequing privileges. A savings account will pay more interest than a chequing account. But the trade-off will usually be higher cheque charges under a savings account than under a chequing account. If in doubt, consult your financial institution who may have someone at your branch who can provide advice.

Maintain a 'no-charge' minimum monthly balance: Chances are your account will have a monthly minimum amount above which you will not incur any service charges related to the maintenance of that account. Of course, you won't earn much interest on that minimum balance, but in this age of low interest rates, what you lose in interest not earned will be more than offset by the savings resulting from the monthly maintenance charge.

Use ATMs when possible: Most financial institutions offer free banking services via their automated banking machines. Check with yours, and you are likely to find you can withdraw cash, make deposits and pay bills, all without incurring transaction fees for those items you transact through ATMs.

Consider a service plan: If you do write a lot of cheques or conduct many non-standard transactions (such as account verifications, certified cheques, or travellers cheques), consider a 'package' of services for a set monthly fee. Most financial institutions now offer such packages. You are likely to find one suited to your purposes, with a little help from the staff.

Use pre-authorized cheques for your frequent periodic payments, such as cable TV, insurance premiums and utilities. These are often processed by a financial institution at less cost to you than if you wrote a cheque and included the cost of postage. But beware that occasionally, pre-authorized transactions get mixed up by the firm who has your authorization to withdraw funds from your account. When that happens, be prepared to spend time unravelling the mess. If you are like many folks and keep a minimum balance in your account, be prepared for NSF cheques to other payees as a result of a screwed up pre-authorized withdrawal you weren't expecting!

Use a credit card to make purchases: Instead of writing cheques to the merchants you patronize, use a credit card issued by your financial institution, such as Visa or Mastercharge. Then pay the charge balance promptly on receipt of your monthly account statement.

Get 'Overdraft' protection: If, despite your best efforts, you occasionally write an NSF cheque, arrange for overdraft protection from your bank. NSF cheques have become quite expensive in recent years, not to mention embarrassing. For a low monthly fee, your financial institution will guarantee to honour NSF cheques up to a certain dollar limit, saving you the cost and hassle of correcting an overdraft situation.

The above are fairly easy ways of minimizing or, at least, reducing bank service charges. They only require time on your part to plan and implement, usually without too much expertise from the financial institution!

34. 'Rebate' Credit Cards

Within the past two years, an explosion of rebate credit cards has occurred. These are credit cards where the issuer has a bonus or rebate of some kind tied specially to the use of the credit card.

An early example was a credit card issued by the now defunct Royal Trust where every one dollar charged to the card earned one mileage of travel 'points' on Canadian International Airlines. (That card and its points scheme are still going strong even if Royal Trust isn't!) Another early offering by some credit card issuers was free medical coverage while travelling outside Canada.

Credit cards have become big business in Canada. Indeed, on a per capita basis, we are the most hungry credit card carriers and users in the world! At the end of 1992, Mastercard and Visa had over $14 Billion in accounts receivable, at an average interest rate of 16%. There were no less than 55 million credit cards floating throughout Canada, a staggering two cards for every man, woman, and child!

With that kind of market saturation, it is no wonder the issuers are looking for more and new ways of encouraging us to use their products. Hence, the premiums such as the ones described above.

Recently, the Bank of Montreal announced that any purchases on its cards will earn a 5% rebate towards the down payment on a new home. Other cards build a 5% of purchases rebate on a new G.M. or Ford auto, with a maximum rebate possible of up to $7,000 after five years of accumulating rebates. If an individual were to take maximum advantage of the latter plan, one would have to spend a minimum of $140,000 on his/her card over those seven years. The auto rebate cards have become an instant hit in Canada with over one million applications during the first two months of their availability.

What consumers must be aware of is that these cards encourage consumption, obviously. But then, the basic cards themselves encourage consumption. So what's new? These cards will be of most use to self-employed people, or people who own their own businesses, who will charge their business expenses on them as well as their personal expenses.

35. Bought a Bust Investment?

Have you made an investment only to have it go sour, and then forgotten about it? Many of my income tax clients have done that only to discover, when we interviewed them, that they were entitled to claim a Business Investment Loss on their tax returns. When in the top tax bracket, such a taxpayer has been able to recoup about 50% of his/her loss through an income tax 'subsidy'. Generally, the rule for deductibility is that the investment must have been made in a qualifying Canadian business or in shares of a Canadian listed company, or in a loan to either one of these. The business, or shares, or loan must have since either gone under, become irreversibly dormant, or become uncollectible. In such a case, 75% of the loss can be claimed as a deduction from taxable income as a Business Investment Loss.

36. Have Your Kids Filed?

Every year we're amazed at how many university age adults who haven't filed a tax return because they, or their parents, didn't think they had to file.

True enough. If a Canadian doesn't have enough income to pay income tax on, there is no requirement to file a tax return. Under the Progressive Conservative government of the past decade, however, Canada's tax system has become a re-distributor of wealth where the rich and middle classes pay tax only to have much of it distributed, through the very same tax system, back to the under-privileged in the form of refundable tax credits.

Anyone over the age of 17 in any province who has less than $10,000 of taxable income not only should file, but is missing out on hundreds of refund dollars by not filing. As parents, we do have an obligation to make sure our children over 17 years of age do file, if they haven't, just as we are under obligation to teach them how to use a bank account, and how to use credit wisely.

37. Car Buyer Arbitration

Buying a new auto and then having to take it back time after time to have it fixed can drive the sanest person insane. We have first-hand experience. The author has at one time or another owned a new Pontiac Fiero and a new Pontiac Astre, and swore he would never buy another new North American car again.

If you live in Ontario, such frustration leading to threatened legal action by you against the manufacturer is now a thing of the past. Thanks to the Ontario Motor Vehicle Arbitration Plan, which brings buyers with complaints together with the manufacturers. A similar plan may soon be in operation across the country. OMVAP was set up in 1986 by representatives from consumer groups, car manufacturers, and the Ontario government as a way to keep disputes out of the law courts. All major auto manufacturers are represented. There are a few conditions to qualify for the program:

- You must be an Ontario resident.
- Your passenger car, light-duty truck or small van must not be used for business.
- The vehicle must be less than 4 years old.
- The deadline for filing a 1992 model vehicle was September 30, 1996.

After filling out an OMVAP application, you will be contacted by one of the Better Business Bureau offices or the Arbitration and Mediation Institute of Ontario, at which point an arbitration hearing will be scheduled. There are 52 accredited arbitrators across Ontario who consider the evidence and then hand down decisions within a month.

In 1992, there were 345 applications for arbitrations. Almost half were awarded repairs, 12% of the vehicles were bought back by the manufacturers, 14% of the buyers were reimbursed for repairs, while close to 25% found the auto manufacturer owed nothing to the buyer. 2% of the complainants had their vehicles replaced.

The program has been so successful in Ontario that at least two other provinces are likely to follow suit. One negative about the program: decisions are confidential, avoiding bad press for the manufacturers, which is probably why the manufacturers are such strong believers in the program!

38.   Purchase or Lease?

Many taxpayers are entitled to deduct the costs of certain equipment or machinery from their otherwise taxable incomes. Self-employed, commissioned, or rental property operators can deduct depreciation for such items as automobiles, computers, and buildings, where such are used in making income.

The question often arises, should I rent or purchase? That is, should the machinery, equipment, or building be purchased with cash or leased from one of the many companies offering leases on just about any depreciable asset?

The question is quite straight-forward from an income tax standpoint: it makes little, if any, difference. Over the useful life of the asset, the total amount of depreciation that can be claimed is the same under both lease and purchase. And if the lease interest rate is similar to what the bank rate would be on a loan to purchase, then the amount of interest deductible over the life of the asset should, also, be roughly similar.

Where leasing does have a very decided advantage over outright purchase is in the question of cash flow and credit. If an asset is purchased outright with no bank loan, then obviously more cash will be required from a bank account than under a lease. On the other hand, if a secured demand loan is obtained from a bank to finance much of the purchase price, then the cash flow under a purchase will amount to the down payment and a monthly loan retirement amount that will usually be less than a lease monthly payment.

Many people who are not otherwise eligible to claim expenses on their tax returns are turning to leases for automobile purchases. About half of all North American cars and light trucks are now sold under a lease, with that percentage expected to rise to two thirds by the end of the decade. With sticker prices now in the $20,000+ range for anything but the least expensive cars (when including sales and GST taxes, as well as the numerous options that are now just about mandatory!), leases now appear more attractive to any buyer who has a good enough credit rating, if only because of the reduced cash flow compared to a more conventional bank loan.

There are two main types of lease: a closed-end lease, where the customer simply walks away from the asset at the end of the lease, and an open-end lease, where the customer has the option of either walking away from the asset at the end of the lease, or can purchase the asset at the end of the lease for a pre-determined 'residual value'. In either type of lease, the customer is usually responsible for maintenance and repairs. For an auto lease, the lessor usually stipulates how much the vehicle can be driven under the basic lease charges, with surcharges applicable if the actual mileage exceeds the limit.

A rule of thumb if you are considering leasing: be prepared to spend as much time and effort into negotiating a lease as you spend in selecting the asset. This is especially true of auto leases! Costs and clauses vary among leasing companies, so it pays to compare and bargain hard! Be certain the final deal you are to sign is acceptable to you in every way, since breaking a lease is often very expensive! Ensure especially that the lease interest rate is spelled out, since there are no consumer laws at present that make that mandatory.

39.   No-Exam Life Insurance Rip-Off

In recent years, several people have reported falling 'victim' to sales pitches for 'no-exam' life insurance. Sold typically to people between the ages of 50 and 75, the life insurance is touted as guaranteed issued without an exam. Thus, people who believe their health histories would preclude getting coverage in the normal way are signing up, usually by mail.

The most pervasive advertiser of such insurance is Norwich Union, of Toronto, although there are several companies who offer such coverage.

In my experience, too many people pay far too much for the limited coverage available when compared to how much traditional coverage costs, even when rated for medical reasons. This coverage is most often purchased by someone who wants to cover the burial costs. It is precisely those people who seldom, if ever, need more life insurance to pay for their final expenses. If such people spent more time detailing their net worths, they would often discover the amount of insurance they are contemplating is negligible, and that the premiums are very hefty.

For a 74-year-old, Norwich Union charges $75 per month, or $900 per year, for only $6,400 of insurance, which is payable only if the insured remains alive for a further two years after taking out the policy. If the insured died in the 25th month, he/she would have paid a minimum of $1,800 in premiums for a $6,400 death claim. If, on the other hand, the insured remained alive to his/her normal life expectancy of at least another ten years, the insured would now have paid no less than $9,000 in premiums for a $6,400 death claim!

The message: if you feel you just must have insurance to pay burial costs, check out conventional policies and rates before committing yourself to 'guaranteed issue' coverage.

40.   Peace of Mind Costly

Ever considered how much you spend buying yourself 'peace of mind', all because of fear of the unknown?

Fear motivates almost all of us into protecting ourselves, which in turn provides peace of mind and, in the event of a calamity, minimizes negative effects. Those who do not protect themselves, either because they do not suffer fear, or 'because it will never happen to me', are idiots at best, and downright irresponsible at worst, for they place their families and themselves in financial jeopardy in the event of an unexpected major loss.

Protecting ourselves and buying peace of mind often involves buying insurance. While obtaining insurance is often prudent, we can sometimes over-react. Here are some examples, culled from the *Financial Post*:

- A couple sold their home in Quebec during the FLQ crisis, obtaining little for it. They moved to Toronto, where they never did accumulate enough money to buy another home.
- Another couple had never invested in anything but Canada Savings Bonds when, in 1987, they agreed to have their money managed by a respected and successful mutual fund manager. During the October '87 Crash, they sold in a panic, losing $10,000 of their original $50,000 stake, reinvesting the remaining $40,000 back into CSBs. Six years later, that same mutual fund has increased by $37,000, after tax. Their CSBs have increased by $13,000. The panic switch cost this couple $24,000!

The challenge, for most of us, is to obtain a balance between paying too much for peace of mind and having adequate protection against calamities. Here are some guidelines on how to keep the cost of fear in balance:

Educate yourself about areas of concern to you: If the couple who took their money out of mutual funds knew how the stock market worked, and if they expected a number of major upward and downward changes over a long period of time, they might have stayed in the fund. Financial education helps remove anxiety and allows you to take prudent risks.

Establish your potential loss, then ask yourself if you can afford to take the loss. For example, many people buy car insurance with a $100 deductible. Why not a deductible of $250? The difference in cost is about 10% of the collision premium. Most people could probably afford a loss of $250. Protect yourself only against losses you cannot afford, such as the possibility of being sued for negligence.

Have faith: You must have a certain amount of faith that things will turn out well. That doesn't mean blind faith. However, many things which at first appear to be disastrous work their way out.

Do not buy or sell out of fear of missed opportunity: Ten years ago, many people lined up to buy gold out of fear they would lose out on a great opportunity. The price finally peaked at around $700US an ounce, but is now down to around $400. Many of the natural resource-based mutual funds on the market today are going through the same gyrations.

Don't buy beyond your means: If you need a replacement fuel tank for your old vehicle, and the vehicle isn't likely to last more than a couple of years, why not buy a second-hand tank, rather than a brand new one?

Get professional advice: Some sales people amplify problems and create fear in order to sell products. The reverse can also happen. For example, a tax-shelter sales person may understate the real risks and concerns. If you are unsure, seek the advice of an investment professional.

Don't say no to something just because there are risks: Lawyers are notorious for pointing out the things that can go wrong in a situation. They do this partly to protect you and themselves if something does go wrong. Ask yourself if you can afford the consequences if something indeed does go wrong.

Shop around before you buy and look for value: If you buy what is the least expensive, you may keep your initial costs down, but end up paying more in the long run. This is reminiscent of the astronaut's reply when asked what he was thinking just before blast-off: 'It suddenly occurred to me I was sitting on top of several thousand parts, each of which were bought by tender at the lowest price'!

41.   Unpaid Overseas Work

Many retirees consider taking up a second career, especially if they've been forced into early retirement by 'buy-outs' at an early age. It's difficult to find a job at age 50+ here in Canada, what with 10%+ unemployment, and especially if having worked for only one employer during a 35-year career. That's why we've seen an increasing number of retirees seek and find employment overseas, even if only for a few years, until they are ready for full retirement.

Since 1967, an organization known as CESO (the Canadian Executive Service Organization) has helped place thousands of older Canadians into meaningful and challenging positions overseas, usually in what used to be known as under-developed countries. Except for travelling and living expenses, and a bit of 'walking-around' money, these positions are unpaid. But they provide the traveller with a unique vantage into other cultures and offer a stimulating way to continue using the skills acquired before retirement. CESO have offices in most provincial capitals. Chances are they are in your telephone directory.

42.   Pre-Paid Funerals

Many older people have pre-paid their funeral arrangements. This makes a lot of sense from an emotional standpoint, since it relieves the person and his/her family of worry both before death, as well as immediately after, when family members are likely overcome with grief.

Pre-paid funerals are often not economical, however, since they usually involve leaving funds on deposit with a funeral home, often in trust, but often with no rate of return. If there is a return, Revenue Canada insists that the administrators of the funds issue T5 slips for any interest, even if that interest is only accrued and not paid out.

If prepaying is of interest to you or a family member, here are some things to watch out for:

- What is your rate of return? How does that compare with a financial institution term deposit?
- How much will you lose in various fees if you cancel the contract? Many people

change their minds about funeral arrangements, especially while they're still alive, and as they approach that big day!

- Suppose you move far away. A large funeral home may let you move to a new funeral home closer to your new address. Will the new funeral home honour the arrangements you made with the old one?

- Does the fine print void the contract if any changes are made? After death, many family members insist on changes to funeral arrangements already made, even if minor. Such changes can render the contract null and void, leaving someone with a hefty second bill on top of what you've already paid, perhaps many years ago.

- Does the contract state whether the funds paid on deposit will pay for the entire funeral, or will they simply be applied on account?

- What happens if items you select today are simply not available when you pass away? Most contracts call for substitution with materials of 'similar or equal quality'. That is as large as a barn door when it comes time for interpretation, particularly when you are no longer around, and your family is upset with your demise.

In 1991, the last year for which figures are available, Canadians spent $8.74 Billion on funerals and arrangements, not counting flowers and other personal expenses. That's big business! So if you are one of the many thousands of Canadians contemplating a pre-paid funeral, and don't quite know how to go about it, there's a book on the market, by Donald Flynn, a second-generation funeral director with 25 years experience in both rural and big-city Ontario locations. *The Truth About Funerals*, self-published, is about $17 at some book stores, or about $20 by writing to Funeral Consultants International, Box 85119, Burlington, Ont., L7R 4K3.

43.   Rental Car Tips

Upset about how expensive insurance cover is when renting a car? I've found the insurance fees to be almost as much as the rental fees on a compact when renting by the week. So I checked with our auto insurance broker and, sure enough, discovered that the drivers listed on my Ontario auto insurance policy are covered when they are driving any car, including rentals. The only catch is that my regular vehicle back in Ottawa not be used by anyone while I am renting another vehicle.

Another 'catch' when renting a vehicle is that only drivers listed at time of rental are covered by the rental insurance. If you have extended rental car coverage on your Canadian auto insurance (known as endorsement OEF 27 in Ontario), then anyone with your permission can drive your rental and still be covered despite what the rental people tell you.

Be careful when renting a car that you really are covered under your 'bank card'. Compare apples to apples, since many bank card insurance plans do not offer the same cover the extended rental coverage under your auto policy does (that OEF 27 business).

Finally, remember that your Canadian auto policy describes coverage in Canadian dollars whereas, when renting a car in, say, the U.S., a different currency is being used, which may lead to far costlier claims than you might have been used to back home.

44.   Tracking Down Life Insurance Records

Several times over the past 16 years we have had to help our clients track down life insurance contracts owned by a recently deceased loved one. Despite the best efforts of some people, transactions occurring decades ago may not have been properly documented, with but little trace left for executors and trustees, not to mention loved ones, to assist in determining whether any amounts are payable on long-ago contracts.

One of the most frequently overlooked sources of life insurance, at least in the Ottawa area, is the Civil Service Mutual Benefit Society, defunct as of last year, whose life insurance policies were taken over by Sun Life. While few of these contracts are worth more than a couple of thousands, few older civil servants ever bothered to keep any documentation, since the cover was provided for pennies a week while working, and since most retired civil servants assume the coverage stopped when they retired. A phone call to the nearest Sun Life branch office will usually suffice to see if there was any coverage on the deceased person.

But, suppose you are looking after the estate of a loved one, and you suspect there might have been life insurance, but you can't find any physical evidence among the deceased's papers. What do you do? Here are some tips based on our experience helping to settle estates:

1. Contact the deceased's advisors: insurance brokers, lawyers, accountants.

2. Go through any surviving papers to see if there has been any record made of contact with any insurance companies or brokers, or agents.

3. Check banking records to see if there are any cancelled cheques or entries in statements or pass books implying premium payments, and to whom payable.

4. Obviously, check safety deposit boxes, strong boxes, or other storage places (the basement and attic are favourites!)

5. Contact the Personnel/Human Resources departments of previous employers.

6. Contact any associations in which your loved one may have been a member. The deceased's occupation may provide a clue to which associations he/she may have belonged.

7. Contact long-standing friends or neighbours to attempt to reminisce about the deceased's favourite occupational/extracurricular pastimes, which may provide clues to the types of pastimes that may have lead to association membership.

8. If the person died while travelling, check with the travel agent/airline/credit card company involved in the arrangements for that last trip. Chances are there may have been free flight or trip life insurance.

9. If you find details of _any_ life insurance, even if lapsed, ask that company for a copy of the deceased's application since all life insurance applicants must record particulars of other life insurance in force at the time of application.

10. If all of the above fails to provide satisfaction in your belief there may have been coverage in effect at the time of your loved one's demise, then contact the Canadian Life and Health Insurance Association, a Toronto-based group representing the majority of companies doing business in Canada. As a service to the public, CLHIA will record pertinent information about the deceased and then, once a month, circulate same to all of its member companies. If

any member company does have a policy still in force, they will contact you directly (but will not contact you if they have nothing on file). Last year, about 20% of all requests resulted in found contract coverage, or 22 out of 94 requests. In 1993, a $200,000 policy was uncovered, although the majority of discoveries are for less than $10,000.

There's currently no charge for this service, but you can imagine that such a request puts a lot of companies to a lot of work. So, the CLHIA insists that you document your case as to why you believe the deceased may have coverage that you have not been able to unearth on your own. They will not, understandably, entertain fishing expeditions.

The above service will not uncover contracts acquired from outside Canada, nor will it uncover coverage obtained under employer group contracts. The former, at least for the United States, can be determined by contacting the CLHIA's American counterpart, the National Insurance Consumer Helpline at 1-800-942-4242. The latter can best be determined by contacting the deceased's former employers.

The CLHIA's number in Toronto is 1-800-268-8099. You'll be sent policy search criteria, and a form to fill out.

45. Check Your Credit File

Have you ever heard of Equifax Canada? You should get to know them, since they are by far the largest collector of financial information in Canada, and they're in business to sell that information back to the financial institutions you deal with who then use that data to determine your credit worthiness. Yes, Equifax probably knows a whole lot about you. Some of it may be wrong, or misunderstood, leading to a less sterling credit rating at a time when you may need a loan or a mortgage.

Have you paid a credit card bill late? Bounced a cheque? Filled out a credit app? Odds are that Equifax Canada knows all about these, and has sold that information not just once, but many times over to all of the organizations you have credit with. And Equifax has cornered 90% of that market in Canada.

Equifax records go back only six years (seven for bankrupts), which will be good news to reformed deadbeats. But even only six years of data can be bad news to a lot of folks! When a CBC public affairs program did a survey, 47 out of 100 people discovered their Equifax files contained errors. Thirteen of those errors could have affected credit ratings. The problem is usually outdated information, rather than outright errors.

You have a legal right to check your Equifax file, to correct any errors, and to add any explanatory notes. You can do this over the phone in most instances. Equifax will mail you a printout of your file, free of charge.

46. You're Going To Live Longer

According to projections by Statistics Canada, most of us are going to live longer than was previously thought. And indeed, many more of us will make it into our 80s and 90s than ever before.

In the first update in five years, Statistics Canada reports that life expectancy has increased, thanks to better health habits, better living habits, and better medical care.

For example, someone presently age 55 has gained about one year of life expectancy since the last life expectancy tables were produced by Statistics Canada five years ago. That 55-year-old can now expect to reach age 78.4. That is the age at which 50% of his peers can expect to already have died, and the remaining 50% to be still alive, even if not kicking!

So, while it's good news that we can all expect to live a little longer, the opposite side of that coin is that it's going to cost us that much more to remain in retirement. How much more it's going to cost can be seen from the probability of reaching advanced age. Five years ago, a man aged 25–50 had about a 9% chance of reaching 90. This year's Statistics Canada tables show that the same 25- to 50-year-old man can now expect an 11% chance of reaching age 90. Two percentage points don't sound like much, but remember that the jump represents a 23% increase in magnitude.

The new tables also confirm that women can continue to expect to outlive men, but that the gap is narrowing. Before, women could generally expect to outlive men of the same age by about seven years. Now, that gap is down to about five years. This is due not so much to men leading better lifestyles, but to increasing numbers of women being in the paid labour force, more women drinking alcohol and driving vehicles, and smoking more.

Here are the new life expectancy figures for selected ages:

	Life Expectancy	
Present Age	**For Men**	**For Women**
25	75.9	81.8
30	76.2	81.9
35	76.5	82.0
40	76.8	82.2
45	77.1	82.4
50	77.7	82.8
55	78.4	83.3
60	79.4	84.0
65	80.7	84.9
70	82.5	86.0
75	84.6	87.5
80	87.2	89.4

47. Canadians to Work Longer

In a recent survey done by the Gallup people, it was discovered that no less than 38% of respondents said they expect to continue working past age 65, at least part-time.

This finding coincides with the views of an increasing number of pension experts who indicate Canadians are going to have to look at remaining active in the workplace well after turning age 65, because Seniors are using more social security benefits than society planned for, thanks to our increasing longevity.

The Gallup survey found that most Canadians still expect to get most of their retirement income from traditional sources, such as the Canada Pension Plan, Old Age Security, company pensions, and private savings. But many also expect they will have to rely on part-time work to help support them financially when they retire from their main careers.

While the survey found that 18% of all Canadians are fully retired, no less than 16% of all people over age 65 are still working!

Over the years, this survey, conducted annually, shows Canadians are increasingly resorting to their own ability to generate income after age 65 rather than relying entirely on government, pensions, and savings/investments.

48. Bank Rate Policy Change

For the past couple of years, the Central Bank rate, the benchmark rate used by financial institutions to set rates on various financial products such as GICs, term deposits, and mortgages, has been set at a weekly auction of Treasury Bills. This auction has been held on Tuesdays, with the result announced usually around 2 o'clock.

This system has been used with great success. However, as we move to an ever more cashless society, where funds are transferred at the speed of light around the country and around the world, the weekly setting of central bank rates is proving to be not quite frequent enough, particularly when foreign currency speculators place pressure on the value of the Canadian dollar relative to other major currencies.

Later this spring (1996), therefore, the Bank of Canada will be moving to a system concentrating on one-day rates, on what is now known on financial markets as the 'call loan rate', the rate charged financial institutions by the Bank of Canada for overnight funds needed by all major financial institutions for the clearing of their cheques through the electronic system.

When this rate changes, the Bank expects to issue a statement indicating the underlying causes and reasons, including any policy shifts. It is further expected that only these periodic statements will be reported by the press. Hence, the anticipation by the public every Tuesday about where the bank rate is headed will soon be a thing of the past.

49. Quebec

I am now convinced Quebec will leave Confederation, and sooner rather than later. I have come around to believing that a separation will be good for all of us, not only for the separatistes, but also for those of us who remain in the Rest of Canada.

I am convinced, now, that Bouchard's missionary zeal is such a powerful force on those who, for generations, have believed themselves second class citizens, that there is little the federal government can do to logically persuade such despondents that they are far better off remaining in a strong Canada. October referendum researchers have discovered that strong separatist leanings exist in high enough concentrations only along a narrow geographic strip running from east-end Montreal along the north shore of the St. Lawrence as far as Quebec City, extending up to the Mauricie and Saguenay valleys. The population in that sector is something less than two million, out of a provincial population of seven million.

Thus, current federalist thinking is to defeat Bouchard using his own logic; ie: if Quebec has the legal and democratic right to secede from Canada (which few doubt), then surely those portions of Quebec containing majorities favouring remaining with Canada should have the legal and democratic right to have their wishes respected. I have become convinced that's exactly what's going to happen, and the sooner the better.

Let's isolate the separatists into a sliver of territory that has little economic consequences to the ROC. Let's fence it off so it doesn't continue to pollute relationships between the rest of us in the ROC.

Radical thinking? As recently as three months ago, yes. But within another six months, I predict that will be official federalist strategy: if separatistes cannot buy our arguments for staying Canadian, then, out you go!

As the federalists evolve such a strategy, foreign investors will become increasingly convinced that Canada is a great place to invest, as it's been for decades. Not only the best place in the world to live, but also the best place in the world to invest!

50.   Ontario Lawsuits Under $25,000

Until earlier this year, any potential Ontario litigant with a lawsuit valued at between $10,000 and $25,000 was generally out of luck because of the high court and legal costs associated with such small actions. On March 11, however, the Ontario Court (general division) began a four-year experiment with 'simplified rules of civil procedure' that makes it a lot easier for small business people and middle-class people to collect money through the courts.

If you have been holding back suing someone in Ontario because you have been intimidated by high costs, you might wish to speak to a lawyer again about the new experiment, and what it might mean to your case.

51.   Bell Canada Pensioners

After almost two years of wrangling, Bell Canada has agreed to a $21 million settlement that will give some 1,800 of its pensioned employees access to money that has been frozen in a voluntary company plan. The agreement puts an end to threatened legal action by the Bell Pensioner's Group. The supplementary plan to which the 1,800 pensioners had belonged had been frozen by the collapse of Confederation Life in the summer of 1994, holding back pensions for retirees who had more than $60,000 in the plan.

Under the deal, Bell will pay out $3 million in each of the next five years to reduce participants' losses. It means policyholders will end up recouping 100% of their capital, plus interest.

The first annual payments are expected later this summer.

Although Bell Canada had no legal liability to pay any funds, Bell recognized that this situation caused many of the 1,800 pensioners prolonged anxiety.

52.   New CDIC Bylaw

Billions of dollars deposited in banks, trust companies and credit unions are not insured, suggesting if one of those institutions goes under, it will take the savings of thousands of Canadians with it.

More than half of all deposits in financial institutions in Canada — $340 billion, or 53% of all deposits — were not covered last year, federal government figures show. Consumers can protect up to the first $60,000 in deposits at any one institution covered by the Canada Deposit Insurance Corporation. But a lot of consumers don't bother with insurance coverage despite the fact that 36 financial institutions have failed since 1970.

Since 1992 alone, 3,794 depositors have lost at least $279 million from the forced closing of eight financial institutions, representing only those deposits exceeding $60,000 and not including unprotected foreign-currency deposits.

But even deposits that are fully insured today may not be two years from now as the big banks continue pushing for co-insurance, in which consumers would bear some of the risk for their savings.

Do you have any joint bank accounts or deposits? Then these may no longer be covered by CDIC insurance, beginning next year, unless you provide the financial institution much more information than is likely on file today.

In a little noted bylaw change last year, the Canada Deposit Insurance Corporation has made it the depositor's responsibility to provide specific information clearly spelling out which account(s) are jointly owned. The information on file must also have an address for each joint owner.

The bylaw change also notes that each joint owner must have a genuine interest in the account; you are no longer allowed to create artificial joint accounts simply for the purpose of increasing the amount of deposit insurance you have with that institution.

Accounts set up 'in trust' require even more disclosure. It is no longer sufficient to simply name 'John Doe as owner in trust . . . '. The names and addresses of each trustee AND beneficiary must be listed. If there is more than one beneficiary, the amounts or percentages held in trust for each must be spelled out.

The bylaw changes come into effect only on 1 January, 1997. So, if you are concerned with depositor protection on joint accounts owned at banks or trust companies, you have plenty of time to revise your banking records to conform with the bylaw's requirements.

For further information, contact your branch, or call CDIC at 1-800-461-2342.

53. Franchises

Over the years, I have been approached with questions about the desirability of opening up franchises as disparate as Tiny Tim Donuts, to paint-and-wallpaper outlets. My answer in every case has been: don't!

It seems that for every successful franchisee, there are at least four or five failures. For every successful franchise, it seems that there is more than another involving Mom, Pop and the whole family working 60 and 70 hours per week, with no holidays, for years before the operation becomes successful.

Why, then, would anyone invest in a franchise? Probably because such people have not yet read a new book: *Opportunity Knocks: The Truth about Canada's Franchise Industry*, by John Lorinc; Prentice Hall; 367 pages; $22.95.

This is a thoroughly researched book that looks at the myriad of franchises that have opened up across the country in the past decade. Lorinc has produced an account that is both engaging and which charts both spectacular successes and dismal failures. Indeed, his book should act as a primer for anyone thinking of getting into a franchise.

Canada now boasts 25,000 franchise establishments with annual revenues of about $30 billion. Although proponents of franchising paint the industry as an opportunity for laid-off managers to run their own businesses, Lorinc has found a different picture: recent immigrants to Canada and young people seeking to 'buy a job' are the prime sources of new franchisees fuelling the continued rapid growth of the industry.

While franchise proponents claim the failure rate is less than in small business start-ups, Lorinc quotes from a Detroit University study that shows failures within franchises actually run at a larger percentage (35%) than among small business start-ups (28%).

The tension between franchiser and franchisee is a constant theme of Lorinc's book, and well before the end of it, it's clear the typical franchise system is stacked in favour of the franchiser.

If you are thinking about investing in a franchise, here are some tips:

- Read all the fine print in the contract, and be on the lookout for oddities. These agreements can be daunting, but you need to read and understand them thoroughly if you are to avoid pitfalls.

- Shop around; look at how other franchisees balance the needs of the company with their own. For example, the Body Shop says it's keen to grow, but not if you get in over your head. They won't let you buy a second store until you've paid off the first.

- Consider ongoing costs as well as the initial costs of the investment. Be realistic about the profit you need from your investment. Buying yourself (and members of your family) a minimum-wage (or less!) job with long hours is not your average daydream!

- Don't rely on the franchiser for information. Talk to other franchisees, including people who have left the system.

- Ask about territories. What protection will you have from new stores? And what will happen if your sales start to slip?

- If you're buying an existing store, ask the present owner how long he's had it, and why he's selling; talk to previous owners of the same location.

- Consult an accountant/lawyer with franchise experience. A fee of $2,000 now could save you much more down the road in time and money.

- Most franchisers want owner/managers. Consider whether you want to be the one who is always roused at 2 a.m., when a rock goes through the front window, or the burglar/fire alarm goes off without cause.

- What kind of support are you being offered for your investment? Royalties and fees usually entitle you to more than just the trademarks, logos or systems. Every month, for example, The Second Cup holds an intensive three-week training and retraining 'Coffee College' at its Toronto headquarters, covering everything from the latest in coffee-bean technology to improving customer service and staff morale.

- Don't be afraid to walk away! Franchise lawyers say its common for potential buyers to be caught up in the excitement of owning their own business.

54. Playing Safe Can Result In Shortfall

Canadians, especially older ones, should learn a few new tricks if they want their retirement nest eggs to live as long as they do.

Traditional financial planning wisdom has held that as a person gets closer to retirement age, their investments should be shifted more into 'safe' investments, such as bonds, GICs, treasury bills, or bond-based mutual funds, instead of stocks or stock-based mutual funds.

In the past, such fixed-income investments have been considered conservative, safe, and secure. They pay interest in regular instalments, providing a steady income.

But the old wisdom has become an old wives' tale, according to three York University professors who are studying retirement strategies. They say stocks (equities; or equity-based mutual funds) offer a better alternative than fixed-income investments because such stocks will grow faster, and they'll keep growing for as long as you live.

'People should have a lot more equity in their portfolios' says Chris Robinson, an associate professor of finance at York's Schulich School of Business.

'Zero equity is a bad idea for most people'.

That's because historical data shows the returns on equities has been much higher than recent returns on treasury bills and government bonds. With such fixed-income investments, 'the risk of outliving the money becomes greater'.

Inflation erodes the value of fixed-income investments, while a mixed bag of equities will likely grow faster than inflation over time, he explained.

So, the very financial instruments that are often considered low-risk could be riskier than most people think, if only because their growth rates aren't keeping up with inflation the way equities usually do.

'Women, in fact, by taking the so-called safe route, put themselves at higher risk often times,' Robinson says.

55. Ontario Auto Insurance

In at least the fifth time in as many years, Ontario is about to pass legislation that will affect premiums drivers must pay.

The legislation aims at catching fraudulent drivers by increasing fines from the present $2,500 for those caught without insurance, to $25,000 on first conviction, and double that on subsequent convictions. New offenses are being recognized by the legislation, which aims to curb fraud by auto accident insurance claimants, car repair shops and health care providers.

People who suffer 'catastrophic impairments' will be able to sue for health care costs that exceed the current no-fault limit of $1 million, while accident victims with injuries that meet a specified threshold will be able to sue for pain and suffering.

These changes are expected to allow auto insurance companies to become more profitable, which means drivers with good records may see their premiums fall by up to 5% beginning this fall.

56.   Ontario Rent Controls

Ontario plans to scrap rent controls on units when they become vacant. Landlords will now be able to charge what the market will bear once a tenant leaves. There will be no rent controls on new buildings.

It will also become easier for landlords to evict tenants, and to convert their rental properties to condominiums. Disputes between landlords and tenants, which now must go to court, will be referred to quasi-judicial tribunals.

For further information, call Ontario's Ministry of Municipal Affairs at 416-585-7041.

57.   Ontario Prescription Drug User Fees

In yet another example of Ontario's belt-tightening, the government has announced that those who once received prescription drugs free of charge will now pay a $2 user fee per prescription, if their incomes are below a certain level. Specifically, seniors with a single income of less than $16,018, or combined joint income of less than $24,175, or welfare recipients, family benefit recipients, home care recipients, or residents of nursing homes will have to fork over $2 per prescription.

Seniors with income over the amounts quoted will have to pay the first $100 of annual prescription costs, and $6.11 for each prescription thereafter.

It is not yet known how these changes will be handled administratively, although the obvious place to do the means testing, and adjustments of fees, is in the income tax system. It will, of course, be quite important for anyone affected by these changes to keep receipts for income tax purposes.

58.   Legal Chat Line

The availability of '900' toll lines has spread into the legal community. Now comes word that you can call a lawyer at a set rate per minute of telephone conversation, which will be collected by your phone company, who keep a percentage before remitting the balance to the lawyer offering such service.

'900' toll numbers have been available for a number of years, being particularly popular in areas such as psychic predictions and sex chat lines. Now, lawyers are joining in. Toronto lawyer Marlene Kazman has had her Law Chat Line up and running for several months, now, and reports getting about 20 calls a day, at $3.33 per minute. The phone company in Ontario insists on a maximum $50 charge per call, but Ms Kazman reports most calls last about 15 minutes.

'People call when they have a pressing legal problem but don't want to go through the anxiety of contacting a lawyer', says Ms Kazman. Often, such people have been served with papers they don't understand, or they have a question about their legal rights and need a quick answer. For example, many women call wanting to know how much they might expect in child support if they left their husbands!

The phone company takes about 20% of the revenues, while the operator of the chat line has to pay set up costs and advertising.

A more ambitious 900 service, Lawyers Direct, will begin operations in Ottawa early in the new year, and charge $2.99 per minute for specialized advice and lawyer referrals.

These two services are effectively competing with the huge lawyer referral service operated by the Law Society of Upper Canada, which has been around since the early 1970s, and having more than 4,000 participating lawyers. That service is free, as is the first 30 minutes of a lawyer's time in consultation with callers who are referred. The Law Society says it does not feel threatened by the new '900' telephone services, since it claims it looks favourably on anything that improves the public's access to lawyers and legal advice.

59. Banks and Insurance

For several years, a debate has raged over whether chartered banks in Canada should be allowed to sell insurance. Up to now, banks have been prohibited from selling insurance through their branch teller networks. In recent years, banks have been pressuring the Finance Minister to be permitted to sell insurance products directly to their clients at their branches.

The federal Finance Minister last year commissioned a task force to study the matter, and to report its findings by Spring of 1996. However, in his last (1996) Budget, the Finance Minister unilaterally ruled out, for the time being, the banks being able to sell insurance products through their branch networks. He made this determination even before the task force had issued its report!

Needless to say, the chartered banks are furious at the decision while the insurance industry is ecstatic.

But how does the decision not to allow banks to compete with insurance companies affect us as consumers? And should we even care?

A new report issued by the respected C.D. Howe Institute in the summer of 1996, states flatly that consumers would benefit by allowing banks into the insurance business. The Toronto-based research think tank says international experience suggests concerns voiced by the Canadian insurance industry about banks using the confidential data bases they have created while building their banking business in selling insurance simply are groundless. And experience in other jurisdictions shows that insurance companies will not disappear as a result of new competition from banks.

But the insurance industry mounted a huge lobbying campaign in the months leading up to the Finance Minister's decision not to allow banks into the insurance business, and we can be sure they will mount an even more vigourous campaign next time the banks start lobbying for the right to compete with insurance companies. Just what are the insurance industry's concerns?

According to the Insurance Brokers Association of Canada, their concerns centre primarily around the potential loss of privacy for the consumer, the rates consumers would end up paying, and consumers' choices for getting the best insurance to suit their needs. Furthermore, according to the Brokers Association, letting the banks sell insurance could also mean lost jobs (presumably by those who work in the insurance industry), and end up making the banks even more dominant than they already are.

Specifically, the Brokers Association voices the following points:

1. Can a bank pressure you into buying insurance from them? Let's say you're trying to negotiate a mortgage at a bank. Could that bank pressure you into buying insurance from them, even if it were not in your best interests to do so?

2. Many of your policy options will disappear. Banks will <u>not</u> offer a broad range of products from which you can choose, whereas brokers can and do offer products from hundreds of insurance companies.

3. With a bank, the level of service will deteriorate. When you think of the words 'personal service' ... do the banks pop into your mind? When filing an insurance claim, who in the bank would you see? Would you merely get shuffled to an automatic teller machine for service?

4. You are unlikely to get the correct and unbiased advice for making important decisions. Bankers are <u>not</u> insurance experts. They will offer a limited range of services and insurance products ... standardized policies that offer them, not you the consumer, the greatest return and convenience.

5. You cannot be properly protected from invasion of privacy. Imagine how much more information the bank would have on you if they <u>also</u> had your insurance business. Could that be misused?

6. The Brokers Association says also that if banks are permitted to sell insurance, customers will pay more, independent insurance brokers will be driven out of business, and people will lose their jobs.

Stevens Financial Services is perhaps the largest independent investment brokers in Eastern Ontario dealing exclusively with life companies. I frankly believe the discussion between the banks and insurance companies is just so much posturing to influence federal regulators and politicians. I not only have been selling life insurance products for some 17 years with little or no competition, but have specialized in investment products, supposedly the bailiwick of the banks.

In other words, I have competed in selling life insurance products that the banks themselves claim exclusivity to, and quite successfully. As an unabashed capitalist, I say: let market forces and competition determine the fittest, and let the weak perish. The consumer should be the ultimate decision maker, even if the consumer prefers to deal with incompetent banks.

!THE END!

Glossary

The following is meant to explain some of the terms used in the text of this book. It is not meant as an exhaustive glossary of the more common terms found in the financial services marketplace.

CSB: Canada Savings Bonds. A bond, cashable at any time, offered by the Government of Canada, intended for savers, not investors. Offered in small denominations; offered in either annual interest payment version or compounded interest payable on maturity version. Registered to owner; not available in bearer form. Considered a poor investment because of the low rate of return. Interest fully taxable at owner's top marginal tax bracket.

C/QPP: Canada/Quebec Pension Plan. Savings plans offered by the Government of Canada or the Province of Quebec. Mandatory membership for all workers over the age of 18. Contributions based on earnings. Benefits available as early as age 60, based on years of contributions and amount of premiums paid. Contributions only partially tax assisted; benefits fully taxable at recipient's top marginal tax bracket. Plan operated by Government of Canada for residents of all provinces except Quebec, where that province operates a scheme almost identical to that operated by Canada.

OAS: Old Age Security. Operated by the Government of Canada and funded by general tax revenues; provides a minimum income to those over the age of 65. Means tested. Income fully taxable to the recipient at the recipient's top marginal tax bracket. Can be eaten away by a Clawback tax at the rate of 15% when taxable income exceeds approximately $53,000. Being replaced by the year 2001 by a new Seniors Benefit for those who won't have reached age 65 by then.

UI: Unemployment Insurance. An insurance scheme operated by the Government of Canada whereby unemployment, when as the result of certain factors, results in a benefit payable for up to a year while the unemployed looks for other work. Now known as 'Employment Insurance'. Premiums get some income tax assistance, while benefits are fully taxed at the recipient's top marginal tax rate.

RSP/RRSP: Retirement Savings Plan or Registered Retirement Savings Plan. Terms are used interchangeably. A savings program recognized by the Government of Canada and the provinces whereby deposits (or premiums) are fully income tax deductible, but where withdrawals are fully taxable in the year of receipt. A scheme supposedly designed to encourage Canadians to save for their retirements. However, affluent Canadians are slowly waking up to the realization that the tax 'savings' during deposit years do not outweigh the crippling taxes (of as much as 70%) levied on withdrawal.

RIF: Retirement Income Fund. An income-producing extension of RSPs, when a person, typically retired, begins an 'income stream' from his/her accumulated RSPs. An RIF is not needed, indeed in some cases, undesirable, until latest possible date allowed by government (currently calendar year following 69th birthday). RIFs have replaced annuities as the most popular method of getting incomes from accumulated RSPs at retirement.

GIC: Guaranteed Income Certificate. A fancy name for term deposits offered by financial institutions whereby savers lend money for specific periods in return for guaranteed interest earnings. GICs offered by banks, trust companies, investment dealers and caisses populaires/credit unions are typically not cashable before the due date; those offered by life insurance companies are (albeit sometimes with early-cashout penalties). Interest on GICs fully taxable at recipient's top marginal tax bracket, except interest on GICs with life insurance companies, where the first $1,000 per year for those over the age of 65 can be considered pension income not subject to income tax.

IRS: Internal Revenue Service. The American equivalent to Canada's Revenue Canada — Taxation.

OHIP: Ontario Health Insurance Plan. A program insuring most residents of Ontario for health care costs. Similar plans operated by all Canadian provinces offer similar protection. As operated by Ontario, premiums collected by a tax on employer payrolls. But premiums may also be collected from employees or from income tax payers, depending on the province.

PA: Pension Adjustment. An amount calculated according to formulas set by the Government of Canada, that represent the value of an employer's contributions to employee pension plans. The PA is used by individuals to calculate how much they are entitled to contribute to their personal Retirement Savings Plans (see RSPs, elsewhere).

CDIC: Canada Deposit Insurance Corporation. An organization that insures qualifying deposits and GICs at savings institutions who belong to the CDIC, for amounts of up to $60,000 and for terms of up to five years. Many types of deposits are not insured, such as mortgage-backed deposits, annuities of duration of more than five years, and mutual funds. Similar but better coverage offered by life insurance companies through their own deposit-protection company, CompCorp.

TC: Travellers Cheques. A bearer bond, cashable at any time by institutions recognizing the seller of the bond, for face value in the currency of the bond if locally available, otherwise in local currency equivalent; does not earn interest. An inefficient and costly, but nonetheless very popular, way of transporting cash equivalents across international borders by travellers wishing more security than offered by cash.

NSF: Non-Sufficient Funds. A term used mainly by North American banks to denote that not enough funds exist in a bank account to be able to honour demand for payment upon presentation of a bank draft such as a cheque. In the U.S., NSFs are considered criminal offenses punishable on summary convictions as demeanours; in Canada, usually results in the cheque being sent back to the presenter with fees charged to both presenter and the one who issued the NSF instrument.

ACB: Adjusted Cost Base. A term used by Revenue Canada — Taxation to denote the cost of an asset when determining how much income tax is due on an asset when that asset is disposed of. Usually, it is the acquisition cost of that asset, plus any ongoing costs in maintaining that asset, such as annual upkeep.

CNIL: Cumulative Net Investment Losses. An accounting term dreamed up by Revenue Canada — Taxation to keep track of an individual's year-by-year investment expenses and losses. Used to reduce the amount of lifetime capital gains exemptions that could be claimed before the lifetime gains exemption was repealed in 1994.

LIF: Life Income Fund. A withdrawal or income-producing plan similar to Retirement Income Funds (see RIFs, elsewhere in this glossary), but applicable to pension plan accumulations as opposed to Retirement Savings Plan accumulations.

ECU: European Currency Unit. A currency offered by the European Union. Not often yet seen in public transactions, this currency is used mainly by European governments as a medium of exchange crossing international currency boundaries.

CAHBB: Canadian Association of Home-Based Businesses. See chap. 6 for more details.